PORTEUS MAZE TEST
Fifty Years' Application

PORTEUS MAZE TEST

Fifty Years' Application

By

STANLEY D. PORTEUS

PACIFIC BOOKS
Publishers
Palo Alto, California

Second printing, 1973

International Standard Book Number 0-87015-139-8.
Library of Congress Catalog Card Number 65-18125.
Printed and bound in the United States of America.

PACIFIC BOOKS, PUBLISHERS
P. O. Box 558
Palo Alto, California 94302

Preface

The Maze Test has been so inextricably tangled with the author's doings that the personal note cannot be avoided in these pages. However, it is hoped that this volume will not be regarded solely as history, either personal or professional. It has a much broader purpose. It is intended as an account and discussion of the psychological problems with which the author has been concerned over a fifty-year period, with special reference to the application of the Porteus Maze. These problems include, among others, the various types of mental deficiency and antisocial behavior; measurement of ethnic and sex differences; and the effects upon mentality of psychosurgery, vitamins, and drugs.

Many perplexing questions remain in the social, medical, and psychological fields. Unfortunately, human perspicacity and skill have not been able to untie the Gordian knots of delinquency, incompetency, and mental abnormality, nor have the shears of man's thought and effort been sharp enough to sever these bonds and set him free. How little any of us know of the workings of the human mind is a compelling reason for deep humility on the part of all those who put themselves forward as psychologists.

But the comparative failure of intuitional approaches to the solution of social problems renders it all the more necessary for the wise investigator to make use of the most satisfactory objective evidence available. The unexpected significance of Porteus Maze scores, under such a variety of experimental conditions as described in this volume, more than justifies the setting up of a new criterion of the significance of any psychological tool—namely, wide range of sensitivity.

For the period of its half-century of competition with other "measures," it can, I believe, be fairly claimed that no other test, or scale of tests, meets this criterion more satisfactorily.

S. D. PORTEUS

Honolulu, Hawaii
January 12, 1965

Contents

CHAPTER ONE

Historical Beginnings

In 1913 the educational world was excited by news of the work of Maria Montessori (1912) with mentally retarded children in Italy, using a special training approach, mainly sensory. The degree of retardation was not made apparent, but the idea quickly spread that subjects definitely feebleminded were responding so well that they had narrowed the gap between them and normal individuals. These reports of progress were, if verified, truly remarkable. It looked like a major educational breakthrough.

The Victorian Education Department in Melbourne, Australia, was so interested that plans were made to convert a city school into a center where the Montessori system, or modifications thereof, would be applied to the training of mental defectives. It was hoped that their development would be stimulated to the point where many of them could take their place in the normal community. Professor Witmer's work in the Psychological Clinic at the University of Pennsylvania also seemed to offer great encouragement to educators interested in the special education of the retarded.

In 1913 I was given the responsibility for selecting children out of the ordinary state schools for attendance at the center at Bell Street, Fitzroy, then undergoing rebuilding and redecoration as a special school. This work was under the general direction of Dr. Harvey Sutton, Chief Medical School Officer, but the extent of his other duties soon compelled him to leave the preparatory work in my hands.

The inevitable difficulty that had to be faced was that of the mental diagnosis of potential pupils. This was my initial acquaintance with a psychological problem that demanded attention. Its solution is still, after 50 years, a matter for disagreement among so-called experts. Educators, social workers, psychologists, and psychia-

1

trists are still uncertain as to the definition of feeblemindedness and the means of differentiating it from normality. A definition proposed by Porteus and Corbett (1953) reads: "Feebleminded persons are those who by reason of permanently retarded or arrested mental development existing from an early age are incapable of independent self-management and self-support."

As could be readily imagined, the situation in 1913 was confused, almost chaotic. Feeblemindedness was almost inextricably mixed up in people's minds with delinquency and general social inadequacy. In America it had been declared the root cause of most social problems. When Victorian school principals were asked to list the mental defectives in their classes, they promptly reported most of their troublesome pupils. Some more objective method of selection was evidently necessary, and the newly publicized Binet-Simon Scale seemed to offer a solution. The Goddard Revision, the application of which was described in a booklet by Dr. Edmund Huey of Baltimore, came into my hands and was applied for the purpose of better segregation of the educational sheep from the goats. It was undoubtedly helpful in distinguishing the mentally retarded from the ill-disciplined.

But unfortunately, the diagnostic inadequacy of any form of the Binet Scale was soon apparent, as it has been demonstrated hundreds of times since. Even at that early date the too great dependence of such tests on previous educational experience and the severe limitations of a predominantly verbal measure were beginning to be realized. True, the recognition of these overriding considerations came slowly to psychologists, whose experience with individuals was limited to brief clinical experiences, or, as the term implied, "bedside" observation. The tests did not cover, as Thorndike afterward put it, the problems of the laboratory, the field, and the office—including many situations dealt with by individuals outside the schoolroom. Thus, to some critical students it became apparent that what was called "practical intelligence," the ability to deal with things rather than words, was in many cases of crucial importance, and that this was not well measured by the Binet Tests.

At first this distrust of any simple means of assessing intelligence was founded on theories of the complexity of mental functions, and took a very long time to infect the rank and file of mental testers. Their prestige had been greatly inflated at finding in their hands a new instrument, the application of which promised to enable them in three-quarters of an hour to determine not only the present mental level of a child, but his intelligence status for the rest of his life.

This unwarranted faith was bolstered by the pronouncements of the leaders of the new movement. Goddard was so impressed by the degree of agreement between test verdicts and the judgments of people in charge of the training of mental defectives that he once declared the Binet Tests to be "a perfect instrument of research." Having found so many cases of positive agreement, he was inclined to sweep to one side the negative instances, believing that any errors of individual appraisal were on the side of the raters of intelligence and not due to any inadequacies of the tests. Everyone was disposed to agree that a measurement was more accurate than an estimate, but few were bold enough to say that the Binet Scale was not a complete measurement but a composite of judgments based on a variety of tests of very unequal validity and significance. Just as was the case in regard to feeblemindedness, the lack of a satisfactory definition of intelligence was a great hindrance to controlled experiment. If this book were an attempt to write a history of mental testing— which it is not—we should have to present a much more searching analysis of the contributions, not only of Binet but also of leading psychologists who did so much to launch a worldwide program of psychological examining. Terman, for example, did his work in a more refined academic atmosphere than Goddard, with the focus of effort centered in a progressive university instead of a training school for feebleminded. The former's work and that of his associates embodied a better selection of subtests and used more thorough methods of standardization than did Goddard's pioneer efforts, but suffered the same handicap of unjustified faith in the accuracy and practical application of the new psychological "measurements."

As new world-leaders in this field, Terman, together with Kuhlmann, was responsible for the establishment in educational favor of the intelligence quotient (IQ) and for the setting up of 70 IQ as the lower limit of mental normality. Just as was the case with Goddard's mental age limits, the IQ criterion—if one took no notice of the exceptions—was reliable enough, but there were too many exceptions. The happy truth was that many individuals who had been designated feebleminded by the 70 IQ criterion were able to prove that they were quite capable of supporting and managing themselves in the community and certainly should be freed of the stigma attached to the label "moron" or even "high grade feebleminded." It is surely one of the ironies of history that from the greatest mental testing experiment in clinical psychology, the army examinations of 1917–18, practically nothing was learned as to the value of the tests used and the standards of mentality they set up.

Nowadays, the term "feeblemindedness," a condition for which mental limits were on the way toward being established, has gone out of fashion. Instead, people now speak of the mentally retarded, the diagnosis of which condition seems to have no proper criteria, either practical or psychometric. This fact puts the problem beyond any estimate of social gravity or significance. How could this situation be appraised for any educational or therapeutic purpose when it is realized that we are all, in some direction or degree, retarded? This lack of established criteria has resulted in estimates of the number of mentally retarded ranging from one-half of one per cent to twelve per cent of the population, with no possibility of determining which estimate should be accepted. I find myself in complete disagreement with one psychologist who, in a review of one of my books, condemned discussion of these fundamental issues as a recital of psychologists' "tribal conflicts" that should be quietly swept under the carpet and forgotten by the psychological housekeeper.

Since this is an historical summary of long experimentation with one psychological test or test series, it is necessary to return to the quandary in which I found myself in 1913. Out of the several hundreds of children classified by school principals in Melbourne as being feebleminded, it was not very difficult to pick out 150 for whom the Goddard-Binet Test confirmed the teachers' judgments of serious scholastic defects. But my contact with such cases was more than a brief office visit for each child, an application of a standardized Binet Test, and an announced diagnosis, followed by a disappearance from view of the individual to whom a label had been attached. I did not have to wait a number of years before having the opportunity of discovering whether or not the label was deserved.

Again, the experience of Goddard and Terman in America and of Cyril Burt in England befell me. In the majority of instances, if the children were functioning in an ordinary school environment, the verdict of the tests was reasonably correct. But in a special school where manual skills were more important than scholastic abilities, and where the adjustment of cases was geared to competition with the dull rather than with the bright or even normal, the status of the individual was more easily determined. It was soon quite apparent that there was more than a sprinkling of cases in which the ordinary scholastic progress was a very poor measure of social competence.

It was fortunate for me that, in a country so far removed from the rest of the civilized world and in an academically limited situation, the roles of educator and psychologist were perforce combined into one. In a very few months I realized that to apply the blanket term "feebleminded" to all those segregated by the Binet Scale as belonging in what was already called "the silly school" was a rank injustice. To a young enquirer, somewhat critical of the whole educational setup from kindergarten to university, all teaching practices seemed a little silly, but that did not make the test situation any better. In some individual cases, I found myself increasingly dissatisfied with a system of testing that used a hodgepodge of tests with, as far as I could learn, arbitrarily assigned values in reckoning a so-called mental age. Unless one accepted the unitary nature of intelligence, how could one adopt a scoring method that gave equal credit to each and every item of success? Was a Chinese puzzle of equal significance to a sentence completion test, even though the former was more difficult? What, too, were some of the distinguishing marks of the mentality of the defective, especially those that were not specifically examined nor weighted in the application of the Binet Scale?

Observation of the behavior and progress of the Bell Street pupils under our somewhat haphazard attempts at their more effective training led to the conclusion that teaching efforts, including the much vaunted Montessori system, suffered from a wrong emphasis. It seemed to me that it was useless to teach a child how to do something when he had no clear ideas as to what had to be done. We were training boys to use a saw, to hammer nails, to fit parts together when they had only the vaguest mental image of what the job would look like when all these operations were finished. Acting without purpose and prevision seemed to me pointless. Function and structure were mutually dependent, and function was the expression of purpose.

The realization of these principles led to the development of a series of mazes to be solved by the individual. These were so arranged as to allow an evaluation of the individual's ability to carry out in proper sequence and prescribed fashion the various steps to be taken in the achievement of a goal, in this case finding his way out of a printed labyrinth. It was convenient to score these efforts in terms of chronological age performance, the test ages being based on a system of deductions for entries into blind alleys. The method, perhaps, is difficult to describe but simple in application. Because prehearsal,[1] or planning is essential to success, the tests were claimed to be approximate measures of planning capacity and foresight at ordinary levels. It was not then assumed, nor was it ever expected to occur that a single series of graduated mazes would be sufficient to measure planning at all levels. That disclaimer is probably hardly necessary, but it should be remembered that the original purpose of the Porteus Maze was the differential diagnosis of those individuals who could neither support nor manage themselves in community life. What other applications could be made, or higher levels tapped, was not at first apparent.

The early steps at working out such measures were naturally fumbling or inept, but there was no doubt that a lack of practical foresight was critical in the case of the defective. Whether it was a matter of making and fitting together parts of wooden toys, or achieving economy of effort in painting them, or delivering footwear from the shoe-mending class, or managing simple household tasks, prevision, or what I have called prehearsal, was essential to success. In constructive effort, what seemed to be lacking was memory images of objects in spatial and functional relationship. Much training time was devoted to fitting insets into a formboard and then complicating the process by placing the insets at some distance from the board, allowing distractibility to interfere with correct performance. This focusing of attention on the goal to be reached while at the same time allowing perception to range over alternative courses in order to select the relevant response was the most significant feature of maze threading.

Early alternative experiments in the choice of test material involved some work with the Fernald-Healy Puzzle Box, in which the problem was to open the contrivance through releasing various cords by manipulating a button hook through a small hole in the side of the box, the proper sequence having been planned by preliminary study of the device, using the glass front of the box. This test could

---

[1] Since "rehearsal" applies to the repetition of an activity already planned, we need a term for mental trial-and-error anticipation. For this the writer has devised the word *prehearsal*.

be neither graded in difficulty nor scored consistently for performance, because too much manual dexterity was required.

Drawing between the guidelines of a maze design required much
less manual dexterity, and by varying the position and number of
exit openings difficulty could be graded and sustained attention
called for. The present-day form of the nine-year test in the series resembles a map of city streets with blind alleys, and this harks back
to early experiences with a twelve-year-old boy who appeared defective as far as ordinary school learning was concerned. However,
he showed normal ability in shoe-repairing work and was particularly reliable in delivering the footwear once a simple plan of the
school's immediate neighborhood had been shown to him and been
memorized.

Incidentally, the claim that the Porteus Maze can be considered
to be 50 years old is based in part on the fact that the series of designs still closely resembles the earliest forms; that the mental traits
involved in performance remain the same; and that the instructions
have varied to a minimal extent, although some changes have come
about in the standardized scoring. Thus, both content and application have remained fairly constant. On the other hand, the substance
of the various forms of the Binet is now almost unrecognizable when
compared with former series, and the diagnostic significance has
been radically amended. Naturally, a nonverbal test would retain
much more of its original character. Other test scales have been so
often revised that, like a well-darned sock, little of the original
material remains.

Thus, by the end of 1913 the new test series was ready for experimental use. But in arranging the test designs in order of graded
difficulty, one problem was to devise meaningful trials of the ability
of very young normal children or of older cases of low mental levels
of development. It had been observed that such children had difficulty in following with the finger the outline of shapes of objects
as used in the Montessori "didactic material," but the conclusion had
been soon reached that this was not due to any bluntness or deficiency of the tactile sense but to a mental incapacity to anticipate
changes in direction of movement. Hence, while individuals succeeded in roughly following a general shape, corners were cut or
rounded. The more right-angle turns there were to be negotiated,
the more inexact the finger tracing was. This was the reason for
using the Maltese Cross as a four-year test and a simpler diamond

as a three-year design. It is interesting to note that later on, a child's disregard of the structuring of the maze manifested by crossing lines and cutting corners was used to reveal tendencies in the delinquent temperament. Not until the five-year age-level was the principle of choice of pathways leading to an exit introduced. Since this ability also depends on prehearsal and the anticipation of changes in direction, the psychological unity of planning or carrying out a preconceived purpose throughout the whole series was preserved.

The tests for the younger children were then tried out with success in city kindergartens. A fairly accurate standardization for three, four, and five years was achieved; and failure to pass at these levels accorded in almost all instances with teachers' estimates of pupil disability, not only to learn simple kindergarten plays but also to adjust socially to other children of their own age group.

At a somewhat later time, after the tests had been published in America, confirmation of the usefulness of low-age-level tests with normal kindergarten children was forthcoming. I can well remember the encouragement I got from this first instance of someone else finding the Maze Test of value. Because of the seeming break in continuity of the scale after the four-year design, I was particularly pleased to receive this verification of my limited experience. E. R. Shaw (1917) wrote as follows:

A surprisingly correct view of individual differences can be gained through such a test. The slow child who habitually leaves his work half-done, the child who is prone to misunderstand spoken directions, the child who makes careless mistakes but quickly corrects them himself, the child who improves with practice, the child who tires or loses interest and hence does worse instead of better in a second trial—all these and many more types that we all know, reveal their everyday traits in this five-minute test as clearly as in a year's work.

It was opinions such as these, evidently based on considerable experience with the tests, that supported my opinion that temperamental traits of pride and self-satisfaction in a good job, close attention, perseverance, and sustained interest were extremely important for everyday adaptation and should certainly be given weight in any psychological appraisal of the individual.

My own failure to foresee the wide use of the Maze Tests and their significance was the main reason for not subjecting the data to proper statistical treatment followed by publication of results. It must be remembered that at this time my concern was with the classification of mental defectives, with little thought of other uses.

The next step in the verification of value of Maze Tests for this purpose was undertaken at what were then known as the "Idiot Cottages" at the Insane Asylum at Kew, a suburb of Melbourne. Dr. Gamble, medical superintendent, picked out for examination those cases who ranked highest in matters of self-help. These seemed to be singled out by the tests with surprising agreement and accuracy. This perhaps should not have been surprising since the tests were of a practical measure, but at that time and place the idea of any objective appraisal or classification of ability was new.

By early 1914, through talks and demonstrations of the tests, pediatricians in Melbourne had become acquainted with the methods. They began to refer parents with defective children to the Bell Street School for examinations that would correct or supplement their own diagnostic suspicions. Dr. Douglas Stephens and Dr. Hobill Cole, leading child specialists, referred all doubtful cases to Bell Street as a routine procedure. Word spread to other capital cities, and it was not long before a psychological clinic, undoubtedly the first in Australia, was operating, though without official recognition, special funds, or staff.

By midyear 1914, I was so convinced that the graduated mazes had exceptional diagnostic value that I made a proposal to Dr. John Smyth, professor of education at Melbourne University, to submit the tests to a trial under the most severe conditions possible. The question to be answered was: out of a group of children entirely unknown to the examiner and with whom he could not communicate except by signs and of whose mentality he had no means of judging other than by their Maze Test response, how successfully could the examiner select those whose mental deficiency had been already adjudged by other criteria?

There was at that time an excellent residential school for deaf and dumb children who were being subjected to intensive training, both through lip reading and the alphabetical sign language. Out of 140 pupils, many of whom had been for several years at the school, there was a group of children with regard to whom long study and experience on the part of both teachers and home supervisors had forced the conclusion that they were not only deaf but feebleminded. For the purposes of the experiment, these cases were mixed in with a large number of others with estimated normal learning capacity. The problem was to discover how many of the defective group could be segregated by the tests without any information beyond their names and chronological ages. At that time the highest age attainable, or ceiling of the Maze, was 13 years, although the design then alloted to age thirteen may now earn maximum fifteen-year credit. Out of 36 cases judged by teachers to be "normal," only two tested three years below chronological level, and one of these had been noted by the teachers as being of "doubtful mentality." On the other hand, of 12 adjudged defective, all tested three or more years below age. Actually, the average chronological age of this group was 13.35, and their mean test age eight years. The "normal" group averaged 13 years also, but their mean test age was 10.6 years. In other terms, the normal group scored 2.4 years below age in test level, the defective group 5.35 years. These results were reported by Porteus (1917).

In 1918, the results of a similar examination of deaf children were included in another article (Porteus, 1918). Neither of these studies was included as sub-titles of the published articles.

Professor Smyth, who observed the experiment and checked the results, was so impressed that he decided to arrange for me to present a paper to the British Association for the Advancement of Science, which was scheduled to visit Australia for a meeting in August 1914. The program at the University of Melbourne had already been arranged with Smyth as local chairman, and the only way to ensure the inclusion of my paper was by cutting his own allotted time in half and transfering the rest to me. I decided that unless I distributed in advance mimeographed copies of the mazes, there would be barely time for a discussion of the nature of the tests, their purpose, and the obtained results. The timing of my paper was so opportune that I was accorded most unusual attention.

Our overseas visitors, mainly British with a sprinkling of other European notables, showed a rather impolite degree of disinterest in the offerings of Australian educators. This was a not uncommon characteristic under conditions of colonialism at that time and was no doubt generally justifiable. There were, however, very few Australian psychologists, and for a rather devious reason my paper was given extended time and greeted quite enthusiastically.

The Goddard Revision of the Binet had been standardized in America about two years previously and from there had quickly spread to England where the claims made on its behalf received a cool reception. In scientific matters generally, as well as in the educational field, American contributions were not at that time highly regarded. It was probably true that much transatlantic social research was supported by hurried and uncritical experiments. The British tendency was to poke holes in the weak fabric of research rather than to get to work and improve its texture and durability. In matters psychological, this attitude remains somewhat apparent. "Not made in Britain" still tends to be an effective discriminatory slogan.

This statement may savor of rank ingratitude, for my effort was given an excellent reception. In order to indicate the validity of the Maze Test, I had to proceed through a process of correction and devaluation of the Binet, and this criticism fell on grateful ears. Actually, distrust of any claim, from whatever quarter, that a 45-minute examination by the Binet Test was sufficient to establish an individual's present and future intelligence level was very well founded. My test at least offered the opportunity to supplement the exploration of mental capacity in what I contended were untested but potentially significant directions. The addition of the Maze Test to the psychologist's repertoire did not make assessment and prediction entirely reliable—but it helped.

There appeared in the BAAS Proceedings only a listing of my paper by title, and even then it was wrongly attributed to some other person. Nevertheless, Professor Green of Sheffield University, editor of the *Journal of Experimental Pedagogy,* asked me to send it to him for publication. It appeared in due course (1915) and was also published in the same month (June, 1915) in the *American Journal of Psycho-Asthenics.* The test itself has outlived both journals.

About this time I became closely associated with Dr. R. J. A. Berry, Professor of Anatomy at the University, who was greatly interested in work on the brain capacity of the feebleminded. He invited me to transfer my headquarters from Bell Street to the Anatomy Department of the Medical School at the University. Mr. Frank Tate, State Director of Education, influenced no doubt by the interest of our overseas visitors, arranged for me to be "seconded" from his department so that I could devote all my time to study and research. I was given the title of Government Scholar in Anatomy, the position and duties being happily undefined. This allowed me opportunities to attend lectures and to carry out as many dissections of the central nervous system as I wished. This experience, together with extensive readings in physiology, enabled me to speak at least the language of neuroanatomy. More than this, Professor Berry was able to obtain a small grant for research, and we set up what he called a Laboratory of Educational Anthropology, of which I was co-director. One of the first jobs I undertook was to attempt to test the correctness of Lee's Formula 14 for calculating brain capacity from head measurements. This was done by measuring the water displacement of brains before injection with formalin. Dr. Robertson was associated with me in this work, and a series of 40 fresh post-mortem brains gave about a 6 per cent error in calculated head size, if subjects were chosen within the normal range. Unfortunately, when I left Melbourne for America, the study lapsed and was never published. Some time previous to my departure, Berry and I had accumulated measurements of head capacity of almost 10,000 subjects, mainly school students ranging from 6 to over 20 years. These measurements were then converted by means of Lee's formula into brain capacities. Despite Berry's hopes, our published tables (Berry and Porteus, 1920), though they showed a crowding of feeble-minded cases into the extremes of brain size due to the inclusion of macrocephalic and microcephalic idiots, did not prove to be of any value in individual mental diagnosis.

My appointment as Lecturer in Experimental Education established my status at the University, and as the teaching duties were light this gave me ample time for research and publication. Through the courtesy of Professor Terman, I received a copy of the Stanford Revision of the Binet scale, and with two assistants, aided by members of my University class, I was able to undertake what was at that time a very extensive study involving the testing of 1,000 school children by both the Binet and the Maze Tests. The results of this investigation showed that the Maze Test standardization was too easy for the earlier years, but too difficult for the upper levels. Up to 10 years of age the Maze Test mean scores were above the Stanford-Binet Test, but decreasingly so, while at age levels 12 and 13 the Maze Test averages were below the Binet. The number of cases tabulated was 970.

On the basis of these results, the Maze Test standardization was revised. The original three-year design became a practice test and the four- and five-year tests were each devalued by a year, while new tests were devised for six and seven years. The old thirteen-year test was raised in test value to 14 years, and four trials were allowed for the two upper tests (twelve and fourteen). This eased the difficulty at the upper end of the scale.

In 1918 (Porteus 1920) this revised series was applied to another large group (N 1,255; 623 boys, 632 girls). The scores of combined sex groups agreed with age up to 9.5 years, but after that showed about a half-year discrepancy up to 12.5 years. Children over 13 years also scored below age but were a somewhat selected group, since the brighter children were beginning to drop out of elementary classes and to go on to high school.

The difficulties of standardization were realized when we considered the effects of various differences in sampling. Schools were classified by residential areas into lower and middle class social grades, and differences in performance were duly noted. It was apparent that sex also made some difference in level of performance. For the Binet Test the matter was even more complicated by differences in level between city and rural children of equal age. Apparently urban residence had less effect on Maze Test scores.

The above findings are cited as being of some historic interest and as showing that mere increase of numbers of cases did not guarantee accuracy, but that the nature of the sample was of overriding importance. Thus, there was even in those days awareness of the difficulty of allowing for social grade, urban, or rural environment, etc., but little attempt to solve it. Unfortunately, the lesson has not yet been properly learned. Statements of negro-white mental differences, for example, are meaningful only if the samples are equated for age, sex, social class, and education, and that very attempt at equation may make the samples unrepresentative of either ethnic group.

The advent of the United States into World War I gave, as we all know, tremendous impetus to mental testing. The committee of psychologists which drew up the Army examinations met for some time at Vineland and, no doubt, learned from Goddard of the value of the Maze Test in the diagnosis of mental deficiency. It had been in use there since 1915, and Doll (1917) illustrated the performance of "a potentially normal" boy by showing his performance throughout the whole series of Maze Tests from three years to 13 years.

As a result, two mazes were included in the Beta, or Performance Scale, and the test as a whole was used (when there was time) for examining doubtful cases. Its application by Navy psychologists in individual examinations was later reported by Goddard.

In Ohio, the newly established Bureau of Juvenile Research needed a director of national stature, and the position was offered to Dr. Goddard. The field of choice as regards his successor at Vineland was narrowed through the demand for psychologists in miltary service, and he recommended me. Possibly some disappointment with the Vineland administrative committee,[2] which made no special effort to keep him as director of research, may have influenced Goddard in suggesting that they must go to the ends of the earth to select a man to take his place. Dr. Milton Greenman, director of the Wistar Institute of Anatomy in Philadelphia knew something of my research activities and approved my appointment. In any case, when I arrived in America in January 1919, I was received most cordially by my psychological confreres, and my program of research was accepted by Mr. Fels and his committee. For the first time he gave assurance that his financial support of the Vineland Laboratory would be continued on a yearly basis. In Goddard's time, the research program operated only on a quarterly grant.

SUMMARY

This chapter sets forth the early history of the Maze Test and the search for a psychological measure that would give a fairer index of the social sufficiency of the mentally retarded child than could be afforded by the Binet Scale. This was the writer's first experience with the problem of adequate mental diagnosis that is still a matter for concern today.

The responsibility of selecting children from elementary grades in Melbourne, Australia, for special education in a school for the mentally defective brought this matter under my immediate attention. Further experience with the Binet Scale showed that except for ordinary academic classification it was much overweighted with verbal tests and responses, and that an area in which the subnormal were often less deficient had been left unexplored. Initiative and practical foresight were being neglected, and a test of "planfulness" was urgently needed. The program of special school training was directed toward helping individuals to support and manage themselves, but these goals seemed to have little to do with academic progress. Hence, the Binet, for practical purposes, had no predictive value. The provision of tests of ability suitable for the lowest levels of intelligence presented special difficulties, but measures of hand and eye coordination seemed to meet this requirement very well.

---

2 Samuel Fels, well known for his philanthropy, was chairman of the committee and the financial supporter of the Vineland Research Department.

A crucial experiment of the test's value in mental diagnosis was then arranged. Deaf and dumb pupils in an excellent residential school in Melbourne were examined, with test instructions given by pantomime, the object being to discover whether the test could pick out individuals already adjudged to be feebleminded on the basis of the teachers' experience. Almost complete accord was achieved.

Shortly after, in 1914, the tests were first publicly demonstrated, and their results set forth. Following their favorable reception by members of the education section of the British Association for the Advancement of Science at its Melbourne University meeting, the writer began his first mental survey of 1,000 elementary school children, the tests used being the Goddard Revision of the Binet, the Stanford Revision, and the Porteus Maze Test. This and another examination of over 1,200 cases provided standardization data.

As a result of publication of the results of these studies in England and America, the writer was invited to direct the Research Department at Vineland, New Jersey, in succession to Dr. H. H. Goddard.

CHAPTER TWO

Early Experimental Studies

The previous chapter dealt in large part with the writer's first work with the feebleminded. Some of the succeeding studies overlap in chronology with these investigations and suffer from the same deficiencies as regards reporting data, partly attributable to inexperience and the inadequacy of statistical treatment common at that time. They are briefly described here mainly because they foreshadowed my future interests with regard to juvenile delinquency, racial differences, and, more specifically sex differences in performance in the Maze Test. The first published investigation (Porteus, 1917) concerned twenty-two boys committed to a Boys' Home at Burwood, Victoria, some on account of parental neglect, others because of mild delinquency. The average Maze Test age was 10.33, 2.33 years below their chronological mean, a much less serious loss than had been found for the high-grade feebleminded. Scores were compared with ratings of conduct as supplied by the superintendent of the Home. Seven cases who had favorable ratings tested only a half year below age, whereas another group of six boys, who were rated unfavorably in conduct, scored three years below the level assigned by the test to normals.

Another group committed to a Reformatory for more serious crimes, such as assaults (including one murder) and housebreaking, were more than 3.4 years below standard, several scoring so low as to suggest that they were feebleminded. Again, it must be remembered that the ceiling of the test was then 13 years. It was noted that the housebreakers ranked somewhat higher than those convicted of crimes of violence. The boy who murdered a companion tested nine years and was considered mentally defective. These results indicated that although the low planning capacity uncovered by the Maze Test was often associated with delinquency, this was not characteristic of all, or even the majority of cases.

16

Another brief study, which was a forerunner of later cross-cultural investigations, was carried out in 1915 at an aboriginal mission station situated on Point McLeay near the mouth of the Murray River in South Australia. This mission had been established for more than 50 years. Very few of the school children were reputed to be full-bloods, the great majority of the 28 cases examined being part-whites. The average chronological age was 10.2 years and the mean test age was 9.75 years, thus indicating a near-normal intelligence status. I noted, however, that the older the cases, the less well they performed, a finding that agreed with the teacher's reports that he had great difficulty in educating his pupils beyond the fourth grade in school (Porteus, 1917, p. 37 ff). The tests of mental alertness seemed to correspond with this conclusion. Twelve cases over 11 years of age were retarded 1.35 years, while 16 younger children had scores slightly above the white levels. However, any suggestion that cases with aboriginal blood tended to slow down in mental development at puberty was likely to be uncertain. The assumption was inherent in this and other test scales that annual increments in age corresponded with similar units of intellectual growth. It is comparatively easy to differentiate, mentally, children of five years from those of a year older, but difficult indeed to prove the assumption that progress from, say, 14 to 15 years is equally apparent. At these older ages, three months of measurable improvement in ability might easily require a year of chronological age to achieve. There may even be a positive mental change between 23 and 24 years of age, but this difference is too slight to be represented in standardization. Thus, what might be considered a slowing down in aboriginal development might be a general phenomenon of decreasing correspondence between mental and actual age.

Publication of Binet-Maze Test correlations, in a study that involved 200 mentally deficient cases and 453 nondefectives (Porteus, 1918), provided a good illustration of what today would seem to competent clinical psychologists to be a curious form of validation of a test. Those who are inclined to use this type of criterion today conceal its irrelevancy behind the term "concurrent validity." In justification it has been said that any good test of intelligence must be related to all other good tests of intelligence. To the writer this seems to be a naive view of intelligence as a unitary function. It is like representing intelligence by the color white and its opposite or absence by black. If this were an accepted analogy, it would then be possible to arrange all tests on a scale of "whiteness" from black through all shades of grey to the pure color. If, then, it were agreed that the Binet afforded the best reflection of white, the correlation of a new test with the Binet would be indeed "concurrent validation." Unfortunately, the color spectrum is not limited to gradations of white. Generally speaking, a degree of agreement can be reasonably expected between tests, but to elevate the Binet Scale into the supreme criterion of test "goodness" was psychologically unsound. Actually, too high a correlation would indicate duplication in measurement.

Nevertheless, comparison with the Binet Test came close to being at one time standard practice. The present writer followed the fashion in terms of reporting numbers or percentages of cases who tested by the Maze Test below or above Binet mental ages. For example, the very earliest comparison, cited in the previous chapter, showed that 120 mental defectives at Bell Street averaged 6.23 years by the Goddard-Binet, 8.13 by the Maze. It was rather triumphantly recorded that 75 per cent of the whole group tested by the Maze within one year of their Binet age. Since, at that time, the main problem was the differentiation of the dull from the feebleminded, the higher mental ranking by the new test was diagnostically useful. It was considered very probable that a verbal measure would do less than justice to dull children, whereas a performance scale would better reflect their practical abilities.

Two of Goddard's chief publications (1913, 1916) emphasized the close relationship of social conditions, such as illegitimacy, delinquency, prostitution, and poverty, to feeblemindedness, and many other psychologists were also regarding these handicaps as evidence of mental defect. As a result, the incidence of such deficiency has always been grossly exaggerated. At the present time, the almost general use of the designation "mentally retarded" and its lack of definition make it difficult to challenge any extravagant estimate of its social importance.[1]

That extreme caution should have been exercised by psychologists in accepting results founded on a Binet diagnosis is the lesson that can be learned from a study by Baller (1936). He followed up into later life the social histories of 206 children from Lincoln, Nebraska,

---

[1] The magazine *Time* recently put the number of retarded persons at almost six million. If this classification includes the tone-deaf, color-blind, slow readers, and nonmechanically minded, there are probably many more.

with IQ's below 70. Only 6.5 per cent were in institutions for the feebleminded, though 25 per cent had had Juvenile Court records and 19 per cent had been in jail or reformatory. But 33 cases finished the eighth grade, three cases finished high school, and one entered college. In any case, for 56 per cent of these individuals, segregation in any type of institution had not been necessary, while 83 per cent were either partially or wholly self-supporting. These facts together emphasize the serious uncertainty of school psychologists' judgments.

Apparently little notice was paid to such an indictment, and high correlations with the Binet were accepted as evidence of "concurrent validity." Fortunately for its viability, the Maze not only correlated well with the Binet but showed rather catholic relationships with a whole list of other tests. In some studies workers were frankly puzzled by the figures they obtained.

For example, far back in the early days of the test, Morgenthau (1922) reported correlations of .54 with the Binet, over .70 with the Healy Picture Completion II and Alpha II, and .45 with a Learning Test, but only .36 with the Pintner-Paterson, another performance test scale. Peterson and Telford (1928), whose subjects were 12-year-old Negro children at St. Helena Island off the coast of South Carolina, found a correlation of .53 with the Goodenough Drawing and .51 with the Digit-Symbol Test. Moreover, these authors reported that the Maze correlated with the total battery higher (r .42) than any of the other tests used, the next highest being the Two Figure Form Board (r .29). Similarly Lincoln, who tried out the Army Performance Scale at Vineland (Porteus, 1919), found that the Maze correlated .63 with the total Performance Scale, whereas the Binet correlation with the total was only .44. The Maze Test correlated with the Binet only .21, one of the lowest coefficients reported. Weisenberg, Roe, and McBride (1936) admitted the correlations they found with the Maze to be "puzzling." They cite as examples .62 with the Printed Analogies, .59 with the Binet, .58 with the Pintner Non-language, and .41 with the Gates Spelling Test, their perplexity arising no doubt from the relationship of the Maze that existed with verbal and performance tests alike. Dewey (Porteus, Dewey, and Bernreuter, 1930) obtained correlations of .54 with the Stanford-Binet, .68 with the Kohs Block Design, .69 with Porteus Form and Assembling, and .77 with Social Ratings. These studies and many others have been previously cited by me (Porteus, 1950).

Anyone looking over this array would undoubtedly be puzzled at the variety of results and might be tempted to question the meaningfulness of the correlation approach.

Two features help to account for the confusing nature of the data. The first is the miscellaneous sampling, which includes London school children, inmates of a Jewish Children's Home, feebleminded, behavior problems, Negro children, part-Hawaiians, adult patients in hospitals, Indiana Clinic cases, etc. The departure from expected relationships serves to illustrate the difficulty psychologists experience in interpreting factor analyses, which apparently differ according to the correlational matrices used, the nature of which depends on sampling.

The other possible explanation may lie in the fact that the solution of most mental tests calls for some planning, but the amount and quality of the foresight required differ in each instance. Dealing with a form board, for example, calls for prehearsal involving comparison of objects by shape and size, but since it is scored on speed, physical dexterity also affects results. The Maze Test, on the other hand, requires no judgments of related forms but a more direct prehearsal of possible courses of action. It is, therefore, more general in reference and thus relates to behavior that is called for more frequently in everyday situations. It is my contention that the planning of responses is an essential part of any intelligent activity, and the intercorrelation of the Maze with a wide variety of tests is due to its relation to intelligence in general. I believe a better case can be made out for calling the Maze a basic or even a general intelligence test than can be established for tests such as the Kohs Block Design, Form Boards, vocabulary, rote memory, where the ability that they examine is more specific.

As is made clear in the foregoing pages, the earliest applications of the Maze were in the direction of improving the diagnosis of mental defect. An early appraisal of the value of the test for this purpose was contributed by a medical officer in Manchester, England, Dr. H. Herd, in an article (Herd, 1923) and later in a book (Herd, 1930).

The article was written "to obtain some estimate of the real value of the Porteus Maze Test in assessing the mentality of school children." He writes:

There is general agreement that the Binet scale of mental tests, either in its original form or in any of its modifications, is too purely linguistic in character, and that by the use of it alone an erroneously poor impression may be derived of the capacities of children whose understanding and use of language is limited, but who may have considerable practical ability.

He then proceeds to list as special deficiencies of the Binet its failure to assess the individual's "initiative, his capacity of foresight and planning, his power to conquer difficulties, to grapple with new situations and to carry on a piece of work to its end—all qualities of great importance in everyday life."

Dr. Herd examined 113 children ranging in age from 7 to 14 years, attending a residential special school for mental defectives. Evidently his work as medical officer kept him in close touch with these pupils. As calculated from his table, the Maze Test mean was 7.5 years, the test quotient 59. To provide an external criterion of validity, instructors divided the children into five grades, A to E, according to practical ability. He did not publish any correlations, but test quotients of pupils ranked from most to least efficient were A 77, B 74, C 65, D 59, and E 45.

Herd sums up this diagnostic experience: "The steady-going, dependable defective, with good practical ability, often scores too high (in the Maze) but his Binet score usually compensates, and the Binet-Porteus combined result will be a good index of the adaptability." The danger is that some of these cases could have been mistakenly labeled defective on the basis of their low Binet ratings.

Four years earlier (Porteus, 1919) I had published a very similar statement with regard to this problem of differentiating the merely subnormal from the seriously defective.

There are many individuals who display a relatively low degree of intellectual capacity, especially in regard to tests of range of information and vocabulary, yet who possess practical common-sense attributes and the ability to profit by experience, and who have developed sufficient industrial ability to make themselves self-supporting. Hence, we are faced with the situation that there are individuals who test, by hitherto widely accepted standards, feebleminded, and yet must be considered from the community's standpoint, normal; on the other hand, there are some who test nearly normal per Binet, but who prove themselves socially inefficient. There is a crying need, therefore, for tests which go beyond the ordinary field of mental examinations, and which will assist us to evaluate temperamental characteristics.

Among these assets of temperament are neatness and care in doing a job, persistence in the face of difficulties, resistance to fatigue and distraction, control of emotions, sustained attention, and many others that are only indirectly examined by tests of the Binet type, and are not as specifically demanded as they are in Maze performance.

Undoubtedly a critical attitude toward mental tests, and particularly the Binet, develops largely on the basis of more intimate contact with individuals. Herd's responsibilities apparently were similar to my own. Professor Cyril Burt, the British authority, had been interested more in general than in specific educational guidance; nevertheless, his analysis of what the Maze measures agrees well with those of Herd and myself. In one volume he sums up the test values and at the same time the Binet's limitations (Burt, 1921).

Many borderline cases of suspected mental deficiency, particularly slow and and steady dullards with a manual or industrial bias, fail hopelessly with the Binet-Simon Scale, and yet unexpectedly succeed with the Maze Tests; and, conversely, many of the more unstable type, girls especially, who answer glibly with the former, have not the prudence, the forethought, the maintenance of attention and alertness which the latter demand. The Maze Tests, therefore, supplement though they cannot, I think, supplant the other scales in a profitable way.

In his republication of the Porteus Maze in another book (Burt, 1923), this author repeated his opinion that the test is "chiefly of interest in examinations of mentally deficient or temperamentally unstable persons."

Two other English investigators, Earle and Milner (1929), quote with approval Burt's listing of the different causes, often temperamental, of failure in the Maze:

The cause may be an intellectual one. The child may become confused; his power of systematic attention may be unable to cope with a task so complex; he may be unable to follow with his unaided eye the longer paths and more devious routes, or he may fail to retain the results of his observation so as to guide the movements of his hand; he may be unable to plan, or to profit by his past mistakes. Quite as commonly, the cause is partly emotional. The child may be over-confident, or careless; he seems unable to take thought beforehand, or too dashing and impulsive to carry out his thoughts.

To this summary I would add only one comment. Any clinical psychologist would surely agree that these traits, or trait-complexes, are essential to ordinary life adjustments and must, therefore, in some way or another be taken into account in mental diagnosis, provided they are measurable.

Except for the present-day confusion of counsels as to what validity means, this discussion would indeed be pointless or repetitive. But the practice of clinical psychology is still uncertain as regards mental diagnosis. I believe that there is no longer disagreement among psychologists as to the inadequacy of the Binet Scale, and for proof of this statement there is the increasing popularity of the Wechsler-Bellevue Test, which threatens to supplant in clinical usage the earlier Binet forms. In America there seem to be two types of response to this general situation. The first is to widen the base of attack by including a greater variety of tests. In military terms, this is tantamount to increasing the number of guns in the battery in order to augment the weight of fire. The second tendency is more insidious and in the long run more devastating—to downgrade the whole mental testing process. More and more psychologists seem to turn away from clinical practice, preferring what they feel to be more academically respectable pursuits.

But surely in relation to the first-mentioned development, no one versed in the use of artillery would adopt the plan of adding new weapons without some consideration of their range and hitting power. If increasing the noise was the desired result—and this may conceivably have some military value—that method certainly would be effective. This seems to be the plan followed by some psychologists whose aim was to copy the Binet method by assembling in a performance scale a hodgepodge of tests regardless of their comparative validity. One would think that tests of such short range as the Mare and Foal Test, or the Two-Figure Formboard, or even the Draw-a-Man Test would obviously not add to the effectiveness of any battery. By short range I mean that these test results are of little meaning beyond the middle period of childhood. With an adult they may be almost meaningless, and many adults or adolescents are referred for mental diagnosis. The multiplication of tests merely adds to the noise.

Even such a popular collection as the Wechsler Performance Scale depends for its diagnostic value on each test's individual validity, and this, as far as I know, has not been supported by adequate evidence. To my mind, there are three main questions to be answered with regard to a test's validity: What does it measure? How well does it measure it? What is the significance of the trait when measured?

The third question concerns the relevancy of the material tested.

For example, a test may measure very well the ability of a subject to imitate a given pattern by putting together colored blocks within a certain time. But have we not the duty to try and determine how relevant that ability is to life adjustment? For some individuals the relevancy of a vocabulary test is greater than that of the Kohs Block Design and, possibly, of the Maze; for others, practical rather than verbal ability is more significant.

Admittedly, the proof that success or failure in a test is related to a person's adequate functioning in society may be very hard to come by. Devisers of tests know very well the extreme difficulty involved in setting up any criterion of social efficiency, especially when general judgments are broken up into traits that contribute in different degrees to social functioning. As elsewhere suggested, provision of a reliable social criterion may take as much time and effort as devising the test.

But because a task is difficult and time consuming does not mean that psychologists should avoid it. The situation that seems to provide the best opportunity for working out adjustment ratings is a residential school or institution. There all the facets of individual behavior, the different manifestations of practical ability, the learning rate, and the temperamental traits can be observed. Both the inmate population and the staff are usually stable. In addition, there is the factor noted by Goddard—namely, the slow rate of development of defective subjects. He used the analogy of observing the equipment and content of a freight train in comparison with a fast express, the former activity being relatively easy. Besides, the institution psychologist has the advantage of running the freight train back and forth along the line, giving him many opportunities to check his observation.

The setting up of such a criterion for the Maze was attempted at Vineland with the assistance of Alice M. Nash, the educational and industrial director. The traits commonly attributed to mental defectives were culled from the literature and were combined when the terms seemed to overlap. Ratings were obtained from all institution supervisors who came into contact with the children in job assignments, in school, and in their home cottages. Only children who had been known to the raters for over two years were listed. Each case was assigned a "general social estimate," based on pooled judgments as to their potential ability to adapt to community life if they were to be dismissed from the Training School. Hence, we established a list of traits most frequently observed among "those whose minds have not developed normally," the basis of admission to the Vineland Training School.

Some traits frequently observable did not correlate well with potential social adjustment and were eliminated. In general, ratings gave proof of very careful assessment. For example, "disobedience" was dropped because supervisors did not think that it would seriously interfere with social adjustment outside the institution, their comment being that most of the feebleminded were too suggestible and malleable and that a certain amount of resistance to institution routine was a sign of initiative. Such an attitude was surprising but was characteristic of those who exercised general oversight.

When this preliminary work was finished, there remained seven traits that most closely correlated with the "general social estimate." Each individual was then rated in the separate traits of the scale, weighted according to the size of the correlations.

This whole procedure has been discussed elsewhere (Porteus, 1920), but our present concern is with the correlation of tests with this criterion. No difference was found for males as between Binet and Porteus Test scores, both correlating .60. This equality may have been brought about by the inclusion of younger boys attending ordinary school classes. In the case of girls, the Binet *r* was .69, the Maze .75. Probably female temperamental traits influenced their behavior more, or were more easily observed. It was noteworthy that the highest correlations between tests and social ratings were found when the Binet and Porteus test ages were pooled and averaged for each individual. The boys' *r* was .75, the girls .79 (N 128). Industrial efficiency correlations with tests are reported elsewhere in this volume.

Any summary of the psychometric test movement would be incomplete without mention of Wechsler's contribution. Though the selection of some of the subtests of his scale (Wechsler, 1939) is open to question (e.g., inclusion of his Object Assembly Test), it was he who first had the courage to elevate performance tests to potential equality with verbal tests by providing two sets of IQ's (test quotients). Speaking of his scale, he wrote: "It was constructed on the hypothesis that an individual manifests intelligence by his ability to do things, as well as by the way he can talk about them." This does not differ in substance from the stand taken by the present writer 24 years previously.

In setting up his scale, Wechsler tended to bypass the perplexing problem of validation. Though he expresses his belief that validity is essentially dependent upon proof that a test measures well what it purports to measure, he is able, as regards his performance sub-tests, to present very little evidence of this nature. Instead, like many other test devisers, he relies upon the statement that the tests of his scale are "good" measures of intelligence because "our own experience has shown them to be so." He believes, in regard to the Binet and other tests, that "their final validation rests primarily on the fact that they worked well in practice, and not because of any compelling statistical correlations." The present writer must confess that he has only the vaguest idea of what "working well in practice" really means. In what circumstances does a test not work well?

Though Wechsler is critical of ratings given by teachers and psychiatrists, he does use agreements of their ratings with tests as evidence of the latter's validity. Such relationships, though far from being adequately substantiated, illustrate the paucity of the evidence that psychologists possess to prove that the tests measure what they purport to measure.

Before leaving the subject of mental diagnosis, it should be explained that any criticisms of the Wechsler-Bellevue Scale that are herein contained are far outweighed by its contribution to the status of performance tests in general. Lightening the diagnostic load that has been placed on verbal tests must surely have resulted in keeping thousands of individuals, otherwise accounted mentally defective, out of institutions. In 50 years of application of the Maze, it must have had no inconsiderable effect of a similar nature.

Burt (1921) in England has also cited popularity among psychologists as evidence for validity of the Binet Scale, stating that it has been used to measure "successfully" the intelligence of tens of thousands of individuals. He winds up his discussion with the declaration: "Pending the construction of some more scientific scale, whose validity has been as widely tested and whose authority is as generally revered, the Binet-Simon Scale must, for rough and practical purposes, still hold and monopolize the field."

With a marked change as regards reverence, signified by grave doubts as to its validity as a diagnostic tool, Binet monopoly of the field has disappeared. Fortunately for its validation, the Maze Test relates mainly to one type of demonstration of mental functioning only, rather than consisting of a collection of discrete subtests, involving a wide variety of mental processes. Thus it avoids the questionable assumption of what Wechsler calls "the functional equivalence of the test items . . . implicit not only in the Binet Scale but in any scale which is composed of a variety or pool of intellectual tasks." Does not this also assume the unitary nature of intelligence so that all mental tasks are considered of equal relevancy to the life adjustment of all individuals?

It should be frankly admitted that the validation of the Maze Test is far less satisfactory than is desired. The extent of agreement with external criteria, such as social and industrial rating scales, was demonstrated 40 years ago. Despite the obvious weaknesses of rating scales, the demonstration was successful, and the results showed that the Porteus Maze had correlations equal or superior to those obtained with the Binet Scale. On the other hand, it did not correlate nearly as well with abilities of scholastic reference, such as arithmetical computation, verbal facility, memory, etc. Moreover, these traits are far more easily assessed than is planfulness, by which is meant foresight and practical initiative. This conclusion seems to be well supported by the fact that though the Maze Test was publicly described 50 years ago, it seems to have at present no serious competitors of its own kind.

Various types of validation have been suggested, such as test content, age discrimination value, concurrent validity, and cross-cultural applicability; but these have to do more with the arrangement of subtests into a scale, simplicity of direction for application, and relationship with other tests, none of which seems to have much bearing on whether the tests measure what they purport to measure. If they are successful in this last direction, then surely all these things, including predictive value, will be added.

As previously urged, the fact that such demonstrations by external criteria are inherently most difficult should be no deterrent to continued patient effort in this direction. Apparently, institutions for the mentally defective offer the best opportunities for studying the developing mind. Those merely mentally retarded in certain abilities —which includes most of us—are differentiated from institution cases, and those centers should be designated as existing for the study of inmates as much as for their care. Psychology is a young discipline and the fact that in some directions 50 years' progress has been insignificant is no good reason for refusing to take up the challenge for further assault.

Only by additions to our psychological knowledge can the current downgrading of clinical psychologists by other workers, including their more academic colleagues, be checked and even reversed. Certainly, further labors in the matter of measuring [2] mentality are worth pursuing. My own plan of approach to the problem is in thorough agreement with a statement made to me by Dr. William A. Hunt (1962): "I am convinced that the most valuable attributes of any test are its wide standardization over all sorts of clinical and cultural groups and the repeated demonstration of reliability and validity throughout this standardization.[3]

It is the plan of this volume to present such a demonstration and thus add to psychological knowledge of at least one test.

SUMMARY

Among very early experiments was the application of the new series of tests to juvenile delinquents. It was realized that if the Maze measured planning, reactions of individuals who had shown inferior social foresight should be noted. But it was soon apparent that although as a group delinquents had lower than normal Maze scores, poor practical intelligence was not a main causal factor in misconduct. Similarly, the first experience in testing aboriginal half-castes indicated that their mean scores were considerably higher than expected in spite of their low intelligence and cultural repute.

At that time "concurrent validity," or the process of establishing the value of a test by demonstrating close relationship to other scales, predominantly the Binet, was much in vogue. This tendency was due to a faith which follow-up studies, such as Baller's, showed to be clearly unjustified.

Actually, the magnitude of correlations of the Maze with a wide variety of tests was surprisingly high. However, its validity rested on more direct evidence, as shown by citations from British investigators Herd, Sir Cyril Burt, Earle, and Milner.

The improvement of mental diagnosis does not, however, depend on multiplying tests, but rather on a better selection of sensitive measures.

---

[2] The use of the term *measurement* throughout this volume does not infer that measures of human traits are anything more than approximate. Psychologists, however, try to make them as accurate as possible. If the surveyor's chain is not available, he may be reduced to pacing, which if carefully carried out by an experienced man may have only a relatively small margin of error.

[3] Quoted by permission from a private communication dated January 23, 1962.

The reasons for choosing institutions for mental defectives as the most suitable places for testing validity are pointed out in terms of better observation of retarded developers, together with stability of population, both inmates and staff, resulting in intimate knowledge of the behavior of subjects. A social potentialities rating scale was set up at Vineland in 1920 and is described, together with its test correlations.

The contribution of Wechsler in combining verbal and perform-ance measures so that two sets of test quotients are made available is commended. However, his principles of selection of subtests are criticized, particularly the "works well in practice" criterion, since this feature is founded on psychological popularity and not research.

That the validation of the Porteus Maze is by no means complete constitutes a challenge to further effort on a difficult problem. The fact that in 50 years of use the Maze has no serious competitors in its field is an index of the complexity of the task of providing better measures of planfulness. Psychologists have chosen the easier course of devising educationally and verbally oriented tests.

The writer has followed the plan recommended by William A. Hunt of wide standardization of the Maze by application to dif-ferent clinical and cultural groups and repeated demonstrations of reliability and validity.

CHAPTER THREE

Psychosurgery and the Maze

Some historical accidents, comparatively unnoted in their time, later became the basis for scientific deductions of considerable importance. The brain operations undertaken by Moniz in 1935, for the relief of psychoses, can hardly be called accidental, but the surgery was "blind" and the rationale, according to Partridge (1950) was "most bizarre." "The most logical point of attack," he remarked, "seemed to be the frontal lobes, both since they had no clearly assignable function and might therefore withstand damage with impunity, and because they were at that time generally believed to be the seat of the intellectual life." The idea of removing psychotic ideas and practices by mutilating the brain was indeed extraordinary. Surely, no surgical procedure was ever initiated on such problematical bases. Nevertheless, Moniz boldly injected absolute alcohol into the frontal lobes of mental patients and later cut out large portions of white matter with a leucotome. Shortly after, Freeman and Watts (1942) introduced into America the operation they called lobotomy, in which a "blunt instrument" was inserted bilaterally through trephine holes in the skull and incisions made that severed the nerve pathways between the frontal lobes and the dorsal medial nuclei of the thalamus. Besides damaging the brains of the patients, it stirred up what Partridge called "a psychiatric storm."

Psychologists are not greatly concerned with psychiatric meteorology nor even with the neurosurgical disturbance, but we should be vitally interested in the theory that the frontal lobes are "the seat of the intellectual life." Mental measures are considered, whether by popular description or by psychologists' claims, to be tests of "brain function," and as so much of the brain mass is included within the frontal lobes, it was our bounden duty to try

30

to discover what effect lobotomy or topectomy, or the other more or less controlled "insults" to the human brain, have on mental functioning and ability. Here was a great opportunity for psychologists to align themselves with neurologists, neurosurgeons, and psychiatrists in joint research to discover the relationship of brain and mind.

Happily for the mentally afflicted, but unfortunately for science, the opportunity was brief. The advent of the tranquilizing drugs promised benefits in the relief of psychotic symptoms similar to those attained or partially attained by psychosurgery. These latter have been summed up by Partridge in an appraisal of the therapeutic purposes of the Freeman and Watts neurosurgical procedure: "Thus it has been used to lessen the turbulence of the florid psychotic, to reduce the tension of the obsessional, to allay the agitation of the melancholic, to diminish the histrionic emotionalism of the hysterical psychopath." To those who have worked in a mental hospital, it is soon obivous that such changes can be also effected to a measurable degree by routine medication with a drug, such as chlorpromazine, and much less painlessly and irreversibly than through the knowledge and skill of the neurosurgeon. But it should be noted in this recital of remedial features that there is no mention of the reverse side of the picture—i.e., the intellectual deficits that may attend the emotional benefits. More specifically, the question is whether the patient who has suffered a standard lobotomy, the stripping of the cortex from certain frontal areas, a thalamotomy, venous ligation in the prefrontal area, thermocoagulation, transorbital lobotomy, or temporoparietal topectomy possesses the same mentality as he was blessed or cursed with when his brain was intact.

During the 15 years or so onward from 1936, when such operations were in vogue, a handful of psychologists and psychiatrists addressed themselves to this inquiry, which seemed to them to be crucial with regard to the mind-brain problem. The astonishing thing is not so much the sparsity of laborers in the field, but the indifference with which the results were received. In the case of psychologists it is the more extraordinary since for years they have been concerned with the detection of brain damage and mental defects of various kinds and degrees. How can they ignore the question as to whether the tests they use for this purpose are significantly affected by planned and executed surgical intervention? The main purpose of this section is to examine and report changes that occur in Maze Test performance after psychosurgery. The sensitivity of other tests is not my special problem and will only be referred to incidentally.

Unfortunately, it is too late for extensive and thorough test validation through the use of this unforeseen criterion. When overall comparisons of test responses have been made, losses after operation have been inconsistent or slight except in the Maze, though a qualitative analysis might have yielded more positive results. For example, the Binet vocabulary score in terms of acceptable word definitions may have remained the same, yet an examination of the quality of the definitions and the type of associations might well have revealed marked changes. When invited to the feast of new facts, most of the psychologists were busy elsewhere with rats, cats, and salamanders, and human reactions were neglected. The result was confusion and chaos. For all the thousands of brain-operated cases, the question as to how these brain injuries really affect mental functioning is left undecided except in limited directions. Even as regards the Maze Test, the research design in some respects has been fuzzy and ill-planned.

Since the above generalizations have been presented before, it remains only to outline briefly the studies involved and to bring them up to date, with the realization that this could well be the last word on the subject, not because of the decisiveness of the conclusions but because experimentation has, for dearth of subjects, come to an end. Not that head injuries are diminishing in number and severity, but in such cases we have no base line; the premorbid levels of intelligence are not available for comparison, and the real extent of organic damage can rarely be determined.

The first work on the subject done by the present writer was begun in 1943 when Dr. Ralph Cloward, nationally known neuro-surgeon, carried out a series of standard lobotomies on patients at Kaneohe, now the Hawaii State Mental Hospital. In association with Dr. Richard Kepner, clinical director at the hospital, we attempted an assessment of the psychosurgical results, based on pre-operative mental examinations in which both the Binet and the Porteus Maze were included (Porteus and Kepner, 1944).

Of 17 cases tested by the Maze, only two gained in score after operation in spite of the fact that normally a second repetition of the test shows a marked practice gain. One of these two patients was re-operated upon, and his performance dropped 11 test quotient

(TQ) points. The other patient was the son of a university professor and had graduated from junior college. His scores before and after operation were consistently high, and the conclusion was reached that either the lobotomy cut was too anterior or that the ceiling score of the Maze was too low to demonstrate any decline.

These findings were surprising on two counts. The first was the comparative insensitivity of a "general" intelligence test, in this case the Binet, the mean change being a loss of 3 TQ points, with 56 per cent of cases showing deficits and 39 per cent gaining. Here was early demonstration of the fact that drastic interference with the functioning of the frontal lobes had only ambiguous effects on mentality as ordinarily measured.

In the Maze, on the other hand, 77 per cent had lower scores after operation, while only 6 per cent gained postoperatively. Another surprise was that these results ran counter to expectation, since the Maze had, at least with the feebleminded, been considered a measure of social adaptability; yet in spite of gains, mainly in socialization, their Maze scores declined. This necessitated a reappraisal of what the test measured; a realization that the mentally deficient failed to adjust because of constitutional inadequacy, whereas the psychotic failed because of more positive dynamic factors leading to emotional disturbances, bizarre beliefs, and unreasonable actions. The reasons for therapeutic change were not clearly definable. After lobotomy the patient became less sensitive to his environment, less anxious, less physically restless, or less withdrawing from his fellow beings. Possibly his adjustment could be summed up as one of greater passivity, which in turn was reflected in part by impaired Maze performance. Testwise, impaired planfulness resulted in less tendency to anticipate problems and to work out solutions in advance. Mental alertness had a more immediate and restricted reference or relevancy. At a much later period of experimentation, the conduct of patients undergoing prolonged medication with a tranquilizing drug also demonstrated an improvement in socialization associated with a decline in Maze Test performance.

Even at this stage it was recognized that if practice effects on a second Maze application could not be controlled, they should be allowed for. Of 17 cases drawn at random from the Psychological Clinic files, all mentally retarded, after an average interval of 4.4 years 71 per cent gained almost 2 years on a second Maze testing.

In contrast, only 6 per cent of the lobotomy patients gained, the net *loss* being 1.97 years.

Because of the varied nature of psychoses, it is extremely difficult to obtain meaningful control groups in a hospital population. Porteus and Peters (1947), therefore, compared 55 lobotomy patients with an equal group of 55 criminals who also had been given a second Maze application. The preoperative mean of the former experimental group was 11.29 years (SD .35), but after operation the same thing occurred as previously, a drop to 9.65 years (SD .39), a loss of 1.64 years, or 11 points in TQ level. On the other hand, the criminal unoperated group had a mean on the first application of the Maze of 12 years, while on the second testing after an average time interval of 4½ years it rose to 13.6 years. Thus the gap between operated and nonoperated widened to almost 4 years. Though the experimental group of psychotics had initially a lower Maze average, this was as near a matching as we could make without including prisoners who were mentally retarded.

Dr. Peters and I decided to go on testing, though realizing that the research design was faulty, until we had another form of the Maze that would be practice-controlled to such an extent that it would yield the same score as the original series. Unfortunately, I did not get around to standardizing this second form until 1955, by which time lobotomies were beginning to be rare operations.

Moreover, we determined to investigate the question as to whether the practice improvement rate was related to social improvement. In conference with the medical staff, we divided operated patients into unimproved, moderately improved, and much improved groups, this being done on the basis of hospital clinical reports. In one preoperative and five postoperative repetitions of the Maze the curve for the "unimproved" had a somewhat lessened initial drop and rose gradually so that by the fifth postoperative application they had almost reached their preoperative level.

On the other hand, the "much improved" cases rose consistently and evenly until at the fifth testing they rose from a first postoperative level of 9.47 years to 14.5 years, or 3.2 years above their preoperative level of 11.3 years. Thus difference in ability to profit by practice after operation was clearly demonstrated.

Taking these figures at their face value by disregarding the practice effects, it would appear that the demonstrable ill-effects of lobotomy are transient and in a comparatively short period of time are completely reversible. But taking figures at their face value is exactly what the scientist refuses to do. In this case, it is analogous to measuring a distance in the first instance with a standard foot rule and secondly by a rule that purports to be a foot but has shrunk to ten inches. It is not the distance that has increased but the instrument that has contracted.

This failure to take Maze Test practice effects into consideration was responsible for rendering inconclusive one of the main findings of three of the best equipped investigations in psychological, psychiatric, and neurological history. These were the two Columbia-Greystone projects and the New York Brain Study, which were reported in three books (1949, 1951, 1956). What made them so noteworthy was the imposing array of collaborators whose fields of interest brought them into contact with psychosurgical cases. Some of the best research psychologists in the country were engaged in assessing the results of the various types of psychosurgery involved. Neurologists, neurosurgeons, and psychiatrists were all included and jointly reported their findings. Nevertheless, the psychological research plan at one point was inadequate, in spite of the extreme care exercised in their measurements and the thorough statistical reporting of the data. Investigators did not fully realize that the Maze Test, as they applied it, was not an ordinary standard instrument but one that was intended to measure, among other traits, the ability to profit by experience. Since this actually occurred, scores improved from the first to later applications. Undoubtedly, had the lobotomy and/or topectomy operations continued at the same rate after 1955, when a practice-controlled Maze series became available, the conclusion that surgical brain injury effects were transient would never have been reached. Fortunately, the insight of leaders in this field, such as Landis, Zubin, and Kinder, prompted them to combine hindsight with foresight through their sponsorship of an eight-year follow-up study of patients conducted by Aaron Smith (1960). This proved beyond peradventure that the losses were permanent, though initially almost completely obscured by practice effects.

The findings of the three projects carried out by the Columbia-Greystone Associates have been summarized in several reports, but the fact that their lessons have been almost generally disregarded by psychologists and psychiatrists makes a restatement at this time advisable, if not imperative. One factor not sufficiently recognized at the time was that the incision by the neurosurgeon's knife was only the initial damage. Later came sclerosis or scarring of the surrounding brain tissue so that the mental deficits became cumulative. Porteus and Peters had noted that while 66 per cent of lobotomy patients showed decline in Maze scores immediately after operation, the percentage rose at some later date (up to 7½ weeks' interval) to 82 per cent. It seemed that the effects of the brain damage were postponed so that in some way certain mental functions continued on their own momentum as it were. Evidently physical, physiological, and psychical changes do not have the same temporal sequence.

The results of the first project were summarized by Carney Landis (1951), as chief architect of the psychological research design, at a conference on psychosurgery held in New York in October 1951, when more than twenty experts were assembled by the NIMH to discuss the findings. Landis reported:

> In the test-by-test analysis of the results which were obtained, the only intelligence test which showed a uniform or almost uniform loss during the first month after operation when compared to the preoperative performance in this battery of tests was the Porteus Maze Test. Dr. Porteus had previously reported this sort of loss after lobotomy. We confirmed his finding that a brain operation performed on the frontal lobes gives rise to an immediate postoperative loss in mental age of 1 to 2 years, in some 80 per cent of psychosurgical patients . . . there was nothing which showed itself as a systematic change in the tests of intellectual function, the tests of learning or the tests of memory with the exception of the Porteus Maze Test.

In the presentation of the data in detail, readers could easily be confused, since Wechsler-Bellevue results were given in IQ form, Maze results in mental ages, making the changes in the latter appear much less marked. When Maze scores were converted into test quotients and compared with the other test findings, patients were found to have *gained* 3.9 points in the full Wechsler-Bellevue and 5.0 points in the Wechsler Performance Scale, whereas they *lost* 8.6 points in the Maze. The control group gained 7.1 points in the Maze, indicating a total comparative deficiency of 15.7 TQ points (8.6 + 7.1). This result leaves little doubt as to the comparative sensitivity of the Maze Test.

In justice to the Wechsler-Bellevue Scale, it should be noted that Petrie (1952), working in England with patients operated on because of severe neuroses, found a deficit of 7 IQ points in the Wechsler-

Bellevue full scale. The discrepancy may have been due to the fact that her cases were at a higher preoperative level than the Columbia-Greystone patients. In other words, they had further to fall. Incidentally, she also observed, as I had done, a greater tendency in lobotomy patients to repeat the same error in successive trials in Maze designs.

In the Columbia-Greystone Project II, patients underwent five types of frontal operations—extensive venous ligation, less severe ligation, thermocoagulation, thalamotomy, and transorbital lobotomy. Outstanding Maze losses after operation were 27 TQ points for severe venous ligation as against a Wechsler-Bellevue full score gain of 0.75 points; in thermocoagulation of areas 9 and 10, the loss was 10.7 TQ points compared with a W-B gain of 9.5 points; in thalamotomy the loss was 30 TQ points as against a W-B gain of 4 points. Only in less caudally extended venous ligation and transorbital lobotomy, the site of damage being anterior and inferior, was the Porteus deficit rather small; in the latter, 5.7 TQ points as against a gain of about 2 points in W-B full scale scores; in the anterior operation, a postoperative loss of only 1.4 points. But once again practice effects masked the severity of the Maze Test deficits, for Landis and Zubin remark: "The Porteus Maze test showed an immediate drop after operation with a full recovery in all but the thalamotomy patients by three months after the operation."[1]

However, these investigators also record that after operation "it was as if the patient were sleepy, fatigued or partially drunk, so that there was disinclination to work at his usual level." They believed this was a generalized transient performance deficiency rather than any specific functional loss.

Had all the facts now at our command with regard to the highly differential repetitive Maze performance been then available, I doubt that such experienced investigators would have summed up the situation in those terms.

An analysis of additional New York Brain Study data appeared several years later, in 1956, and confirmed previous findings. In this investigation, operations were classified into orbital or superior topectomy. Once again the Maze showed much greater sensitivity. Whereas the orbital cases lost one IQ point in the W-B full scale, the Maze deficit was over 10 points; for those who suffered superior topectomy, the Maze loss was 20.6 TQ points as against only 1.5

[1] See Chapter 14, *Psychosurgical Problems*, p. 276.

points in the Wechsler. Thus, even if the inevitable increment due to practice were disregarded, the loss due to operation was quite apparent, indicating that foresight is mediated, at least in part, through the frontal lobes.

These results, of course, left in abeyance the important question as to whether the results were permanent or transient. Fortunately, eight years after the operations were performed there were still some of the same patients available for re-examination at Rockland Hospital, N. Y. The work was done and reported by Dr. Aaron Smith. The subjects were 27 operated patients and 23 controls, and the same four tests used in the New York Brain Study eight years previously were reapplied. Since the effects of aging could not be equated for the control and experimental groups, we will disregard the control data for the present.

The four factors of length of interval, site of operation, age at operation, and the particular psychological measure employed were identified as determining the amount of change in mental functioning. Smith offers this comment: "Although all four instruments (Porteus Maze, Homograph, Weigl, and Wechsler-Bellevue Adult Intelligence Form I) showed differences between initial and long-term postoperative effects, the changes in the Porteus Maze scores were unexpectedly definitive and illustrate the importance of the last factor, the nature of the measure." This quotation explains the title of Smith's paper.

For some reason not clear to the present writer, two preoperative Maze examinations were given, ostensibly to measure practice effects, but if so, nothing was done about the demonstration, for the comparison was made, not between the last Maze score just before the operation, but with the earlier, much lower original testing. Hence, the first postoperative test was actually the third Maze application and the eight-year postoperative was the fourth of the series. It was quite obvious that practice effects should be very operant. It will be remembered that Porteus and Peters showed that a group of criminals registered a practice gain of 1.6 years of test age after an average interval of time of 4.7 years. Smith, however, elected to follow the Brain Study procedure and contrasted the results of the latest postoperative examination with the *first* preoperative score instead of with the second preoperative test level, which had been raised through practice. This is analogous with recording a man's position twice while climbing a ladder and deciding that the distance he fell after slipping was to be measured from his first position when he was only part of the way up, instead of from the higher level from which he fell.

Smith's cases were divided into two groups according to site of operation, superior (Brodmann areas 9, part of 10, 8, and 32) and inferior (11, 10, and Walker's 13). His figures showed a mean loss for 17 subjects, who underwent the superior operation, of 3.88 years, while 10 orbital patients lost only .2 of a year. Age of subjects was not a crucial factor in the superior operation. Three older orbital patients lost 2.17 years after eight years.

But when the comparisons are made between the *second* pre-operative and the long-term postoperative testings, the situation is quite different. Porteus and Diamond (1962) analysed Smith's data in this way and found that the deficits indicated by Maze re-examinations were increased in every category. They amounted to 4.74 years for the superior operation group and to 3.10 years for the orbital patients. When classified by age, the younger group, averaging 42 years of age, showed a major postoperative deficit, viz. 4.96 years, while the three older patients who underwent the orbital operation suffered the greatest loss, namely 5.33 years, equivalent to a decrement of 38 TQ points. This much at least seems certain—that patients left in hospital after eight years and therefore likely to represent the more unsuccessful cases exhibit increasingly serious Maze Test deficits, but the amount of loss varies in individual cases.

Since the number of older patients is small, the question as to how much the loss should be ascribed to aging is still not certain. It is possible that the Maze is particularly sensitive to the mental effects of senility. On this point we can offer strongly opposed evidence derived from the examination of other elderly groups.

There have been two recent studies that report the effects of aging on Maze performance. Loranger and Misiak (1960) examined 50 women over 70 years of age resident in eight different homes for the aged, subjects being selected on the basis of absence of neurological, opthalmological, psychiatric symptoms, or other serious illness. The tests used were the Porteus Maze, the Digit-Symbol from the Wechsler Adult Scale, the Primary Abilities Reasoning Test, the Raven Matrices, and the Wisconsin Card Sorting.

Results indicate the greater resistance of Maze Test performance to the inroads of old age. The authors report:

The Porteus Maze yielded a broad range of scores, discriminating better among the elderly subjects than any of the other tests. Although half of the subjects have mental ages below 10 years, 16 per cent have mental ages of 15 years or better . . . On all tests there was a considerable range of scores, but almost none of the aged performed as well as the average adolescent and young adult, except on the Porteus Maze.

It is also interesting to note that on the Raven Progressive Matrices the average was about that of the normal eight-year child, or two years below the Maze mean. Evidently the Maze is less difficult or otherwise better suited for elderly subjects, but unless the general standardization of the test supports the conclusion, it would be hazardous to assume that the higher mean score indicates that the Maze is generally too easy. In the present writer's view, the test does not get progressively easier with age as does, for example, the Mare and Foal Test, which Southwest American Indian tribes also found very easy (Havighurst and Hilkevitch, 1944) when scored on speed. All the evidence available indicates that a Maze score of 14 years is about average for adults. Weisenberg, Roe, and McBride (1936) note that in their study of adults the average for the Maze was 14.1 years, or 6 months below their Stanford-Binet level.

On the evidence at hand, I would conclude that the Maze distribution was what might be expected in the Loranger-Misiak study and that the incidence of 16 per cent of high scores does not indicate a generally easy standardization. It could mean that the habit of considering alternatives and making prudent decisions is required more consistently of the aged but is more irregularly differentiated among the old than among the adolescent. It is a natural expectation that the ability that is used or practised most frequently will remain better preserved. In other words, personality traits "hold" well, so that the cautious, deliberate individual is more likely to remain so to the end of his chapter, rather than to change radically in the type of his reactions. Foresight is more urgently needed in maturity than in youth, though of course some declines of ability in old age are inescapable.

That the situation as regards aged males is similar to that of females has been shown in a paper by Milton Jensen (1961). His subjects were men domiciled at a Veterans' Administration Center and represented what he called a biased sampling of the community in general. Sixty per cent had lived in rural communities,

6 per cent were foreign-born, 98 per cent had been in unskilled and semiskilled vocations, 43 per cent had never married. They were not "unintelligent," 670 of the inmates being about the 50 percentile on the Wesman Personnel Test for Industry, their scores coinciding closely with industrial norms.

From these scores Jensen theorizes that "intellectual decline in populations such as ours is not a product of aging *per se.*" He also believes that sensory and motor impairments cause unwarranted assumptions as to cortical decline, that the old frequently simulate mental ineptness, and that "senescence in man is a very complex and individualistic process"—in short, that the years of a man's life are certainly not in direct relation to his level of abilities. Certainly common observation supports this final conclusion. Jensen's graph for Porteus Maze scores shows little change with age, whereas the curve for verbal IQ's shows a steady decline from age 46 to 66 years.

He makes one very significant observation: "Those who completed less than eight grades (of schooling) evidence the same general decrease in score with advancing age that was shown on the verbal tests. With more than eight grades of schooling the trend is reversed. As age increases, so does Porteus test score." In other terms, the dull grow duller with age but the smart at least hold their own longer. "Our 11 subjects, 70 years of age and older," he says, "actually averaged higher (I.Q. 123.1) on the Porteus than did any other age group." Obviously, in this sample, long survival correlated with level of planfulness. It may well be that intelligent anticipation helps to determine longevity. In other words, it takes sustained mental alertness to remain alive. The results of these two studies suggest that the declines in Maze scores after operation found by Smith are not substantially due to age deterioration.

Since the purpose of this book is not so much the presentation of detailed results of the applications of the Maze Test, but rather the discussion of the larger psychological problems to the understanding of which it has contributed, it seems pertinent to attempt a further historical summary of psychosurgical findings. In 1955 an article in the *British Journal of Medical Psychology* (Porteus, 1955) stressed the confusion of counsels attendant upon consideration of the various surgical insults to the frontal lobes. We may, therefore, list some of the evidence that seems relevant to the problem of localization of brain functions, particularly those ascribed to the frontal lobes.

The above-mentioned article pointed out that the famous experimental work of Fulton and Jacobsen (1935) with the two chimpanzees Becky and Lucy resulted, after brain operation, in marked diminution of manifest anxiety and frustration. This was in agreement with the outcome of Moniz's pioneer efforts to relieve psychotic symptoms in human subjects through frontal operations. These were followed by the full development of the lobotomy program of Freeman and Watts (1942) in the United States. But Jacobsen's study also foreshadowed another significant finding—namely, that frontal lobe surgery brought about an observable loss in planning capacity. Becky and Lucy showed distinct impairment as regards their ability to do the stick-and-double-platform test unless the planning steps were reduced to the simplest levels of gradations of difficulty.

Though in lobotomy patients the loss of foresight and ability for prehearsal of solutions seemed secondary to the practical gains in alleviation of anxiety and social concern, it was outstanding enough for Freeman and Watts to remark that "substantially, the frontal lobes add foresight and insight"; and for Wilder Penfield (1950) to declare unequivocally with regard to the lobotomized patient: "The operation which amputates both frontal lobes does not produce loss of memory, because other parts of the cortex are used for the recording of memory; and no interference is produced with sensory perception nor with motor control, for a similar reason. *But the luckless individual does forfeit capacity for planned initiative.*" (Italics mine.)

In view of Landis's pronouncement of no consistent changes in Binet or Wechsler-Bellevue scores and a similar absence of alteration in continuous problem-solving, word association, memory, or Rorschach performance, there is no need to recite this experience again except to say that the centers for mediating these important abilities must be looked for elsewhere than in the frontal lobes, unwelcome though this conclusion may be to the believers in the total supremacy of this supposedly distinctive human development.

Smith's eight-year follow-up study and its final analysis proves conclusively that the immediate or short-term results of frontal brain injury are by no means the most significant. Deferred effects are also to be reckoned with; but in the meantime memory, association, etc., are carried on by other parts of the brain.

An alternative explanation is that already well-integrated mental functions continue as it were on their own momentum, independent of the intactness of the brain structures through which they were initially acquired. It is true that an early observation (Porteus and Peters, 1947) indicated that in 21 per cent of lobotomy patients there was a gain in postoperative performance followed by a subsequent loss. This phenomenon can hardly be considered evidence for equipotentiality of brain area functions, but rather the reverse. It merely indicates that the deterioration that follows psychosurgery is in some cases gradual rather than immediate. In terms of everyday behavior or of personality, we may say that some individuals, probably on the basis of long-established habits, may continue for a time to be cautious and deliberative in their style of response. Only later are prudential attitudes forgotten and the tendency to be less concerned with the future asserts itself. The situation is well illustrated in some individuals operated upon for intractable pain. Their statement is that they still feel the pain, but it no longer bothers them. It takes time for the memory of constant discomfort to fade and for them to realize that it has left them. Similarly, caution, whether it be in threading a maze design or crossing a busy highway, is still a habit, and habits are not easily broken, even after lobotomy.

We are still, however, confronted by some puzzling facts. One is that the same or approximately the same amount of brain damage occurring in the same site results in very uneven effects. Maze Test losses in identical operations differ in degree from relatively large amounts of test age to much less significant deficits and, in about 20 per cent of cases, to no loss at all. In many of these cases of lesser loss or even postoperative gain, the explanation might well be that psychosurgery, having alleviated some of the psychotic or neurotic attitudes of some patients, enables them to make a better showing in the testing situation. In other words, the Maze represents a task or job, and the removal of various distracting factors allows of more competent or representative performance.[2]

The relation of social improvement to increased Maze scores was demonstrated in the Porteus-Peters (1947) study, in which the "much improved" group showed a more consistent rate of practice gain in the Maze than was registered by the "moderately improved"; and they in turn were decidedly superior to the unimproved. The

2 This viewpoint has been taken from time to time by Hebb.

same tendency was noted in the patients of Columbia-Greystone Project I.

Some had an initial loss in the Maze followed by recovery in a second test at three months, followed by a further gain at a later retesting. Psychiatrists independently selected six subjects who showed the greatest social improvement. Five out of these six belonged in the first-named group who best exhibited the loss-regain Maze pattern; the sixth individual was not rated by the psychiatrists as among the most socially improved but was within a year discharged from the hospital. His successive scores were 11, 9, 11.5, 15, and 13 years. But we are still faced with the fact that other patients who had suffered the same surgical and hospital treatment registered different changes in regard to social adaptation.

On the other hand, it seems undeniable that the pattern of test behavior tends to be related to the generalized pattern of brain damage. For example, Landis, Zubin, and Mettler (1950) reported: "The number of transient changes was greatest near the primary motor area (greatest in cases of ablation of Areas 6 and 8) and decreased in a regular fashion as one moved forward from Area 6 to Area 11—from agranular to granular cortex." Freeman has also remarked that for every millimeter encroached upon by the neurosurgeon's instrument posterior to the coronal suture, the greater the mental change effected.

These observations may be interpreted in two ways: either in relation to the cortical area affected or in terms of interference with the frontothalamic "trunk lines" of communication between cortex, midbrain, brain stem, and the general motor-sensory system. Since lobotomy also interferes with the cingulate-thalamic complex, or what MacLean (1949) calls the visceral brain, this may account for the emotional deadening or "bleaching affect" that follows the operation and its influence on intractable pain.

Since the remedial results of topectomy or ablation of frontal lobe areas seem to be minimal as compared with lobotomy, it would appear that while interference with neural corticothalamic pathways has definite effects, the type of mediation assumed by specific cortical areas is much more certain.

One suggestion by Ritchie Russell (1948), the well-known British neurosurgeon, is worthy of special attention. He stresses the importance during the learning period in childhood of the frontal areas but suggests "that, as age advances, the frontal lobe mechanisms provide an asset of diminishing importance, but this factor must vary enormously from person to person." He believes that the pattern of responses in behavior are mediated in the dominant left temporoparietal area. One observation on Maze Test performance in lobotomized patients (since there is so little firm evidence) may be cited as supporting this theory of a shift in localization. The operated individual often has little difficulty in dealing with the simpler maze designs in which the alternative courses are palinly evident; hence, such simple problems are probably solved on a temporoparietat basis. When, with added complexity of the Maze design, difficult choices are presented, the frontal lobes come into play. If these areas or their neural connections are affected by operation, the individual soon reaches the limit of his ability. The writer has previously described this change in type of performance as "dramatic."

Almost suddenly, with the introduction of greater complexity—usually at about years eleven and above—the subject seems to relax all vigilance, with errors, often repetitive, following in quick succession. Sometimes readjustment after this initial floundering takes place, but is apparently difficult. The change in the approach to the tests seems sometimes dramatic. From an unhurried, easily confident individual, the subject suddenly changes to an unforeseeing, stupid, almost compulsive type of person.

This experience would appear to support Ritchie Russell's theory of dual, possibly multilocal, mediation of functions. Under such a system, problems involving decision-making on the simpler perceptual level—or on what I have called short-term foresight, where all the factors necessary for solution are apparent—can be solved through the activity of the temporoparietal structures. But as soon as wider concepts are involved, the formulation of which depends upon reasoning and inference, then the fontal lobe areas come into play; in military parlance, decisions must be made at the level of higher command. This hypothesis, it will be seen, reverses the role assigned to the cerebral regions by Russell. It would relate learning to the temporoparietal areas and integration or conceptualization to the prefrontal cortex. This would accord better with the results of the Columbia-Greystone findings of no change in learning test after frontal operations, but a decided loss in planned initiative or "planfulness." Phylogenetically, this would assign priority of development to the temporoparietal regions, and support the theory that the frontal lobes are the latest addition to brain architecture. Apparently, man is the only animal that projects his anxieties far into the future, and this he does through an overdeveloped forebrain. We may even speculate that overgrowth and functioning of the frontal lobes may represent one of those specializations that have written *finis* to the evolutionary progress of other animal species. One of the problems of our race is to find the happy medium between laissez faire indifference and eroding anxiety.

But if this theory of brain organization of functions has any validity, then psychosurgery in the temporoparietal region should result in very decided Maze impairment, with a lesser effect as regards memory and learning. On this point there is one piece of positive evidence.

Brown, French, Ogle, and Jahnson (1956) reported the results of surgery on the temporal lobe to bring about relief of the type of epilepsy characterized by psychomotor seizures. Their full report can be drawn upon here only with regard to the test results. Besides the Wechsler-Bellevue and the Maze, tests "whose customary use is for the detection of intellectual deficit due to organic brain damage" were administered. They included the Bender-Gestalt, Weigl, Graham-Kendall Memory, Hunt-Minnesota Test for organic brain damage, and Shipley-Hartford Scale. The mental examiner's overall impressions for individual patients included the notation "no deficit" in most patients. On the other hand, postoperative scores in the Porteus Maze showed an average decrease of 24 test quotient points, a drastic decline. The investigators' summary reads:

Neither pre- nor post-operatively did these patients consistently give test evidence of the kinds of intellectual deficit traditionally associated with organic brain damage. Porteus Maze Test results suggest that temporal lobectomy may result in impaired vigilance and foresight and that this impairment may be larger than the similar impairment which has been found to follow frontal lobe psychosurgery.

If the type of simpler, more fundamental planning is mediated in the temporal lobes, then such marked deficits could be expected.

Thus what evidence is available points toward a wide interregional control of Maze-tested functions rather than through a narrowly localized neural mechanism. The commonsense conclusion seems to be that several brain centers are involved in Maze performance, among them being the reticular formation in the brain stem. For example, Carney Landis (1951) has this comment to offer as regards the type of mental alertness most certainly needed in Maze threading: "By vigilance we mean the opposite of sleepiness; that is, a state of wakefulness. These patients during the first post-operative month (most, but not all of them) showed a marked decrease in vigilance; that is, they were somewhat 'dopey', acting as if they were a little sleepy." Apparently the reticular formation is critically involved in a state of mental alertness.

My own experience leads me to believe that something more than being wide-awake is needed for success. Patients will sometimes recognize the fact that they have previously entered a certain blind alley, but do not seem to be able to inhibit the wrong action. It did not seem to the examiner that the subject had become sleepy, causing deterioration of effort, but rather that an inexperienced pilot had taken over control of the mental machine. Possibly "control" is hardly the word to apply to brain organization. There must be a "chain of command"; otherwise, there would be utter confusion. A chain of command implies levels of responsibility, and this would seem to be inherent in Russell's formulation.

Certainly in the learning process we see many examples of differing levels of integration, so that it would not be at all unreasonable to suggest that one area of the brain could be responsible for solution of a very simple maze, while other levels or areas direct more complex tasks. I would suggest, therefore, a modification of Wilder Penfield's (1950) theory of a "headquarters switchboard" in the brain, to the extent of postulating several switchboards at different levels, the question of which is the headquarters or command center being determined differently for different individuals in accordance with their experience. If, for example, the prefrontal cortex is the decisive level, it can come into play only if the individual has formed the habit of substituting or deferring simple perceptual presentations for more highly integrated conceptual formulations. In the language of aviation, the co-pilot can fly the plane for most of the time, but in any threatened emergency the captain takes over. Thus it will accord with Penfield's conception of the *modus operandi* of the "master motor area" in the upper brain stem. To which he adds: "But it can only function properly by the simultaneous employment of the various areas of the cortex, each contributing to a different aspect of mental activity."

Allowing for the fact that psychologists did not at once mobilize coordinated effort for the study of psychosurgery data and considering that individuals available for investigation were somewhat unsuitable for experimentation by reason of abnormal mental condition, the above statement seems at this stage of human knowledge to sum up most of the lessons that have been learned from the employment of the Maze Test in psychosurgical problems. Research was particularly handicapped when its subjects were already mentally damaged. Pre-existing psychotic conditions contributed to obscuring the picture.

It must be admitted that the rationale of leucotomy or lobotomy seemed to be far-fetched. Those who approved the surgical approach could, of course, point to the fact that operations, even amputations of other parts of the organism, are accepted medical practice. These procedures are not only justifiable but necessary. The difficulty seemed to lie in the fact that brain operations were not being undertaken for physical reasons—e.g., the removal of a brain tumor, pallidectomy, etc.—but to change a mental state. But when it was demonstrated that mental behavior and personality could be altered by the use of the neurosurgeon's leucotome, a whole new area of therapeutic activity was opened up for exploration. Unfortunately, enthusiasm for the operation grew so quickly that exploration soon changed to exploitation. Fundamentally, the use of ataractic drugs was based on the same general purpose—namely, to effect by physiological means changes in the functioning of brain areas. The main difference between psychopharmacology and psychosurgery was that the results of the latter were physically irreversible, whereas the effect of the drugs after a time wore off.

The advent of psychosurgery soon involved its proponents in a climate of rather bitter controversy. Some practising psychologists and psychiatrists, particularly those psychoanalytically oriented, were so convinced of the psychogenic origin of mental disorders that they rejected offhand the evidence that damage to the brain's organic functioning could possibly bring about striking therapeutic changes in the personalities of patients. They were fully aware of the patience and labor involved in the application of Freudian methods and theories to individual mental problems. The neurosurgeon threatened not only to mute their thunder, but to steal from them all the drama of recovery. If the effects of repressed sex traumas, for example, could be erased by eliciting submerged experiences, it seemed to them most bizarre that deliberate injury to the frontal lobes of the brain could possibly cut the Gordian knots of frustration, anxiety, paranoia, unreason, or other abnormal states. But bizarre or not, there was undeniable evidence that in many cases psychosurgery was of benefit, and in a most dramatic fashion. In any case, medically speaking, the psychoanalyst's couch and the surgeon's operating table represented the East and the West of the practice of medicine.

Meanwhile, in spite of bitter questioning and disbelief, the new procedures became increasingly popular, so much so that psychosurgery exceeded its proper bounds. The discovery that frontal surgery could be undertaken with such apparently minor threats to a patient's intellectual functions was so intriguing that brain operations were undertaken for a great variety of mental troubles— constant headaches, deep-seated feelings of inferiority, obsessive fears, chronic euphoria, neurotic depressions, even homosexuality. In some instances the endings were sufficiently happy to justify the means, but the prescription was indeed drastic. Perhaps the greatest contribution of the Maze Test was its demonstration that there was another side to the ledger in which losses might be entered to balance the gains. The fact that it seemed to be the only test in general use that consistently showed deficits in score after operation might have served as a brake on the therapeutic wagon except that the smoother, easier slopes of the tranquilizing drugs intervened to make the brakes not nearly as necessary. True, the same test indicated that in the case of drugs there was also loss as well as profit, so that its lessons might still be needed to slow down the pace of psychopharmacology. But in this latter case, there was no bloodletting as regards patients and hence less concern.

One of the hindrances to an adequate assessment of the results of psychosurgery has been the fact that no data have been available as to patients' premorbid levels of intelligence. Many subjects of this type of research are chronic cases resident in mental hospitals for many years. It is, of course, possible to give such patients preoperative examinations, but this may represent their original level less the deficits that have occurred because of their psychoses. The amount of deterioration, of course, differs according to the individual. It would be of exceptional interest and value if there were available for investigation a group of normal or at least nearnormal cases. The only comparable patients are those who underwent surgery for the relief of intractable pain, but it would be difficult indeed to find a sufficient number of these. Fortunately, one psychiatrist, Dr. Macdonald Tow (1954) of Oxford University Hospital, was sufficiently convinced of the importance of the project to undertake the investigation of 50 cases suffering from what he called "mild encapsulated neurotic illnesses, which did not in any way affect the whole person." These psychosurgical subjects represented the nearest approach to normality that could possibly be achieved.

By the most assiduous efforts, Dr. Tow examined the records of hundreds of patients, and by "sorting and sieving" segregated about 150 individuals who appeared the most normal of those available for clinical examination. From these he selected 50 whom he felt to be definitely normal. The examination of these cases necessitated about three years' travel to mental hospitals and neurological units in the south of England. Personally, I am convinced that no one could now duplicate Macdonald Tow's cases, and they must, therefore, remain a unique group. The only work comparable as regards selective study was that of Rylander in Sweden.

Because of Tow's modifications in method of application of the Maze Test, it will be useful to quote his account in some detail: [3]

Porteus Mazes were used in a modified way designed specially for this work and based upon the writer's previous extensive experience with the test sheets on frontal subjects. Years 6, 7, 8, 9, 10, 12 and 14 were given; the subject told to trace his way from the entrance S, and without lifting his pencil from the sheet to find his way through and out by the shortest possible route. The mazes were explained by analogy with garden mazes. He was to regard the lines as walls which could not be crossed. Similarly, if he went down a blind alley, he would have to retrace his steps by tracing a line back with the pencil, just as if he had to walk back. One sheet of each number, making seven in all, was presented to the subject and he was allowed to continue tracing in this fashion until he found his way out. If he lifted his pencil from the sheet, he was immediately told to put it back and not to do so again. He was not permitted to trace his way ahead with his pencil or finger in the air. He was told also not to draw over his previous lines (as earlier experiences had shown that subjects tended to do this purposely, apparently to try to cover up their mistakes). The subject had to draw a separate and distinct line if he wanted to retrace his steps, so that a loop was formed in the blind alley. Thus a continuous line was formed from the beginning to the end in each maze, giving a permanent record of his actual activity. He was timed from beginning to end of each problem.

The above method, as thus described, differs from the standard method of application. In this, the examiner allows the subject to

[3] Tow's book is out of print. The author himself extracted and forwarded the quoted matter that appears in this chapter.

enter a blind alley and proceed only until he realizes his error. At that point an unsuccessful trial is recorded, the test sheet is withdrawn, and a new sheet substituted. He is allowed the allotted number of necessary trials: two in each year level from 6 to 11 inclusive, four in the 12-, 14-, and adult-year levels.

The advantage of Tow's method, also adopted by Foulds (see Chapter 4), is that the whole process can be easily timed as well as the individual tests. Allowing the subject to retrace his steps possibly draws less attention to the gravity of an error since self-correction is allowed. In the standard application the intervention of the examiner and the substitution of a new sheet serves to emphasize the mistake. We continue to quote Tow's method and his interesting results:

> *Scoring*—Inspection of the post-operative sheets showed that the amount of retracing was considerably greater than before operation. More blind alleys had been entered, some of them twice and three times. Such repeated attempts, by themselves, increase the time taken; but in addition to this measure, the sheets have been marked according to the number of times a blind alley is entered. If a wrong path is entered once, it is marked as a grade I error. Such an error is recognized by one loop within this blind alley. If a wrong pathway is traversed twice, it is marked as a grade II error. If a wrong pathway is entered three or more times, it is marked as a grade III error.

Though this modified method yields very interesting results, the drawback is that we have no data on normal subjects to use in comparison. While preoperative and postoperative tests were given, it is not possible to give the results in terms of difference in test ages before and after operation.

Tow's results show a decided loss postoperatively, in spite of the fact that the second or postoperative application would be affected by practice. This practice effect, as previously pointed out, is not necessarily due to any conscious memory of the traps to be avoided but rather to a different mental set toward the maze problem, which is no longer a novel experience. The subject is now more fully aware of the fact that any lapse in attention may result in an unexpected error. His second experience is attended with the realization that constant vigilance must be exercised to avoid error. Macdonald Tow notes,

> . . . a fairly general increase in grade I errors (Table 3). In many subjects there is also a very large increase in the number of grade II and grade III errors. The mean number of grade I errors before operation is 5.1 (S.D. 4.5), after

operation 7.3 (S.D. 5.0), approximately half as many again. The mean of grade II before is 0.2 (S.D. 0.6), and after 1.4 (S.D. 1.9), a sevenfold increase. Before operation, grade III errors do not occur; after operation they occur in a total of 8 problems.

It is this perseverative tendency to err at the same point that impresses the author of the study. As a comment on his excerpt from his book Tow writes: "I think clinically this is the main, striking behavior, going down alleys where they can *see* they've been before and failed."

The above finding has been reported for the application of the Maze after operation by the standard method. Petrie (1952) stated:

"A significant difference in the number of double mistakes (entering the same blind alley twice) made by the (operated) group as a whole, both at the three- and nine-months investigation. The patients tended to make the same mistake repeatedly after the operation, which did not happen before the operation, suggesting a loss of ability to learn from errors."

Our first report on the mental effects of lobotomy (Porteus and Kepner, 1944) commented as follows on the occurrence of these repetitive errors: "In our case reports reference has been made to the tendency of lobotomized cases to repeat identical errors often in successive trials on the Maze." We then presented a table showing the frequency of this feature. One hundred normal cases, out of a total of 238 blind alley entrances, made 10 repeated errors, or 6.7 per cent. The same number of delinquents out of 408 such errors made 33 repetitions, or 8.1 per cent. Fifty mental defectives totalled 302 errors and repeated 37, or 12.25 per cent. But 18 lobotomy patients made 109 errors, with 32 repetitions, or 29.4 per cent.

Three years later another tabulation of repeated errors was made (Porteus and Peters, 1947) in connection with the summing up of the results of 55 standard lobotomies that Dr. Ralph Cloward had carried out. Out of 50 adult prisoners examined as controls, only four made two or more repeated errors, or 8 per cent. But of 62 patients given postlobotomy tests, 23 or 37 per cent made two or more identical blind alley entrances. When 55 of these were re-examined, the percentage of repetition of error was still 34.5 per cent. Among 46 who were given a third postlobotomy test, there were 32.6 per cent who repeated identical errors. Hence, even with the advantage of increased practice, the inability to profit by previous experience was still constant and marked.

Using Tow's table, I have counted the number who made such repetitive errors and found them to number five, or 13.8 per cent, before operation and eighteen, or 50 per cent, after operation. One of his patients, who made no repetitive errors preoperatively, had eight such errors postoperatively. Three, or 8.5 per cent, entered the same blind alley three or more times. The individual with eight grade II errors actually made four grade III errors, showing most extraordinarily stereotyped wrong choices. In my experience, I met with two cases (Nos. 1 and 3, cited in "Mental Changes After Bilateral Prefrontal Lobotomy," 1944), where I commented on their apparent inability to profit by mistakes or to readjust methods after failure.

Macdonald Tow, in his book, sums up his experience as follows: "The mazes very clearly bring out a severe defect in the frontal subject. There is a moderate increase in time taken, which is statistically significant. There is a great increase in the incidence of gross errors in performance. This increase in errors is associated with an increase in time."

SUMMARY

Psychosurgical operations, despite their seemingly bizarre rationale, resulted in relief of psychotic symptoms in a significant percentage of cases. To psychologists the most surprising finding was that so-called general intelligence and most performance tests were slightly or ambiguously sensitive to most serious surgical brain damage.

The early book of the writer in this field is described, and the deficits in the Maze are shown to be in strong contrast to the results with other tests. Practice gains in repeated applications to non-operated Ss are very marked, and this throws into strong relief the deficits that actually occur in operated cases. The failure of investigators to take into account the effects of practice on the Maze have misled them into the belief that losses after operation were transient. This was the conclusion reached by the Columbia-Greystone investigators. Since the whole subject of psychosurgery threatens to be a closed chapter in medicopsychological history, the results are worth summarizing again, particularly the almost unique situation as regards Maze Test deficits. If both W-B and Maze changes after operation had been reported in test quotient points, a fairer statement of comparative sensitivity could have been made.

Aaron Smith's follow-up study of former New York Brain Study subjects after an eight-year interval shows that deficits not only are not transient, but also actually increase in size. That this greater deterioration in Maze tested abilities is not due to the aging factor is shown by two studies of the test reactions of elderly people, one by Loranger and Misiak for elderly women, the other by Jensen for old men. Both indicate that the Maze Test is singularly resistant to the declines attendant upon old age.

When Smith's data are considered from the standpoint of the Maze examination immediately prior to operation, all deficits regardless of the site of operation are much more marked. Reasons for these deferred consequences are discussed. The social or personality changes that occur necessitate a restatement of the type of improvement following operation, which appears to affect not social efficiency generally, but socializing that is passive rather than dynamic in nature. (This point is discussed in a later chapter.)

The effect of Columbia-Greystone findings on theories of brain localization is set forth, especially multilocal or at least dual control of Maze Test responses. Temporoparietal operations offer evidence on this subject.

The fact that practically all psychosurgical patients are psychotics complicates the problem of properly assessing mental changes after operation. It would obviously add to the value of the experiment if a group of individuals, operated on for reasons other than that they were psychotic, could be studied. Macdonald Tow in England analysed many hundreds of records and segregated 34 Ss who could be considered of normal status. He used a modified Maze Test application, allowing S to retrace his course after entering a blind alley by looping back and continuing his maze threading until the exit was reached. The tendency to enter blind alleys increased greatly after operation as did also the re-entering of the same blind alley on a second trial. These perseverative errors seem to be a feature of postoperative behavior, as this tendency has been noted by Petrie with neurotic operatees, and by Porteus and Peters.

CHAPTER FOUR

Drugs, Vitamins, and the Mentally Abnormal

It may seem somewhat surprising that a scale of graduated mazes, put forward originally as a test to improve the diagnosis of mental defect by including measures of practical intelligence along with verbal abilities, has proceeded slowly but steadily beyond that purpose, further and further into the field of abnormal psychology. That progression now not only includes the reactions of socially maladjusted delinquents and criminals, but also, as we shall see later, extends quite logically into the investigation of primitive mentality. Delay in making these further applications of the Maze Test was due in large part to differences in backgrounds, training, and viewpoints of workers involved in the various disciplines concerned. Fortunately, the tendency of some anthropologists, sociologists, and psychiatrists to regard the psychologist as an intruder seems to be rapidly declining.

More particularly is this the case as regards the field of abnormal psychology, where the worker with psychological training works with medical men with traditionally better grounding than he possesses in the treatment of mental disorders. But here the boundaries of knowledge and practice are not very definitely drawn, particularly in many conditions now generally recognized as psychosomatic in reference and origin. Here the psychologist may be admitted as a junior partner in the curative or alleviatory process. His minor role is, I believe, not so much founded on inferior knowledge of individual psychology, but on the important fact of the great professional prestige of the medically trained. As far as the patient is concerned, all healing is to some degree faith-healing, and his confidence in the practitioner is of considerable importance. Apparently there are enough people who are afraid of doctors to provide livings for many psychologists in private practice.

But there is one area where the psychologist is admitted without question as a major participant. The medical man has come to realize that psychological tools are essential to the appraisal of the results of some of his specific approaches, particularly in the measurement or demonstration of therapeutic changes. The key role played by the Porteus Maze Test has already been amply demonstrated in the case of psychosurgery. But latterly the use of tranquilizing drugs, now an essential item in the doctor's pharmaceutical handbag, demands similar scientific appraisal.

Because the Maze Test samples a portion of the patient's behavior that lies outside merely verbal responses, medical researchers are rapidly growing more percipient of the fact that the test may offer a ray of illumination in evaluation of the total personality, an area that is unfortunately dim. Thus they are beginning to ask that psychological examining should proceed further than the application of a Wechsler-Bellevue or a Binet Scale. The proof of this statement is to be found in the increasing number of hospital and clinic studies in which medical men collaborate with psychologists in research and publication.

Because the doctor rarely is aware that an instrument such as the Rorschach Test, through its dependence on verbal responses, covers a limited section of the psychological field, he appears rather too trustfully to accept its verdicts in the differential diagnosis of neuroses and psychoses. Rorschach validation badly needs critical research.

As regards the Maze, I do not think it too presumptuous to predict that, while it can be expected to do better than hold its own in the educational clinic, it will find increasing use in mental hospitals and psychiatric centers, and may even be found valuable in out-patient groups where psychosomatic features are commonly met with.

As has already been set forth, the present writer, from 1943 onward, had played a part in the measurement of the effects of frontal lobe brain operations, and was one of the first to show that lobotomy brought about objectively demonstrable mental deficits. Thus a clear understanding was finally achieved that permanent losses followed a number of surgical interventions, including frontal topectomies as well as lobotomies. In a considerable proportion of cases, social improvement also was associated with this psychosurgery; about one-third of the patients were greatly improved to the extent of return to community life, while a similar number achieved a marked increase of adjustability within the mental hospitals to which they had been committed.

From this use of the Maze Test to demonstrate mental deficits that helped to counterbalance social gains, it was an obvious step to the consideration of the mental effects of medication by the new tranquilizing drugs that, except in rare cases, displaced psychosurgery, just when the latter threatened to become almost standard mental hospital practice. There was soon abundant evidence of the drugs' remarkable therapeutic values and, if the same results could be achieved painlessly, why not use the simpler, if less dramatic methods of cure or alleviation of psychotic symptoms?

I must confess that I began the work of applying the Porteus Maze before and after routine tranquilizing medication with an expectation opposite to what really occurred. There seemed to be evidence from several directions that the Maze was apparently one of the best measures of social adjustments, and the steady administration of a drug such as chlorpromazine was reported in certain cases to work marvels in social rehabilitation. The evidence of mental hospital administrators, psychiatrists, nurses, and psychiatric aides agreed upon this point. Surely, if as seemed certain, the Maze was a valid measure of social adaptability, this improvement should be reflected in better test performance so that higher Maze scores could be expected to match the better social adjustment.

True, the reverse relationship had been shown in psychosurgical cases. In these the operation had been succeeded not by a rise, but by a decline in test scores. As the deviser of the mental measure in question, I should have been satisfied with the declaration of some of the most competent clinical psychologists of the day that these deficits were merely transient—in short, that the losses were recoverable. Moreover, these experts seemed pleased to be able to demonstrate that there was a relation between the rate of recovery and the degree of rapidity of social rehabilitation.[1]

But unfortunately, I knew too much about the practice effects of repetition of the test to feel satisfied about the transiency of the deficits. I therefore found myself arguing during the 1951 Psychosurgery Conference in New York for the view that postoperative declines, even though they told against the Maze Test as an index

---

[1] See: *Selective Partial Ablation of the Frontal Cortex*, p. 198 ff.

of one type of social adjustment, was permanent and probably greater than the figures appeared to show.

The fact that the therapy in question involved serious injuries to the forebrain probably misled me into believing that the whole relationship constituted a special case. But the situation as regards the mental effects of chlorpromazine stood differently. Brain injury of a most drastic nature was one thing, the daily ingestion of a drug was another. There was little ground for any other expectation than that the change in physiological state induced by the drug would have a favorable effect on Maze performance, quite different from what might be expected to follow extensive brain damage. There was also the possibility, at that time not proved, that the drugs might have a selective effect on subcortical structures such as the hypothalamus and also the reticular formation in the midbrain that seemed to control wakefulness.

The first step in this research, undertaken, like the lobotomy enquiry, at the State Hospital at Kaneohe (about 13 miles from Honolulu) was to verify the nature and degree of the social changes (Porteus, 1957b). The plan was to select two "closed" wards, each housing about 80 male patients, and in a double-blind procedure administer the drug to all patients in one ward and placebos to the inmates of the other. The only information given to patients was that the new medicine would be very good for them, and the psychiatric aides were not told which pilule contained the drug and which the placebo. Both, of course, looked exactly alike.

Undoubtedly, the better plan would have been to have made a random selection of patients from among the populations of both wards, but there were several circumstances that would have militated against the success of this procedure. The first was that, in common with most state hospitals, the staff was inadequate, two psychiatric aides being allotted on day shift to each ward, or a quota of 40 patients per aide. The plan of administering all drugs in one ward and all placebos in the other made for much easier control of medication.

A rating scale of ward behavior had then to be devised and, since neither nurses nor psychiatrists were available for special ward duty, the application of the scale had to be suited to the level of understanding of the psychiatric aides in charge. These were given special training first in rating each other and later selected patients, the former arrangement being necessary to show them that most categories of traits represented a wide normal range. Only hallucinations and delusions belonged entirely in the abnormal behavior exhibited by mental hospital patients, the other descriptive categories differing from normality only in degree. To illustrate this point further, the experimenter gave a self-rating, showing that an absolutely clean record as regards unfavorable traits was unrealistic. Their own self-ratings were also useful in obtaining a proper range of judgments; otherwise the tendency was to give extreme ratings to many patients simply because they were confined to a hospital.

It was found that when aides were asked to justify their individual ratings, the men in charge of H ward were more discriminating, so it was determined that theirs should be, unknown to them, the experimental ward. In a short time, owing to the appearance of common symptoms of drowsiness or other easily observable changes, it became quite apparent to the aides which ward was receiving the drug administration. And since these early symptoms would have been just as noticeable in individually selected cases, the double-blind feature would have been neutralized.

The drugs effecting changes in behavior are inadequately described by the term *tranquilizing*, since in many cases of stupor or withdrawal the drugs have a stimulating effect. Another feature that had to be kept in mind was the occurrence of behavioral cycles. Hence, it was essential that the experiment continued long enough for the rated behavior to appear consistently or become stabilized. In some reported studies the drug was given for a period of days rather than weeks. As far as Maze-tested functions are concerned, our experience was that the effects of medication for less than one month were not readily observable and that a minimum six-week period of drug administration was the most suitable for research, though individual responses differed greatly.

One other factor that may vitiate conclusions is that any treatment introduced with the statement that the drug "will do the patient good" arouses favorable expectations in both patients and raters, so that the more suggestible will report good effects even when a placebo is being administered. Unfortunately, there is as yet no scale of suggestibility that could be used to equate the control and the experimental groups. These and other similar matters are discussed more fully in the reference previously cited.

The ward behavior scale used in the study contained eleven trait complexes. In summing up the changes, we observed a fairly rapid amelioration in six to nine weeks, with a flattening of the curve of changes between twelve and fifteen weeks. The most significant modification of behavior traits over the whole period was the fading of hallucinations and delusions from patient consciousness. After this the most rapid change for the better was observable in aggressiveness and physical restlessness, with the least overall effect for depression. In summary, it was found that 63 per cent of the experimental patients showed significant or marked improvement, as against only 11 per cent of the control group. It will be noted that the scale represented the negative or detrimental facts of behavior.

Unfortunately, there were comparatively few patients who were either responsive to testing or whose premedication test records could be properly scored. All cases had been classified as chronic so that many had been in a "closed" ward for years. Thus only 22 cases were finally available for Maze study. Of these, 68 per cent declined in score in contradistinction with the fact that many of the whole group of over 60 experimental patients improved socially. In this group the mean Maze loss was serious, amounting to 2.06 years of test age. Since for the postmedication examination the Extension Series of mazes was applied, practice effects were presumably eliminated. In the discussion of the results (Porteus, 1957a), comparison of this loss was made with two groups of lobotomy patients whose deficits were respectively 1.91 years and 1.81 years, somewhat lower than the chlorpromazine drop in scores. However, it should be remembered that the lobotomy results came before the devising of the practice-free series. Had the Extension Series been employed, the losses undoubtedly would have been greater for the psychosurgical cases.

This study was supplemented by further work (Porteus and Barclay, 1957), using 35 patients who had taken 300 mg. of chlorpromazine daily for periods from six weeks to six months. No attempt was made to measure in detail the degree of social improvement that followed medication, though there was no doubt that in the majority of instances it was considerable. Again, the Original or Vineland Revision of the Maze was applied prior to medication and the Extension Series after medication.

With considerable mental reservations as to the value of the procedure, it was arranged that a control group of 25 patients, who had not had chlorpromazine at the hospital, should take the same examinations. The uncertainty lay in the fact that since all the controls were also psychotic with a variety of abnormal manifestations, we could not rule out the possibility of having their Maze performances affected by temperamental factors that operated differently at different times. Aggressiveness, anxiety, restlessness, antagonism are all traits that can be expected to affect individual Maze performance, but, as we well know from personal experience, they do not operate consistently at all times, some being episodic in appearance. Tranquilizers diminish the frequency of such fluctuations in mood and conduct in the experimental group so that test responses are likely to be more consistent. The untreated, or control group, show more variability in behavior. Hence, there is no assurance that the test results can be regarded as yielding "representative" scores.

A research design that includes administration of a tranquilizing drug to one group and a comparison of their scores with untreated patients seems to me a misapplication of the term "control." It is analogous to attempting to measure the range of tidal change on an open shore as compared with a sheltered harbor. How would one determine whether the high water mark outside was due to a storm or was a tidal phenomenon? Personally, I am very dubious about the use of "control" groups from a mental hospital population, where behavior is frequently, though often temporarily, disturbed. The essence of proper research is the equation of groups, which under such circumstances is extremely difficult and illustrates the hazards of mental hospital studies.

It should be remembered that the effects of a tranquilizer could ordinarily tend to bring about improved scores among an experimental group, making any decline on their part the more significant. Hebb (1954) has commented "on improvement in 'testability' which offsets a loss due to brain operation."

Porteus and Barclay found the mean Maze of 35 tranquilized patients to be 11.9 years prior to medication, that of the 25 control patients to be 11.96 years, the Original Series having been applied to both groups. The difficulties just previously discussed are well illustrated by the divergence from normal levels of these scores. Equivalent groups outside the hospital could be expected to have a mean score of over 14 years, or two years higher.

After medication, extending six weeks or longer, the experimental group's postdrug mean fell to 10.01 years, a decline of 1.89 years.

This was in the practice-free Extension Series. In the same period the untreated group fell to 11.86 years, a decline of only 0.1 of a year. Thus the "net" comparative change was 1.79 years.

A better comparison could be achieved by a matched individuals procedure. It was found possible to pair by Original Maze scores 20 patients in the two groups, both pairs having an original score of 11.85 years with SD's also exactly the same (3.5).

When the Extension Maze was applied to both groups, the drug-treated fell 2.2 years to 9.65 (SD 3.2), while the "control" groups improved 0.2 of a year to 12.05 (SD 3.6). Thus new evidence was furnished in two directions, both as regards a loss in Maze performance after chlorpromazine and confirming the practice-free feature of the Maze Extension Series.

Emotionally disturbed children have also been the subjects of drug research. Apparently, variations in the experimental procedure have resulted in confusing results, so that any further light, particularly on the effects of chlorpromazine, is very welcome.

Helper, Wilcott, and Garfield (1963) have recently reported such a study, their subjects being 39 children in a psychiatric hospital. Porteus and Ching (1959) had previously reported a loss of one year in Maze Test age for mental defectives after routine administration of chlorpromazine during a six-week period. In common with other investigators, we noted a marked sedative effect with drowsiness as a side effect.

Helper *et al.* cite various findings ranging from impaired retention of verbal material to no effect on serial learning and actually more improvement after placebos than after chlorpromazine. They list also our two studies that demonstrate marked deficits in Maze scores (Porteus, 1957a; Porteus and Barclay, 1957), but note failure by Judson and MacCasland (1960) to confirm this decrement. However, the last named study was concerned with only one month's medication, whereas our results were obtained from a four months' drug application. They found no change in Wechsler-Bellevue, MMPI, or Rorschach scores. Moreover, their paper does not state whether the postdrug examination was made by means of the practice-free (Extension) form of the Maze. If the same form of the test were repeated, then results would not be in line with our own, in which test practice was controlled. Their control group showed a practice gain significant at the 5% level, whereas the experimental group showed only a slight loss. In other words, the practice effects masked any impairment in the test. We have already pointed out that neglect to consider practice gains was responsible for the idea, now controverted by Smith's follow-up study, that Maze losses after psychosurgery were transient.

Helper *et al.* cite improved learning in school subjects found by Freed and Peifer, while Freed also reported therapeutic changes when chlorpromazine was used in psychotherapy. These findings are important as an indication that demonstrations of gains versus losses associated with the use of the same drug are dependent upon what mental measures are used to evaluate changes, and the period of medication. As in psychosurgery, an almost unique value for the Maze is suggested, since there seem to be so few tests that register deficits. In spite of their short period of chlorpromazine medication, the statement of results by Helper, Wilcott, and Garfield seems unequivocal as regards the situation. They say:

> The effects attributable to the administration of chlorpromazine in the present study were selective and specific rather than general and pervasive. Only two of the measures studied, the paired-associate learning task and the Porteus Maze Mental Age score, changed more with the administration of chlorpromazine than with placebo. Selectivity in drug effects was noted within the paired-associate task itself, in that the later trials and slower learning subjects were most affected by chlorpromazine. . . .
>
> The relative decline of about 1 year in Porteus Maze Mental Age following chlorpromazine in the present study was somewhat less than the average deficit of about 2 years reported by Porteus (1957) and Porteus and Barclay (1957), but does indicate negative effects for chlorpromazine on this test in children as well as adults. The present study also revealed a trend toward improved qualitative performance (Q score) on this test under chlorpromazine. This variable has apparently not been studied before in experiments on chlorpromazine, though it could have valuable implications for the nature of the deficit produced by chlorpromazine on the Porteus Mental Age score.

The present writer agrees that changes in Q-scores might be important as relating to the brain area affected by the drugs.[2] If mental alertness is mediated to a large extent by the reticular formation, one could expect a decline in test age scored on entrance into blind alleys, but not in Q-scores scored on careless execution of the Maze tracing.

With regard to the "nature of the deficit," one observation seems to agree with our own experience with the test, especially in regard

---

[2] Aaronson (1963) has reported greater sensitivity of qualitative scores to drug effects.

to the fact that performance on the easier mazes seems to differ in character from solving the more complicated designs. This exemplifies what Brundage called "shatter effects." I have previously suggested that more than one brain organizational area may be involved (possibly the temporoparietal area) for tasks at the simpler perceptual level, but that the frontal cortex (areas 9 and 10) is involved in solution of the higher mazes.

Helper *et al.* imply that "the factor affected by chlorpromazine can vary in importance within the course of a single learning session, as well as from one learning task to the next." They add:

> One possibility is that chlorpromazine impairs the maintenance of active attention to novel and significant details. The paired-associate task, with its continued reshuffling and elimination of items, and the Porteus Maze, with its series of increasingly complicated designs, would seem to share some requirement for such sustained alertness.

They then proceed to cite the experience of Mirsky and Rosvold (1960) with the Continuous Performance Test. These investigators related lapses in attention after chlorpromazine to depressions of functioning in the midbrain reticular formation (MRF), which apparently mediates a condition of "wide-awakeness" essential to good performance in the Maze. It may well be that the reticular formation is much more directly concerned in solving mazes than are other brain areas activated in doing other tests.

Mirsky and Rosvold, on the basis of various studies, suggest that involvement of the MRF structures may affect attention, alertness, and wakefulness, and quote Lindsley, Bowden, and Magoun to the effect that lesions in the midbrain tegmentum render animals permanently somnolent. These investigators then go on to state that certain barbituates, chlorpromazine, meprobamate, and lysergic acid (LSD-25) have a demonstrable effect on MRF functions. After prolonged sleep deprivation, chlorpromazine produced the most significant Continuous Performance Test impairment and meprobamate the least. Since the Columbia-Greystone projects showed definite losses in Maze performance to be much greater than in the Continuous Performance Test, it seemed unfortunate that Mirsky and Rosvold did not use it also in their experiment. Psychologists in the New York projects also noted that the Maze responses after topectomy were characteristic of somnolent persons.

Elsewhere in this volume we have already quoted Landis and

Zubin to the effect that patients doing the Maze after psycho-surgery functioned as if they "were sleepy, fatigued, or partially drunk" and disinclined (or unable) to work at their ordinary level. Evidently the reticular formation depressed by chlorpromazine brings about a similar condition adverse to successful Maze performance.

Dr. Elbert W. Russell has also communicated to me the results of a study presented by him as a Master's thesis at Pennsylvania State University in 1958. He failed to find any decrements in the Porteus Maze. His subjects were mild schizophrenic patients to whom the drug prochlorperazine had been administered, but he notes the fact that this medication, unlike chlorpromazine, does not induce sleepiness and thus suggests that prochlorperazine is not acting on the reticular formation as chlorpromazine does.

In relation to therapeutic changes, we are still confronted with the puzzling lack of correlation of social improvement and Maze score so many times demonstrated in other groups of maladjusted individuals. Could it be that the social adjustment that follows psychosurgery and chlorpromazine medication is of a different type to the adjustments observable in in normal untreated persons who are neither psychotic nor delinquent? This may illustrate the misleading use of convenient blanket terms in describing personality.

Consideration of these problems of test interpretation has forced recognition of the fact that maladjusted persons are often dynamic individuals who actively reject the restraints that society imposes on their conduct. They are what might be called ultra-extraverts, or superegotists. If the physical restlessness, the spirit of antagonism, the aggressively resistant attitude, the personal irritability of the individual could be reduced, then his reaction to the rules imposed with respect to the convenience, safety, or good will of other people would be improved. Although inner rebellion or protest may still be present, it may partake of a more passive nature. The person then becomes less objectionable to his fellows, more outwardly conformist, and easier to live with. Becoming compliant or easier to live with may make the individual also easier to work with, a condition often essential to earning a living. This type of social adjustment was mentioned in the previous chapter.

In studying the effects of lobotomy, this soft-pedaling or blunting of emotion is very noticeable. One of the cases first observed by the writer was a Negro whose assaultive disposition had got him into serious trouble in five different states of the Union. The slightest reference to his race was enough to throw him into a paroxysm of fury in which he violently attacked the offender. In his conduct he showed the kind of foresight that I have tried to describe as immediate or proximate, as compared with distant planning. Before operation, distant foresight was shown by his realization that he might readily commit murder in one of these sudden outbursts of hostility; hence, he guarded against this by filing down the blade of his pocketknife so as to make it a less lethal weapon. He thus avoided charges of going offensively armed, and at the same time he lessened his chances of committing homicide. That this was effective was shown by his having inflicted 43 stab wounds on an opponent and yet avoided a manslaughter charge, since his victim recovered. His picking of a fight showed immediate impulsivity, his choice of a less dangerous weapon, long-range planning. After lobotomy he lost both types of planning, falling from an eleven-year Maze score to seven years, with a greatly increased tendency to enter the same blind alley repeatedly.

To make the distinction clearer, we might say that proximate foresight concerns problems in which all the factors necessary for solution are present and more or less easily apparent; in the other type of foresight, which we have called distant foresight, all the factors are not easily apprehensible but in many cases can be inferred. Proximate foresight is simpler so that immediate decisions can be made. Thus the mental operation is in the nature of what Guilford has called perceptual foresight. In the other type of ability, since the factors are not plainly set forth, immediate actions are inhibited and the attempt at solution is deferred. A temporal factor enters the problem; time must be allowed for situations to develop. For example, in a chess game an opponent's moves cannot be foretold exactly. What he logically should do and what he does do differ. Stock market operations provide another example of what Guilford (1958) calls conceptual foresight. But the variable factors in such situations cannot always be foreseen and weighed and balanced against each other. I do not believe that any objective test can take account of uncertainties. Certainly the Maze is bound by structural necessities, in which there is only one correct course. Wrong alternatives are easily perceived and avoided. If accidental errors occur, they may arise from personality defects in the person examined.

My formulation differs from that of Guilford in that I do not envisage two *independent* kinds of foresight, but rather a single mental trait operating at different levels; in other words, there are different degrees of planning—simple and complex. I cannot conceive of an individual's being able to develop the more complex ability unless he is capable of planning on a simple level. It may be taken for granted that everyday life is full of situations, from driving a car in traffic to managing one's ordinary affairs, where more immediate or proximate foresight is in demand. Hence, the testing of planning on this common, everyday level is of importance.

Unfortunately, even psychologists are prone to accept and use such blanket terms as motivation, adjustment, compulsions, and planning without reference to social values and effects. These words not only cover a multitude of sins, but also extend over a great number of virtues. An individual may be strongly motivated toward good or evil ends; compulsions may be socially purposeless or, on the other hand, useful, the direction of adjustment may be toward right or wrong; successful planning may be as characteristic of a Hitler as it is of a Lincoln. If these things be true, then we may expect that any operation or drug that diminishes initiative will change behavior. Anxiety *per se* may be not so much diminished by chlorpromazine as may be the *capacity to feel anxious*. Passivity, unconcern, dullness in anticipation may result in greater social acceptability merely through the reduction of the aggressive features of personality that we designate as initiative. Similarly, a blunting of mental alertness may also bring about decrements in Maze Test proficiency. Perhaps instead of claiming that the Maze is a measure of planning in general, it would be better to admit that the specificity of the situation affects performance. In some situations initiative is exercised in antisocial directions. Under the influence of tranquilizers, or as a result of psychosurgery, the inner dynamic pressures are reduced, antagonism may be succeeded by indifference, supersensitivity changed to unresponsiveness, rebellion to acceptance of the *status quo*. All of these quite conceivably reduce Maze Test scores but aid socialization of a passive type. In short, it becomes necessary to re-emphasize the overriding importance of sampling on test performance. When we group together for the purposes of mental measurement, psychosurgical cases, neurotics, drug addicts, Australian aborigines, or persons we designate "normals," the test scores are affected greatly by this process of selec-

tion. But it is the fact of human variability that makes testing interesting and, provided we examine critically the basis of sampling,
scientifically rewarding.

Another study that had as one of its purposes a check on the
chlorpromazine findings was reported in a paper presented at the
Eastern Psychological Association (Margolis, Englehardt, Freedman, Hankoff and Mann, 1960). These investigators, however, modified my research plan in several directions. They did not administer
chlorpromazine as a fixed dosage, but the psychiatrists responsible
for treatment (who visited the ward eight or more times during the
experiment) determined the amount of the drug to be administered.
Hence, the dosage ranged from 50 mgs. to 800 mgs. daily, with a
modal amount of 150 mgs., half that given in our experiment. Lack
of information as to the basis of psychiatric decisions with regard to
the drug dosage makes comparison of the two studies difficult.

Another factor that quite conceivably affected the representative
nature of the sampling is that patients were able to leave the clinical
problem at will. In some treatments, where voluntary participation
enters into the project, the sample may become biased thereby.
But far more important is the question whether or not the same
series of the Maze was used for predrug and postdrug application.
A careful reading of the contributors' APA paper does not indicate
whether the practice-controlled Extension Series was used for postdrug evaluation. If not, then the practice effects would effectively
conceal drug-induced impairment.

Margolis *et al.* divided their cases on the basis of Rorschach responses into what they call amorphous, ideational complex, and
mediocre groups. The first group showed an improvement in Porteus
score, increase in clarity of role perception, increase in obsessional
symptoms, and no change in perseveration. The ideationally complex group declined on the Maze and in obsessive symptoms and
decreased in role perception and perseveration. The mediocre
group, along with moderate Maze improvement, showed decrease
in obsessional symptoms but increased role perception and perseveration. Without knowledge of which Maze series were applied, it
is impossible to evaluate these results adequately.

Another very significant study in the field of psychopharmacology
was reported from the Psychiatric Institute of the Maryland University Hospital at Baltimore. The investigators were H. Aronson
and G. D. Klee (1960). Their research concerned the effect of lyser-

gic acid diethylamide (LSD-25) in changing intellectual function, so that "capacity is lowered but by no means completely destroyed." They note that psychosurgery also reduces "the ability to foresee the consequences of an action and to modify behavior accordingly." These investigators also cite their clinical observation that there are some features of LSD reaction that resemble the effects of prefrontal lobotomy.

Frequently observed in both states are reactions which show a basic indifference to ordinary environmental events. Coupled to this is a tendency to poorly planned, impulsive action. In both states it is often necessary to increase external control or supervision as a substitute for a control from within, which the patient is less able or willing to achieve. . . . Since the Porteus Maze is purported to measure such a change and since it apparently does so in the case of frontal surgery, the test was chosen to evaluate the state of the function under LSD. It was our hypothesis that LSD, through its interference with critical judgment, would impair performance on the Porteus Maze Test.

Whether it was critical judgment or planning or some other trait-complex that was affected by the drug cannot be now discussed, but the Maze impairment was unequivocal. Aronson and Klee's subjects were 68 male volunteers declared to be within normal limits on the basis of physical examination, psychiatric interview, and group psychological tests. They were randomly divided into a control group of 34 cases and the same number of cases who took the drug. Six of these were tested 2 to 3½ hours after ingestion of 100 mcg. LSD, 28 subjects 1¼ to 2¼ hours after ingestion of 75 mcg. of the drug. The Original (Vineland Revision) series was administered in the standard way. No placebos were given the control group, but the Maze performances in the normal state were approximately the same in the two groups. The experimental group members were slightly older and more educated than the controls so that educational advantage favored, if anything, the experimental group.

The investigators sum up their study by stating that the drugless group were superior to the 75-mcg. group, which in turn were superior to the 100-mcg. subjects. By the Mann-Whitney Test, the differences were significant at the following levels: Control versus 75-mcg. group $p < .005$, controls versus 100-mcg. group $p < .0005$, and 75 mcg. versus 100 mcg. $p < .05$. By taking the range of Mazes between the lowest and highest tests in which errors occurred, it was assumed that the greater the variability score the less the subject was functioning at his greatest capacity, since he had succeeded in higher tests after failing simpler ones. Compared in this way, the drug group had higher variability scores than the controls, the Mann-Whitney level of confidence being p < .005.

Aronson and Klee offer the following comment:

> The results are consistent with the clinical observation of a detrimental influence of LSD-25 upon the ability to exercise critical control over behavior. The highly significant difference between normal function and that obtained with only 75 mcg. would indicate that "anticipatory planning" is a function which is extremely sensitive to the action of LSD-25; and it is likely that considerably milder doses than those studied may be sufficient to produce a change. Only one other drug, chlorpromazine, has been reported as showing an effect on maze performance. Like the results found here, the effect appears to be detrimental.

On the basis of deficits that were found to follow administration of chlorpromazine for an extended period to chronic psychotic patients (Porteus and Barclay, 1957), the authors state that this loss "is comparable to that of our 100 mcg. patients."

The purpose in quoting these findings, which admittedly are not final, is not so much to show the effects of drugs such as LSD-25, but to provide additional evidence of the sensitivity of the Maze Test. Unlike psychosurgery, the administration of LSD-25 does not have effects limited to the Maze. As Aronson and Klee report, the Maze shares this sensitivity with other tests. All Wechsler-Bellevue subtests with the exception of two, tests of immediate memory, abstract reasoning, and probably many others could be adversely affected. Both in chlorpromazine medication and psychosurgery the associated mental decrements are by no means as easily visible in test performance as in the Maze. However, as I have suggested elsewhere, too much importance is ascribed by psychologists to *statistically significant* differences in test results. The differences may be too small to reach a high *t*-test level, but if they consistently appear in the same direction, they may be quite significant. Fortunately, the psychologist's choice of measures is not limited, and it may be possible to demonstrate a reduction in mental alertness in a variety of experimental situations. However, he would be wise to include in a selected repertoire of tests those that are the most consistently sensitive. Of this essential battery, the Maze Test appears to be one.

In some of these experimental results an unusual sensitivity has been demonstrated for the Maze. No doubt the advent of tranquilizing drugs on the psychiatric scene is responsible for the fact that editors of psychological journals no longer give space to articles dealing with psychosurgery patients. This may account for the non-appearance in published form of an article that seemed to dispose rather effectively of the suggested parallel between chlorpromazine effects and psychosurgery. Its conclusions do affect the question of the comparative sensitivity of the Maze, a matter with which we are concerned. This paper was written by Dr. Bernard L. Bloom in 1959 on work done at the State Mental Hospital at Kaneohe and is entitled "Ataractic Drugs and Psychosurgery: Psychological Test Parallels." As far as the writer knows it is as yet unpublished.[3]

Briefly described, this study involved application of a battery of tests before and after six weeks' medication in which either thorazine, compazine, or pacatal was administered. Since no test differences as between specific drug usage were found, all subjects (N 22) were combined into one group.

The tests used fell into two groups, the first consisting of three previously found to be sensitive to psychosurgery—Porteus Maze, Capps Homograph, and Weigl Color-Form Sorting. This sensitivity was on the basis of Columbia-Greystone research projects previously cited. The second group included tests previously found *insensitive*—Information, Picture Completion, and Digit-Symbol, all subtests of the Wechsler-Bellevue Scale—with the addition of two other tests that have recently been shown to be sensitive to intracranial pathology. These were Partington's Pathways and Spiral After-effects. As far as the Maze Test results were concerned, there was one weakness in the research design: the same form of the test was repeated after therapy as before, thus disregarding its well-known practice effects. This procedure was followed because it was the method used in the Columbia-Greystone topectomy project, the findings of which the author wished to check. At the time of the Columbia-Greystone project neither the practice-free Extension Series nor the Extension Supplement form was available.

The author notes that although the decrements in the Maze "did not achieve statistical significance, since the practice-free form was not used, the decrease is undoubtedly significant." Actually, the decrement amounted to 0.73 of a year (*t*-test 1.55). Since in several investigations controls gained over 1.6 years on a repetition of the same form of the Maze, the actual or net loss approximated 2.3

---

[3] Tests were administered by John Barclay.

years. None of the other seven tests used gave such a clear picture of decline. The two tests that after psychosurgery had shown previous decrements again registered small losses; one, the Capps Homograph, had a drop of 0.1 of a year in mean score; the other, the Weigl Test, a drop of 0.23 in raw score, neither decrement being statistically significant.

The three tests previously found insensitive all showed slight *gains*. These were the W-B Information Test, the W-B Picture Completion and the W-B Digit Symbol. Both the Spiral After-effect and Partington's Pathways showed an insignificant gain. The net result of the whole study was to demonstrate once again a peculiar sensitivity in the Maze.

In sum, the conclusion supported by this study was that the administration of a tranquilizing drug was followed by a definite decline in Maze-tested functions, a decrement not nearly as apparent in other test performances, and with a reverse tendency in some.

I have mentioned earlier that some studies, in spite of the difficulty of setting up a statistically admirable design in regard to numbers of cases, may yet be of great value. Their illuminative scope may be limited, but where all is dark even a flashlight may be extremely helpful.

One such study (O'Shea, Elsom, and Higbe, 1942) has been cited in several of my publications and cannot be left out of any exposition of the sensitivity of the Maze. The reason for its inclusion is the unlikelihood of there being any attempted replication of this investigation. Its research design included obtaining subjects to suffer voluntarily long-continued acute vitamin-B deficiency through restrictions of the daily diet, which, however, contained "an adequate quantity" of all dietary factors except the B-vitamins.

The vitamin-B deprivation continued for various periods until clinical manifestations were apparent, in one case for as long as 98 days. When one considers that those manifestations included easy fatigue, anorexia, marked epigastric discomfort, malnutrition, muscular tenderness, nausea, irritability, neuritic pains, etc., it is easy to understand why the experimental group had to be limited in number to four middle-aged women. These volunteers unfortunately remain anonymous since they are undoubtedly among the heroines of science. The four controls "had it easy," proceeding with their normal diets at the Thompson Vitamin Ward of the Philadelphia General Hospital where they were employed. Their only inconvenience was the comparatively minor one of undergoing the psychological tests at the same times as the unfortunate experimental group. These tests were applied to the latter when severe clinical manifestations appeared. At that time thiamine was added to their diet, with the result that all cases improved; and, finally, when the B-complex was also given, all cases completely recovered, and the investigation ended.

The battery of tests included the Whipple–Healy Tapping Test, the Henmon-Nelson Test of Mental Ability (Forms A, B, and C), the Otis Quick Scoring Mental Ability Test (Beta Forms A and B), the Thorndike-McCall Reading Scale for reasoning ability (Forms 1, 2, 3, 4, and 5), the Healy-Bronner Picture Memory Test of visual and auditory memory, and the Porteus Maze Test, presented in ordinary and inverted positions. Perhaps on the basis of mental cruelty even the repeatedly tested control group of subjects should also be commiserated with. The authors' object in rotating the mazes to an inverted position was to diminish practice effects.

Following my suggestion, the Mazes were used as a point scale, both groups being approximately equal at the beginning of the experiment with Ss averaging 68.6 points in the upright mazes, 69.3 in the inverted positions. The Otis Tests were used only in a preliminary exploration of Ss' mental ability and were then dropped from the research design.

The impairment that accompanied vitamin-B deficiency was marked when measured by the two alternative Maze series—the one applied in the usual position, the second inverted. The experimental group's Maze scores in the series A and B were 40 and 54.5, while the controls averaged 65.8 and 73.4, respectively, showing considerable cumulative practice effect. However, once thiamine feeding was established, the experimentals improved from 40 to 78.7 points in one Maze series (ordinary position), and when the B-complex was added to the diet, from 54.5 to 81.75 points. On the other hand, the controls improved slightly, evidently through additional practice effects, by 5.12 and 10 points in each corresponding testing.

The authors sum up the situation thus:

Furthermore, a definite relationship existed between the degree of deficiency and the degree of impairment of Maze performance. These results indicate that deficiency of the B-vitamins is associated with impaired ability to solve a series of mazes, that this impairment begins early in the deficiency and progresses as the deficiency deepens and that it may be restored by the administration of either thiamine alone or the B-complex.

Another of the authors' tables shows that when the results of the two series of mazes are combined, the deficiency during the deprivation period amounted to 22.31 points for the experimental group, but after the vitamin-B deficiency was corrected by re-enforced diets, they caught up to and finally exceeded the control group by 3.12 points. Both initial loss and improvement after therapy were consistent for each individual in the experimental group. The authors quote other studies to show that general inanition does not reduce maze-running performance in rats, but a specific B-vitamin deficiency does.

That the Maze is peculiarly sensitive to vitamin-B human deficiency seemed to be proved. O'Shea *et al.* conclude: "General intelligence, reasoning ability (reading) and speed of hand muscle coordination (tapping) show no measurable deterioration when the subjects are deficient in the B-vitamins and no improvement after therapy with thiamine or with the B-complex."

There was one attempt made to check O'Shea's results (Gruetzow and Brozek, 1946), but unfortunately the investigators apparently made no allowance for the very considerable practice effects in the Maze when it is repeated. We have already emphasized the fact that neglect to take this factor into account was responsible for the mistaken conclusion in the Columbia-Greystone project that the Maze deficits that followed were transient. Gruetzow and Brozek in describing their procedure state that "the mazes in their original upright position were repeated, each time following the administration of a rotated 'alternative' form." Since these alternative forms merely consisted of three clockwise rotations of 90°, this means that there were at least eight applications of the Maze Test. Only the four most difficult mazes were used so that bright subjects soon reached the ceiling of the test. Hence, all scores were very high. Obviously the practice effects in eight repetitions of the Maze Test to subjects with near-ceiling scores would effectively mask any objectively measurable deficits associated with vitamin deficiency. In addition, the research design differed so much from the O'Shea procedure that it cannot be considered a replicative study. These variations extended as far as the dietary program, for the Gruetzow-Brozek investigation employed a *restricted* instead of a vitamin-free diet, and apparently no mazes were given during the "acute deficiency stage," the symtoms of which are not described.

This demonstration of the effects on mental level as measured by the Maze may possibly have an important bearing on the low comparative status of some primitive ethnic groups such as the South African Bushmen or the Sakai Jeram, coastal dwellers in Malaya. If through nutritional analysis of their foodstuffs it could be shown that vitamin deficiencies are more likely in certain habitats, great variations in Maze scores might be in part explained. Undoubtedly the Bushmen's diet is likely to contain more protein due to the greater abundance of game, whereas the enforced supplementation of Australid sustenance with vegetable food stuffs may give them a better balanced diet. The gathering and preparation for cooking of grass seeds, roots, etc., are laborious tasks, and if meat were really plentiful as it is when eland, giraffe, and the larger antelope are killed by the African hunters, there is not the same dependence on finding "veldtkos" as they term vegetable food. An eland would feed the Bushmen for a week, whereas a large kangaroo would last an Australid group for little more than a day. The effects of diet on vitamin deficiency among some primitive peoples, of course, are purely speculative until proper nutritional studies can be made.[4]

Turning again to abnormal Caucasian subjects, we can cite two studies; these were undertaken with the object of testing the possible value of the Maze for differentiating psychiatrically classified psychotic or psychopathic cases. The first was submitted by Marian S. Webster (1949) as an M.A. thesis in psychology at the University of Maine. Its title was "A Comparison of the Qualitative Performance of Manic and Depressive Patients on the Porteus Maze Test."

The author's general conclusion reads: "From the results obtained by Porteus in testing normal boys and girls, delinquent boys and girls, adult criminals and bus drivers, and the results obtained in the present study, it appears that the Maze, when scored qualitatively, differentiates between general classes of behavior, but is not sensitive enough to measure small, but possibly significant variations within the (abnormal) classes."

The significance of the last conclusion may depend, however, on the validity of the classification as applied to Webster's cases.

---

[4] On the basis of observations of Bushman mentality, especially those reported by Vander Post (1958), the present writer is disposed to look for such special explanations of their low Maze scores. Though called Bushmen, not all were purebloods.

Unfortunately, such classes are often very uncertainly defined, and it would be too much to expect that the test would be independent of the uncertainties of the psychiatrists. Agreement among psychiatrists as to the nature of schizophrenia, for example, is anything but marked. As to the classification "manic-depressive," the situation seems to be confused, as it is likely to be when the term "manic" refers mainly to outgoing physical activities and "depressive" to a mental state. Thus, when research is concerned with manic versus depressive groups, the two classes are found not to be mutually exclusive. This is shown by the fact that two opposed descriptive adjectives are hyphenated or combined to describe the one group.

Any student concerned with the setting up of symptom rating scales is soon faced with the difficulty that though two mental states are opposite they may express the two extremes or poles of an emotional condition or continuum. This is particularly the case with depression and its behavioral opposite, elation. Normal people are well aware of their very variable mood-swings, which seem to occur independently of specific stimuli, possibly related to the autonomic nervous system. Occasionally we begin our day with much less than our ordinary ambition, optimism, euphoria, happiness, confidence, etc. Then without sufficient reason our moods change drastically to good humor, satisfaction, loss of anxiety, and the feeling, often ill-founded, that all is well with ourselves and our world. The feeling of depression finds social expression by inaction or withdrawal. On the other hand, euphoria is often accompanied by desire for social cooperation. Thus it is obvious that somatic and mental reactions are rather inextricably mixed. The bipolar nature of personality descriptive terms is discussed further in a later chapter.

Webster recognized this difficulty in differentiation when she says: "The lack of difference found in the present study may be due to the fact that fundamentally mania and depression may be behavioral manifestations of the same fundamental disorder." She then quotes Cameron (1947) on this point:

Mania must be looked upon as one of the mood disorders which appear under certain environmental and organismic conditions. These conditions, and indeed the whole behavioral picture, are obviously in need of further analysis. It is well known, for instance, that when a mood disorder arises under circumstances of personal disaster, this can be in the form of a manic attack as well as in the commoner depressive form. The conclusion is suggested by this and other clinical evidence that it is useful to regard mania as an equivalent of depression rather than its opposite pole.

I believe that the situation can be better understood when it is recognized that there is a great disparity between verbal and physical expression. Our repertoire as regards the latter is limited; frowning, crying, smiling, laughing, wringing or clenching the hands, setting the jaws, general physical restlessness, and violence make up a fairly limited inventory of emotionally expressive acts. But some of these are subject to different interpretation. With some people, smiling is not a sign of pleasure but embarrassment, and among the Oriental peoples it may be considered the proper accompaniment of fear or grief.

Enough has been said to indicate that the manic-depressive descriptive classification is necessarily confused, so that in default of an adequate dichotomy, test responses would be unlikely to be differentiated. Actually, as Webster notes, "results do, however, support the theory that mania and depressions are behavioral manifestations of the same fundamental disorder."

With regard to the applications of the Porteus Maze in the field of abnormal psychology, reference should be made to a study carried out in England, in which reactions of different groups of psychoneurotic patients are compared (Foulds, 1951). Before making this comparison, this author had studied two groups of normal subjects with some interesting sex differences, which are listed in another section. The chief interest in Fould's study lies in the reactions of certain psychoneurotic groups.

These results are comparable with Macdonald Tow's study as previously described. Both Foulds and Tow employed modifications of the Maze testing procedure and scoring. In Foulds' study if S entered a blind alley he was not stopped but allowed to continue until he realized that he was wrong. He was instructed when this happened to retrace his course and then proceed through the rest of the maze. This obviously may have had a marked result on the final score. The reason for making S start again from the beginning as soon as he enters a blind alley is to give him the opportunity to make other mistakes earlier in the test design or even repeat the same errors, a repetition of which not infrequently occurs. Thus Foulds' results are not strictly comparable with scores made in qualitative performance nor in the quantitative or test age procedure.

Foulds calls these entrances to blind alleys W.D. or "wrong directions," an error that has a very minor weighting in my qualitative scoring. For W.D. in that case merely means a wrong direction, self-corrected before S crosses an imaginary line across the entrance to a blind alley. This very infrequently happens and would better be called C. D., a changed direction. Foulds is evidently confused for he notes that I state that a majority of investigators show a correlation of .6 to .7 between Binet and Maze scores. But these scores are not based on a self-corrected change in direction of line but on a half-year penalty imposed for each actual entry into a blind alley. As I use this term, I would be surprised if there were any correlation at all between W.D. and either Binet or Maze test ages.

Despite these changes in procedure, Foulds' contribution added new knowledge regarding psychoneurotic reactions, a very difficult subject to study, since individuals in this classification are not proportionally represented in a mental hospital population. His subjects, 190 in number, were divided into five groups—psychopaths, hysterics, anxiety states, reactive depressives, and obsessionals. Among the scored items, besides some of the ordinary qualitative features such as lift pencils, crossing lines, and wavy lines, were two with temporal significance. He included St.T. (starting time), or the number of seconds elapsing between giving the standard instructions and the subject's beginning the test, while T.T. (total time) was the time taken from the beginning to the end of the Maze tracing, recorded in units of 15 seconds. His table 6 shows that St.T. differentiated psychopaths from depressives and hysterics from depressives, while T.T. (total time) differentiated significantly psychopaths and depressives, hysterics and depressives, but these temporal items do not differentiate psychopaths and hysterics. A conclusion reached was that the "test was found to differentiate more clearly between the psychoneurotic groups than between psychoneurotics and normals."

Foulds' summary of observed differences in Maze reactions is most informative. I have selected from his paper for citation some of his most illuminating comments. Fould's findings were:

(1) *Psychopathics and hysterics* "start without prolonged delay and proceed rapidly with a relatively smooth, evenly flowing line. . . . not quite adequately under control since they cross a relatively large number of lines. They might be said to be somewhat impulsive and careless. . . . They have a low score for lifted pencils."

(2) *Patients with anxiety states,* perhaps because of their inability readily to make decisions, start slowly and then work reasonably quickly with a very tremulous line tracing, crossing many lines. Foulds noticed that the lines tend to become more wavy after an error has been committed. He also mentions, in relation to this latter characteristic, a finding by Brundage, cited by me in 1946 and discussed elsewhere in this volume, but this refers to quantitative, not qualitative scores. Brundage comments that some subjects exercised normal forethought and vigilance in the early tests until they made a mistake by entering a blind alley. Thereafter, their performance changed quickly to a more impulsive type of response. He called this a "shatter effect," which I have also often noticed, particularly with psychosurgical cases. Changes in qualitative performance were not so apparent.

(3) In *reactive depressives,* Foulds stated that the tempo is slow throughout. This enables patients to avoid crossing an undue number of lines, but they make rather frequent errors in the early stages and forget to heed the instruction about not lifting the pencil. There is a slight tendency of depressives to proceed further up blocked roads than other subjects. Many subjects seem to gain "added enjoyment" from the test after they have made an error, though this is less frequent in the case of the depressives. Foulds also notes that the anxious and depressed have a slight tendency to enter blind alleys in the first third of the maze design and to make other qualitative errors in the simpler mazes.

(5) *Obsessionals* show "rather slow tempo throughout, relative freedom from very gross errors of direction, few lifted pencils, firm straight lines down the center of the channel and careful, right-angled cornering, with consequently very few crossed lines."

This last observation is very important, as the habit of making careful right angles usually results in achieving a high consistency-variability (C-V) score, which has been described in another publication.

In view of the idea frequently advanced by psychiatrists that juvenile delinquents are mentally disturbed, it would be instructive to undertake a detailed analysis of their Maze performances along the lines followed by Foulds. Unfortunately, our delinquent records were not timed in any way, but this feature could be introduced in future research. Total times were recorded also by Macdonald Tow for leucotomized normal cases.

Shapiro, Kessell, and Maxwell (1960) also used Fould's method of scoring with three groups of subjects, normals, schizophrenics, and brain-damaged, with 16 cases in each group. They found that in speed of performance the normals were faster than the other two groups. With regard to entering blind alleys, the brain-damaged had the worst records. These results accord with Tow's findings.

A very recent study (Conners, Eisenberg, and Sharpe, 1963) is both timely and extremely interesting from the point of view of this present volume. It concerns the effects of methylphenidate administered in a double-blind, placebo-controlled study over a ten-day period to children in two institutions. On the basis of reports of other studies and an unpublished report from their own clinic, the authors' expectation was that the administration of this drug might diminish the overactivity of brain-damaged children of low intelligence and might bring about beneficial clinical effects in delinquent cases with behavior disorders. They believe that both groups of cases share some common features. The behavior disorder group exhibit high incidence of EEG abnormality, labile emotional characteristics, and hyperkinesis, as do also the organic cases. "These children," they say, "function as though they lacked central cortical inhibitory capacity over their internal drives and the external stimuli impinging upon them."

The authors further theorize that a drug that acts as a central stimulant "should result in a greater ability to attend to relevant task dimensions, to inhibit irrelevant stimuli, and to inhibit impulsive responding."

All those whose work brings them into close contact with juvenile delinquents become discouraged at the apparent ineffectiveness of measures of social reform. If those measures could be reenforced by the use of drugs of proved value in reducing impulsivity, such a discovery could easily pave the way for a breakthrough in the treatment of those cases whose persistent law-breaking is an indication of poor inhibitory capacity. Any demonstration by the use of the Maze Test that a stimulant drug is effective in the above-mentioned directions is of great importance. The study by Conners *et al.* is regarded by these investigators as being at present of only tentative value, yet its indications are definite enough to appear very promising. They suggest that these subjects with low levels of intelligence would be likely to benefit most from the stimulation.

Their subjects were resident at the two institutions, one (A) be-

ing a center for children awaiting foster home placement in permanent homes. In general, they may be described as deprived, having
had very unsatisfactory home surroundings, and many were somewhat emotionally maladjusted. In the second institution (B) were
children undergoing psychiatric treatment directed toward reducing serious emotional disturbances. They were more seriously disturbed, however, than the children in Institution A, though none
was diagnosed as psychotic, mentally retarded, or brain-damaged.

At the outset the authors comment on a factor affecting success
of a drug experiment, which the present writer has previously mentioned. This is the expectation of improvement that a new pill administered *en masse* occasions. The placebo feature is supposed
to equalize the groups in this respect, but a random sampling, unless with very large numbers of cases, does not equate them on the
basis of suggestibility. However, such an equalizing process is not
at present possible. Another point is that if the pill occasions self-
evident changes, these are likely to be interpreted very favorably
by the more suggestible cases.

The two divisions, drug and placebo groups were then classified
in three categories of low, medium, or higher IQ's. With regard to
the effects on Maze performance, the study indicated that the lower
IQ subjects gained most from the drug, the increase being at the
.05 level of confidence, while the middle group's gain was less significant ($p < .10$). The investigators noted that this change in Maze
performance brought them almost to about the same level as the
higher IQ group. They suggest that possibly the re-enforcing effect
of the drug was not as apparent in children already performing at
their optimal level. The learning tasks that were also set for the
groups showed a similar interaction with intelligence, the lower
level subjects, as expected, contributing most of the variance in effects. There was no relation between drug action and the anxiety
and impulsivity measures also applied.

Conners, Eisenberg, and Sharpe cite an article by Helper *et al.*,
already summarized in this chapter, which supports the hypothesis
that the functions depressed by chlorpromazine are conversely stimulated by methylphenidate. They comment as follows:

"These behavioral findings are in keeping with the fact that the
amphetamines and chlorpromazine have reciprocally antagonistic
effects on EEG and general behavior, possibly because of opposite
effects on the reticular system (Elkes, 1958)." But they also point

out that neither the Maze nor the learning tests used are "pure measures of alerting or inhibiting activity." To clarify the problem, Conners *et al.* commend a method by which distracting factors may be filtered out better under the influence of the drug.

Since this study raised the question of a relationship between intelligence level and drug therapy, indicating that a stimulant such as methylphenidate had an important effect of raising the Maze level of children of lower intelligence, it would be interesting to contrast this result with the use of chlorpromazine with similar low level cases. In particular, it would be interesting to discover whether with children supposedly feebleminded, chlorpromazine still has the same effect of depressing Maze scores as seems to occur with psychotic patients.

Following two studies (Porteus and Barclay, 1957), previously cited, which deal with the effects on psychotics of a period of about four months' medication with chlorpromazine at the State Hospital at Kaneohe, Oahu, the investigation was transferred to the Waimano Home for defectives near Honolulu. Some mainland United States' studies had recorded gains in IQs., as measured by general intelligence scores after chlorpromazine, but apparently there were no investigations of Maze reactions with defectives.

Dr. Edward T. Ching, physician at the hospital, and the present writer (Porteus and Ching, 1959) carried out a small study with 20 high grade defectives at Waimano Home. One hundred milligrams of thorazine, or one-third of the daily dosage administered to chronic psychotics at the Kaneohe Mental Hospital, were given daily for six weeks, or about one-third of the duration of the drug therapy with the psychotic patients.

Clinically, there was noticed a decrease in mental alertness, vigilance, and initiative, changes that were expressed objectively by a decline of Maze scores from a mean of 11.2 years in the Original Maze Series to 10.2 in the practice-controlled Extension form of the test. The decline in the adult psychotics, using the same test procedure, was 2.06 years (N 22), slightly more than double the deficit, but results for defectives were for one-third of the dosage and a much shorter period of medication. In a second study of 35 psychotic subjects, the loss in the Extension Maze was 1.89 years, significant at the .05 level. A third comparison, using 20 pairs matched for Original Maze scores, yielded a decline of 2.2 years for the experimental group, a gain of 0.2 of a year for the controls. These studies have been summarized previously but are repeated here for contrast with the lesser decline in mental defectives.

It seems impossible to postulate any relation of drug effect to individual level of intelligence. As set forth above, the premedication Maze level of the first chlorpromazine study was 12.2 years, while the premedication mean of the defectives was 11.2 years, not so much below the psychotic level. Moreover, the examination of our data does not reveal any lesser deficits for individuals with high premedication scores, but rather a reverse tendency. Apparently gains or losses in psychotics are not directly related to the premedication Maze level, but are determined on an individual physiological basis, as yet uncertain. They may, however, be related to the premorbid level that except in rare cases, cannot be determined in psychotic patients. In cases of mental deficiency the case stands differently, since that condition has existed from an early age.

In the children studied by Conners, Eisenberg, and Sharpe, a high degree of consistency of mental level except as affected by age may be assumed. In short, they differ from psychotics whose Maze levels have been affected by their mental pathology. Confusion in the published results underlines the fact that individual differences are of overriding importance. Whether subjects are psychosurgical patients or drug cases, the effects of the therapy usually differ widely. Some day enough may be known of functional localization to enable research workers to anticipate the varying effects of operations and drugs as reflected in specific test reactions. Until then, theorizing is interesting but hazardous.

The only circumstance consoling to investigators is that all these procedures are comparatively new. After 50 years of experience with the Porteus Maze, I am far from completely understanding the rationale of its application and results. As to prediction in individual cases, that is even more hazardous. Fifty years is a short span of time, especially when workers are few, investigators having many interests other than that of exploring Maze Test results and interpretations. Fortunately in the last 15 years more students have been attracted by the potential values of Maze applications so that the body of research, both in America and elsewhere, has considerably increased. In clinical practice many psychologists have been disposed to accept uncritically test claims. For example, the journals are full of articles assuming that brain damage can be reliably indicated by certain tests, such as the Bender-Gestalt, Rorschach, and Wechsler-Bellevue, when the evidence from research indicates that these scores are insignificantly affected, even after the most drastic damage. It seems strange to the writer that so much care and labor is expended on reporting investigations with little regard paid to the fundamental question as to whether the selection of tests on which the study is based is really promising for the purpose for which they are being used. Neither the popularity of the measures nor their usefulness in other situations, nor in fact the claims of their authors, can rightfully take the place of critical research. Two psychologists, Carney Landis and Harriet Babcock, have emphasized the importance of first-hand experience with and knowledge of tests. Their independent counsels offered in two articles, entitled respecively "Psychologists Should Study Psychology" (Babcock, 1948) and "Experimental Methods in Psychopathology" (Landis, 1949), are deserving of very careful attention.

The latest summary of results achieved by Conners and Eisenberg has been reported to me by letter.[5] Their findings read as follows:

The children for this study were out-patients in a Children's Psychiatric Service with the diagnosis of hyperkinetic behavior disorder. The children were given an extensive battery of psychological and clinical appraisal procedures. These included anxiety scales, mood scales, parent, school and psychiatric ratings, and family evaluations by a social worker.

The children were randomly assigned to dextro-amphetamine or its matched placebo with an average dose of 10 mg. per day over an 8-week period on a double-blind design. The Porteus mazes and other tests were administered prior to treatment and on the last day of treatment. The results show highly significant increase in Porteus test quotients in the drug treated group (see accompanying table). The qualitative scores did not show significant changes. The results were further substantiated by highly significant ratings of improvement by teachers who had no knowledge of the treatment conditions. The clinician's ratings also showed improvement in the drug-treated group. Improvement in motor control under stress was also noted in the drug group, using a modified Luria tremorgraph procedure.

These findings confirm results from an earlier experiment with the use of a stimulant in treating disturbed children.

[5] Quoted by permission from a letter from Dr. C. Keith Conners, dated July 17, 1964.

Porteus Maze Test Quotient Scores Before and After Treatment

	DEXEDRINE			PLACEBO	
	Pre	Post		Pre	Post
N	19	19		19	17
X	102.79	118.63		105.63	107.59
σ	16.37	10.41		17.14	18.66
σ_D		17.97			6.96
σ_{DD}			4.77		

$$t \ (df = 34) = 3.32, \ p < .01$$

SUMMARY

The increasing use of the Maze Test in problems of abnormal psychology is noted, as proved by the number of research reports in which medical men and psychologists have collaborated. This has been apparent not only as regards the effects of psychosurgery —now likely to disappear as a topic in the literature—but with regard to therapeutic drugs, which have displaced lobotomy, leucotomy, and other neurosurgical approaches in medical favor.

Because of the observable social improvement following the use of "tranquilizing" drugs, such as chlorpromazine, the writer began his investigations in this field with the expectation that increased Maze Test scores would be found. The parallel with the results of psychosurgery was discounted at first as a special case.

The research design set up at the Hawaii State Hospital indicated that, while socializing was improved, there was a serious loss in Maze performance. Dubiety with regard to the value of control groups in mental hospitals was expressed. However, individually matched patients in groups of "on-drug" and "no-drug" groups showed a decline after medication of over 2 years in Maze Test scores.

Results of studies with mental defectives are reported, variations in reported results being due probably to variance in the duration of drug administration. In one investigation loss in learning task ability was also noted, but other tests failed to register any decline. Another team of researchers (Mirsky and Rosvold, 1960) suggest that the reticular formation of the midbrain mediates awakeness, or mental alertness, and if so, drugs that affect the midbrain are likely also to affect certain test activities.

The present writer theorizes that blunting of emotion assists the socializing process, making the individual easier to work and live with. Thus tranquilizers and psychosurgery may logically be expected to improve that type of passive adjustment without increasing planning capacity. Capacity to entertain anxiety may be the trait that is changed.

Other studies are cited which, however, neglected the practice effect apparent in repetition of the same Maze Test series, a procedure that masks any deteriorating trend.

A very important side light is thrown on Maze functions by an inquiry into behavior under the influence of LSD in a study by Aronson and Klee (1960). Significant differences were exhibited by groups who took the drug in doses of 75 and 100 mcg., and much more significant differences for the drugless control group compared with those who took the drug, thus illustrating how ability to exercise critical control was affected.

One study almost unique in its field has to do with the effect of B-complex vitamin deficiency on test performance. Out of a number of psychological measures applied by O'Shea *et al.*, the Maze stood out as showing that scores declined with severity of avitaminosis and rose in almost direct proportion to therapeutic measures. This suggests a possible relation between inferior Maze performance in primitive groups, such as the Kalahari Bushmen. If this is a valid connection, it could have a profound effect on the interpretation of racial differences.

Attention is drawn to studies in England, one by Foulds and the other by Macdonald Tow, who used a different method of application and scoring of the Maze. The first study related to the differentiation of psychoneurotic groups, the second to Maze reactions of normal subjects who had undergone leucotomy while enthusiasm in England for the operation was at its height. Total time taken by subjects for the test increased as did also the number of entrances into blind alleys. This was confirmed by an American investigation.

One psychiatrist-psychologist team has been busy at Johns Hopkins Hospital in experimenting with the use of a central stimulant drug in the inhibiting of impulsive reactions. The Maze means of contrasted groups indicate a therapeutic effect of the drug as measured by Maze scores, the favorable changes being more marked in emotionally disturbed children of lower intelligence levels than in those with higher mental ratings. The authors point out also that

the amphetamines and chlorpromazine have reciprocally antagonistic effects. The Maze is thus seen to be sensitive to this type of
therapy.

The ambiguous nature of a few current findings serves to accentu-
ate the novelty of the above approaches and the youthfulness of
clinical psychology.

CHAPTER FIVE

Juvenile Delinquency and Crime

The first and most obvious obligation of those whose responsibility it is to investigate a violent crime is to look for clues. The time, the manner of the deed, the weapon, objects left on the scene, fingerprints, the victim's background are all carefully considered in the hope that they may reveal the identity of the perpetrator. On the other hand, the psychologist, interested in the field of scientific investigation, must center consideration on the criminal rather than on the crime. Specifically, he wants to know whether there is such a thing as a delinquent style of reaction that marks behavior and thus provide clues for recognition or prediction.

A great deal of effort has already been expended on advancing the theory that the social offender is *sui generis,* an individual mentally, temperamentally, or even physically apart from the rest of us. The last assumption is an extension of the old notion of the mark of the cloven hoof or the brand of Cain. Unfortunately, this type of endeavor brought results of little worth. Physical types and stigmata when studied seemed to show tendencies to be somewhat concentrated among prison populations, but further inquiry proved that their incidence was characteristic of different social classes rather than of deviant moral status. The relationships that appeared to exist between conduct and physical characteristics proved to be extremely tenuous.

The question resolves itself into this sort of dilemma—is an individual untrustworthy because his eyes are too closely set together, or has their setting nothing to do with honesty? This type of speculation has, of course, no scientific merit. Phrenology and physiognomy and bodily typology seem to have had their day. On the other hand, unwillingness to meet another person's direct gaze may be indicative of some kind of conscious inadequacy or personality defect. The question as to whether certain temperamental trends possibly associated with crime are more common among Italians and Negroes is as yet unresolved.

Since delinquency is in the last legal resort entirely a matter of overt behavior, the study of criminal reactions would seem to offer the reward of better understanding of one of the most perplexing human problems. If the psychiatrists are right in claiming that crime is a disease, then its symptoms should be carefully noted and tabulated. But the warning must at once be given that such psychiatric claims are not necessarily true. Their case is not yet proved and will not be until they can list the specific ways in which delinquents tend to act alike and which are different to the ways of the rest of us. In other words, the symptoms of a legal disorder are indeed difficult to specify, as witness the confusion in the definition of insanity. Being in prison does not necessarily determine criminality any more than living in a feebleminded institution constitutes a diagnosis of mental deficiency. Laws are man-made, and men are liable to error. The difficulty of diagnosis of criminal tendencies must be a worry to the psychiatrist. For many years political prisoners were usually considered to be of a different stripe from their fellow-prisoners even though their treatment was the same. How, then, should they be classified? If the psychiatrist insists that a delinquent is sick, he should be able to tell us how sick he is and the site of his illness. "Sick in the mind" is a very vague diagnosis.

The basic difficulty, apart from the problem of an exclusive definition of a criminal or delinquent, is that the causes of law-breaking are so many and various that to speak of wrongdoing in the legal sense as "a disease" would savor strongly of irrelevancy. The trouble with the analysis of moral behavior is that the good overlaps so widely with the bad that it is impossible, except in extreme instances, to say who is sick and who is well. In attempting to determine distinctive behavior patterns, the psychologist as well as the psychiatrist is faced with the immense variability of human conduct. Because of the overlap, or the existence of a thickly populated zone of moral "shadiness," the best that the student can do is to recognize marked *trends* or patterns of action and reaction. There is a large group of symptoms shown by the "bad actor," none of which is pathognomic.

With regard to trends in Maze Test reactions, I learned long ago that poor quality of performance rather than inferior test age characterizes the performance of delinquents. Even as early as 1922, while carrying out research among the inmates of the Vineland Training School, an institution "devoted to the interests of those whose minds have not developed normally," problems of differentiation were complicated by inability to describe adequately the term "normally." Among the mentally retarded or subnormal were included some whose behavior was either delinquent or psychopathic. The best I could do in the way of differentiation by analogy was to represent subnormality as a small circle, indicating an area of intellectual constriction within the larger circle of normality; delinquency by a somewhat larger inside sphere, the circumference of which was irregular; psychopathy by a star-shape with a very jagged outline drawn roughly inside the circle of normality, the points of which could reach to and even extend beyond the range of ordinary intelligence.

My early task was to discover whether Maze reactions were different in the delinquents, the expectation being that when misconduct was related to constitutional weaknesses these would be reflected in the test record. In the phraseology of that time, these inadequacies were ascribed to "weakness of will" as though "will power" was a unit character, overlooking the fact that inhibitions are very selective in operation; one may be poorly inhibited in one set of circumstances, strongly resistant in others.

But the psychopathic individuals, so-called, show even greater irregularities of conduct than the delinquent. Their moral deviations seem to have a different point of origin or etiology. Under a given set of environmental pressures, the delinquent's actions present some indication of socially adaptive response, if only to the standards of his peers. But the reaction of the psychopathic to environment seems out of all reasonable proportion or relevancy. The matter appears to boil down to predictability of response to environmental factors. The well-adjusted individual, even though intellectually defective, can be relied upon to act consistently at a low level of efficiency; on the other hand, the delinquent's behavior is less predictable, and psychopathic conduct is so unpredictable as to be quite unreasonable or bizarre. The psychologist himself is in some situations inept and can therefore understand the inadequacy of the mental defective. He is not immune to temptation and can therefore put himself in the situation of any wrongdoer. But in relation to psychopathy, this seems so far outside the orbit of ordinary conduct that he cannot from his own experience account for it. In spite of wide differences as regards what is personally permissible in conduct, most of us would agree as to general standards of right and wrong. A mind that sees those standards as seriously inoperative is insane.

Psychologists' knowledge of the two conditions of delinquency and psychopathy cannot be expressed in positive terms but in degrees of ignorance. We know a little about the basis of delinquency but practically nothing at all about the causation of mental abnormality. Under such circumstances, I cannot see why members of my own profession should invade the field of mental abnormality, either as regards diagnosis or treatment. The only justification for so doing may arise from recognition of the fact no one can claim to have really expert knowledge; both the psychologist and his medical confreres are very poorly armed with the weapons of research and understanding and must enter the field with limited confidence. This chapter will attempt to sum up some results of an objective measure used also in somewhat limited investigations of delinquent and psychopathic persons.

Forty-one years ago writers such as myself could be forgiven some rather naïve formulations, characterized by the rather glib use of general terms such as motivation, the full meaning and application of which is so uncertain as to leave the problem as vaguely defined as ever. There was then, as now, a tendency to believe that when we had invented a blanket term, we knew what was underneath it. In attempting to differentiate psychopathic from delinquent behavior, I wrote:

> It is probably true that some of the delinquencies have a psychopathic basis. The only criterion which we can apply is that of motivation. If the action seems to proceed from normal motivation and is proportionate (relevant?) to the aims of the individual, then there is no reason for regarding such action as psychopathic. It is when the conduct is ill-founded or disproportionate in respect to motivation that we regard it as psychopathic (Porteus, 1922).

Unfortunately, judgments of motivation with regard to our own actions as well as those of others are often "ill-founded," so that the criterion is not of easy application. Only when the individual has progressed in his psychopathy to the point of hallucinations or delusions, or extreme variability of conduct, can we be sure of the abnormality of his motivation.

The practical question is whether the Maze reactions provide clues to a delinquent "diagnosis." In the book already quoted, I have this to say:

It is noteworthy, however, that even though the test age credited to many delinquents may be relatively high, their mental alertness as shown in quickness of perception and readiness of action being often in evidence, their responses to the tests may show qualitative differences from those of normals of equal test age. In other words, observation of the test response may bring to light important temperamental differences which are not to be expressed in terms of mental or test age. (Porteus, 1922, p. 85.)

In the light of later experience, this statement should be modified. As we shall see later, studies of groups of maladjusted children do reveal some test-age differences.

However, although qualitative differences in reaction were duly noted, no attempt was made for nearly 20 years to measure them, though I listed (Porteus, 1941) as characteristic of delinquent reactions the crossing of lines, cutting of corners, underestimation of the difficulty of the task resulting in initial errors or overconfidence, impulsive changes in direction, disregard of instructions, such as not to lift the pencil during the course of the tracing of a single design. Later, a numerical scoring was devised that took account of the frequency of these errors in execution among various delinquent and nondelinquent populations and was described in monograph form. These various errors were summated and weighted to provide a numerical qualitative score (Q-score) (Porteus, 1942, 1954).

A degree of relationship with more serious and more habitual delinquent careers was indicated by a Q-score of 57 for adult criminals, whereas 100 Honolulu bus-drivers scored 18 points, a better showing than that of (younger) high school students. There were low negative correlations between Q-scores and Maze Test mental ages, indicating an insignificant relationship between quality of workmanship and ability to avoid the major mistakes of entering blind alleys.

A follow-up study was undertaken three years later (Porteus, 1945), which neatly confirmed previous results; 50 delinquent boys averaged 48 points, almost exactly the same as the earlier group. Another group of 100 prison inmates scored 58 points. Then, to test the suspicion that it was not actually declared delinquency that was responsible for high Q-scores but rather a wide complex of habitual reactions not necessarily issuing in overt offences, another study was undertaken.

Teachers were asked to select the lazy, undependable pupils who refused to conform faithfully to the school's standards and, though by no means unintelligent, failed in achievement commensurate with their mentality. To my surprise their Q-score mean was also 48 points, while the record of the industrious, reliable pupils was 23 points, thus proving that the label "delinquent" had no magic significance in dividing the sheep from the goats. This left the investigator still puzzling over the question—what is a delinquent?

The close correspondence between these successive studies seemed to me to be a little too good to be true, but other psychologists working independently made similar findings. Catherine Wright (1944), working at the Nelles School in Whittier, Calif., examined 54 delinquent boys, and they scored 49 Q-score points. Only the Grajales (1948) study differed to any noticeable extent. His 60 subjects, being children who had appeared before the Children's Court of New York and then were referred for psychiatric treatment, scored 56 points. It was noteworthy that when he segregated 25 scores of Negro boys, their average was 49 points. Unfortunately, neither Wright nor Grajales had any nondelinquents to serve as controls, and so they accepted my Q-score figures for normal boys. However, this deficit in investigation was later repaired by Docter and Winder (1954). They went back to the Nelles School and examined 60 boys whom they compared with an equal number of nondelinquents "matched for age, sex, mental ability, race and, for the most part, socio-economic level." This latter group had been selected from the ninth and tenth grades of California schools.

The results were confirmatory of the previous studies to a quite extraordinary degree. The mean qualitative score of the delinquents was 47 points as against 48 and 49 points obtained in previous studies. The control group of nondelinquents averaged 25 points as against the previously reported mean score of 22 for male students in Honolulu. The critical ratio of the difference being 5, the difference would be considered statistically reliable.

The present writer had found a critical or cut-off score of 29 to be exceeded by 80 per cent of delinquent males. For girls the cut-off score was 32 points. Docter and Winder found that 70 per cent of the delinquents and 20 per cent of the nondelinquents had scores above 29 Q-score points. Thus their qualitative error scoring was not as discriminatory as I had found.

These investigators arrived at some other very interesting conclusions. If the various categories of errors were left unweighted and a cut-off score of 16 points adopted, the critical ratio of the differences between experimental and control groups was still 5.18 and the percentages above and below the cutoff were about the same. As regards the reliability of two persons scoring the tests, a correlation of .98 was found, which, considering the rather subjective nature of the judgment of "wavy lines," seems to me to be almost incredibly high.

As previously mentioned, Grajales (1948) had no control group, but he noted that 94 per cent of his delinquent group had scores above, (i.e., worse than) my nondelinquent average. He states that the Maze "used as a qualitative scale discriminates clearly between normal and delinquent adolescent boys. . . . The difference between the averages of the two groups is absolutely significant since the critical ratio is 8.6." Also worth quoting is Grajales' statement as to the interest of his subjects in taking the test, a point of extreme importance when any segregated groups, such as delinquents or untutored primitive peoples, are concerned. He says: "The boys liked the test; they wanted to be tested. If at times we had to interrupt our work because of the requirements of the Hospital or because of a visit of the parents, usually the boys came back willingly and without being called. Boys who have recently arrived at the Hospital asked to be given the test." Oddly enough this readiness to take the test was noted in almost the same terms with Australian aborigines in 1962.

In passing, I would say that I wish I could be as optimistic as Grajales that the Maze "discriminates clearly" the delinquent. If we could be sure that the latter's temperamental inadequacies are unfailingly demonstrated by the test, it would be a great advance toward a better understanding of the problem. Unfortunately there is an overlap of at least 20 per cent. As we have previously stated, although temperamental inadequacies are clearly demonstrable, it is still true that they do not always issue in delinquency. Thus we are in a quandary analogous to that of the social worker who observes so frequently that the delinquent is the product of an unsatisfactory or broken home, but cannot explain why some of the offender's siblings escape the blight of declared delinquency. In other words, a bad environment is not the crucial determinant. Neither, apparently in our experience, is the presence in the delinquent's makeup of deviant characteristics. In short, delinquent tendencies do not always fulfil themselves.

The most probable theory is that temperamental weaknesses and an unfavorable environment are predisposing co-factors. It may, however, be the case that environmental factors may sometimes have a reverse effect. Some individuals with strongly self-determined goals prefer to swim against the current rather than be swept headlong downstream.

If we could center our research attention on the less explicable cases—the nondelinquents who have poor Q-scores and the delinquents who demonstrate the possession of good work habits in the test—then we might help to resolve our problem. If, for example, we found that the first-mentioned types, namely, nondelinquents with poor Q-scores, are bolstered or supported by favorable environmental influences, and that, conversely, the delinquents who have good test records are the victims of unusually corrupting influences, then some of the anomalies of the situation might disappear. Inevitably the problem will not be found to have too definite a relationship with nurtural factors, otherwise all the "underprivileged" would tend to be delinquent. The whole personality of these selected deviates must be studied and analysed. Quite possibly a boy may have the desire to steal but has so timorous a disposition that he is afraid to venture into wrongdoing. The girl may have unusually strong sex propensities but yet is so keenly aware of the social consequences that she fears to indulge. Fear may not be the most admirable factor in behavior, but a lively anticipation of consequences is an effective deterrent. Personality differences demand careful study of all the individual checks and balances. The great danger lies in oversimplification of the problem.

So far, of course, these are assumptions, more or less likely ones. But my own belief is that it is the borderline cases that will best repay intensive study. In the present state of our knowledge, we have to be content with noting the overlap in test performance and await the research that will enable us to interpret it adequately. Once it has been agreed that the nondelinquents who possess deviant tendencies offer the best promise for intensive study, new tests would surely be forthcoming.

Many years ago I devised a set of questions that plainly demonstrated a tendency of delinquents toward self-indulgent habits (Porteus, 1941). A number of situations of frequent occurrence in youth were categorized according to the choices of three hypothetical individual boys. Each situation represented three degrees of self-indulgence, one ordinary, another somewhat marked, and the third excessive. None of these character traits, however, was actually very extraordinary or reprehensible. They concerned frequency of attendance at movies, amount of ice cream consumed, etc., and the subjects were asked to indicate which choice they themselves would like to make.

But it was found to be difficult in such a questionnaire to cover adequately the gamut of juvenile pleasurable experiences or to weight choices in such varied situations. The chief problem was, however, to assess the truth of such self-estimates, a weak point in all self-evaluation, the tendency being to regard oneself as moderate in reactions. There was no means of deciding whether the individual would actually exercise the choice he indicated as the one he would like to make. Nevertheless, the percentage number of extreme reactions was much greater for the delinquents than nondelinquents. The self-indulgency score for all delinquent boys was 27.07 (SD 11.87), for 248 nondelinquents 16.43 points (SD 8.4), the critical ratio being 6.81. This was a significant difference, but again the overlap was considerable.

My experience in this field leads me to believe that self-indulgence is not nearly as critical in determining delinquent behavior as is proneness to make decisions that a certain course of action either will not have untoward results or that those consequences can be avoided—in other words, that events can be manipulated. So often the misdoer is confident that carelessness or poor planning is responsible for his detection. His theory is that only the stupid individual is caught. Then, too, the criminal or delinquent has considerable faith in his luck. This confidence, which has, of course, no real basis, is not confined to misdoing. The soldier in battle is often upheld by the belief that while others may be hit, his time has not yet come. In other words, his fate is predetermined. However, this faith is far from complete, so he takes every possible precaution, seeking every bit of shelter that is available.

If it were possible to obtain some measure of the tendency "to take a chance," it should provide a very good index of actual and potential delinquency in both boys and girls. For example, though the strength of the sex impulse differs greatly in individuals, I believe that the crucial factor in successful inhibition of the impulse is based upon the ability clearly to forsee and imaginatively experience the possible consequences of sex indulgence. I fear, however, that the test, if devised, would have to be general rather than specific. Sex behavior, for instance, is so subject to conditioning that what we are examining is not a developing but an already developed trend. It might be possible, therefore, to invent a game or test that would apply to financial investments but would not be as subject to emotional crises that so strongly affect sex behavior. But it would be of advantage no doubt to obtain an index of adventurousness in general, and a test of this kind should not unduly strain the 'ingenuity of psychologists. Meanwhile the high Q-scores of female sex offenders would seem to provide an indication of impulsivity that could be related to sex proclivities. Possibly masculine disregard of consequences in certain sex activities arises from the fact that those consequences seem milder in comparison, more easily avoided, and are longer deferred.

Some other phenomena belonging in the field under discussion have been studied. One is the possible relation of Q-scores to ethnic constitution. People who have lived and worked in Hawaii are prone to see racial groups in terms of stereotypes. Actually, there is nothing at all scientifically wrong with stereotypical classifications. Many of these beliefs are true in the main, but break down in their application to individuals. It may be true, for example, that Hawaiians are as a group easy-going, uncalculating, generous, and very permissive as regards behavior of people of other groups whom they know well. The danger arises when the generalism is applied to the individual. Actually, stereotypes are very useful; it is when they threaten to hinder original observations, or to become too universal in reference that they become dangerous.

In any case, the Hawaiian mold of temperament is so consistently recognizable that in applying the Q-score technique to delinquents, among whom there is a disproportion of part-Hawaiians, we laid ourselves open to the accusation that we were not setting forth delinquent tendencies so much as examining the Hawaiian disposition; or, in other words, that our delinquent scores would not be so high if groups of a different blood and social background were to be studied. At an early stage in the application of Q-scores, studies elsewhere were not available in sufficient numbers to discount this theory. Hence we decided to have a further look at the Maze reactions of nondelinquent Hawaiians.

The availability of the students of Kamehameha Schools, a well-endowed residential institution for the education of the progeny of Hawaii's original people, admission to which was dependent on possessing some admixture of Hawaiian blood, gave an opportunity to apply the Maze Test and score it qulaitatively. There is no doubt that the student body represents a highly selected group, the moral, educational, and social standards for pupils being high. Kamehameha Schools' chief aim was undoubtedly to develop potential leaders of the Hawaiian people. Supported by funds from the Bishop Estate, originally donated by Princess Pauahi Bishop and supplemented by her husband, Charles Reed Bishop, the schools possess a fine campus, excellent buildings, and a healthy school spirit in both student body and staff. An additional advantage is that it is coeducational, thus emphasizing the relatively high status of women in Polynesian societies. A rather interesting fact is that Kamehameha Schools present an example of segregation in reverse, since non-Caucasian blood is a requisite for admission and not a reason for exclusion. Whether any pure Hawaiians are left is extremely doubtful.

Under such conditions it would have been surprising if students' qualitative scores were not very good; nevertheless, the level of performance was beyond all anticipation. The boys (N 31) had 13.66 qualitative error points as against a mean for predominantly part-Hawaiian delinquents of about 48 points; 25 girls averaged 15.8 points as against the delinquent girls' mean of 53 points. This really tremendous difference between delinquents and nondelinquents of similar racial blends is a rather striking, if indirect, validation of the Q-scores, but at the same time it underscores emphatically the importance of the factor of selection as regards interracial group comparisons.

Obviously, racial comparisons are most meaningful when they apply to representative groups. If further demonstration of the truism is needed, then the individual and group ranges of Maze scores are so wide as to prove that the ethnic label which is worn by anyone does not and cannot determine his intellectual status as an individual. Actually, no impartial student holds this view. Nevertheless, racial differences may be very real and significant if their range and distribution is taken into account. In other words, the question is not whether Hawaiian, Negro or Australid men of high degree occur, but how often they appear. The inclusion of individuals of mixed blood complicates the situation. Apparently the range and distribution of Maze Q-scores are even more varied than Maze test ages.

A testing survey, which was carried out with pupils of ordinary schools in Hawaii, enabled us to obtain representative samples. This placed Japanese (N 219) in the lead with 21 points; Chinese (N 72) second with 22 points; part-Hawaiians (N 83) third with 30 points; Portuguese and Koreans had worse Q-scores, but the number of cases were too few to be considered representative. Again, it must be remembered that the lower the Q-score, the better the performance.

One other more recent study (Porteus and Gregor, 1963) pin-points the problem of definition of delinquency. During the process of establishing the comparative standardization of the third (Supplement) series of Mazes, all the students of the ninth grade in a Honolulu intermediate high school were examined by both the Extension and Supplement series. Males numbered 249, females 259. It so happened that besides standardization data, the material included some other features, such as Q-scores, conformity-flexibility indices, sex differences, etc., and that delinquent tendencies also offered themselves for investigation. Hence the staff members who were applying the tests decided on their own initiative to try to discover whether the group, supposedly nondelinquent, was actually so. Accordingly, at the end of the testing they asked four apparently innocuous questions regarding the boys' favorite subjects of instruction, special school difficulties, etc., and then suddenly confronted them with the direct query—have you ever been in any trouble with the police? Subjects had been previously assured that nothing that transpired in the interview or testing would be communicated to the school or other authorities.

The question met with varied receptions. Some answered immediately in the negative, others hesitated before answering, either negatively or affirmatively. The significant thing was that, after disregarding minor traffic offenses, such as riding a bicycle at night without lights, etc., 48 out of 160 boys questioned admitted more or less serious offenses. Later the records of the Crime Prevention Department were consulted and 16 others were added to the list.

Since none had been committed to the Detention Home nor a training school, they could be designated a mildly delinquent group. Their mean Q-score (N 64) was found to be 44, whereas the mean for the 201 nondelinquents was 28.

The lesson to be learned from this study is that it is unwise for investigators to assume that their subjects can be declared to be exclusive of delinquents without special inquiry as to their history. It also indicates the sensitivity of the qualitative scores and the need for special study of those individuals with deviant temperaments who nevertheless escape the label "delinquent."

The number of studies in which the mean delinquent Q-score was very close to 49 points would indicate a definite trend. Whenever, however, the group investigated consists of specially classified delinquent cases, a variation occurs. For example, Fooks and Thomas (1957) carried out a study involving 50 cases (25 boys, 25 girls) in Connecticut institutions. These had been diagnosed by psychiatrists as delinquent psychopaths or as having psychopathic tendencies. They were then matched with students from the New London High School on the basis of age, sex, intelligence, and socio-economic status of parents. Hence, members of this experimental group were somewhat selected, representing those whose delinquencies were complicated by psychopathy. Both the Original (Vineland Revision) form of the Maze (Porteus, 1919) and the Extension Series (Porteus, 1955) were applied.

The investigators found a mean Q-score of 40 in the Original Series (SD 18) as against the nondelinquents' mean of 22, the latter very close to that found in several other studies. Those cited by Fooks and Thomas included two studies by myself (Porteus, 1942, 1945), in which the nondelinquents averaged 22 (N 100) and 19 points (N 179) respectively.

The Q-scores for the Extension Series, gave a nondelinquent mean (both sexes combined) of 24 points (N 300). In a later study (Porteus, 1959), the Extension Series was given first, followed by the Supplement. The mean on both series combined was 30 points (N 508). The score obtained by Fooks and Thomas on the Extension Series was 28 points as compared with their psychopathic delinquents' mean of 46 points in the same test series. The similarity of these scores is very close, though the delinquents were selected on a different basis.

With this consideration in view, we may quote the Fooks-Thomas conclusion with regard to their findings. "Qualitative (Q) scores on both tests (Original and Extension) significantly differentiate between delinquents and nondelinquents (p < .001)." To this they add the following notes: "No sex difference in the Q-score, no significant relationship between intelligence as represented by the test age or quantitative score, a nonweighted system of scoring (as suggested by Docter and Winder) almost as efficient as the present system; an inter-scorers reliability of r .98."

A blanket term such as delinquency, which certainly covers a multitude of specific sins, is difficult to correlate with test responses because there is no quantitative measure of the degrees of delinquency. How many burglaries, for example, should be balanced against one rape? Frequency of offenses may be used as an index, but there are some crimes the gravity of which draws such condign punishment that the criminal has little chance of repeating such offenses. Thus a common prison classification such as "recidivist" may not have much real significance. It should, however, be interesting to inquire whether the type of offense has any relation to Maze Q-scores.

According to the 1945 study, those convicted of the more violent crimes, such as murder, rape, or assault with a dangerous weapon (N 56), had a mean Q-score of 67 points. Their impulsive personalities are reflected in their type of test performance, indicating lack of deliberation and social inhibitions. In Hawaii, because of the excess of males in certain ethnic classifications, there is heavy incidence of the less serious sexual crimes, such as intercourse with a female under 16 years. Frequency of female sex offenses is probably related to lax family supervision among the part-Hawaiian groups. Persons who possess these low standards of behavior, whether as regards a job or social behavior, are likely to betray the tendency in Maze performance. Sex offenders' mean (N 59) was 57 points of Q-score. A group which can be expected to exhibit better planning—often at a skilled level—are the burglars, 55 of whom scored on an average 54 points. Embezzlers and forgers often manage to avoid detection for long periods of time; 29 men in this category had the relatively low Q-score of 44 points, or 23 points better than the impulse-driven, extremely aggressive, socially dangerous criminals.

But again we must emphasize that individuals are found who may be free from demonstrable test deviations. Some murders are deliberately and carefully planned; shop-lifting may be the specific outcome of inner compulsions, not exhibited in the offenders' generalized behavior trends. Modern genetics has shown what grave changes can result from a single gene substitution, and the key to much abnormal conduct may be so concealed that it is easily overlooked, or is actually indetectible.

In default of rating scales for delinquent behavior, we must fall back on group data to discover whether younger, less seriously committed cases show any relationship between their habits of social misconduct and their Maze reactions. Admittedly, the twofold classification of well-adjusted and ill-adjusted children is not very discriminatory and so lacks critical determination, but in default of any other yardstick, we must rely on such comparisons. We can cite two very early investigations.

The most significant of these researches were two studies, the first by Poull and Montgomery (1929), the second by Karpeles (1932), the subjects of both investigations being cases resident at a youth facility on Randall's Island, New York. This housed delinquents as well as nondelinquents so that two types of cases were available, thus enabling comparisons of the Maze Test ages of both groups. The qualitative scoring had not then been devised.

In the Poull-Montgomery study there were 72 cases considered maladjusted because of "stealing, boisterous behavior, teasing, fighting and inability to get along with companions, parents or guardians." The second group of 81 cases were reported to be "law-abiding, self-controlled, diligent and cooperative individuals." Perhaps one note of caution should be inserted here. Just as we have found that unrecognized delinquents occasionally are included among supposedly delinquency-free cases, so also institution supervisors tend to overrate the individuals in their charge who conform to rules and regulations. There may be a distinction between socially and institutionally well-adjusted cases, so that some model inmates finally prove they lack self-control outside.

Though the Stanford-Binet showed no average differences between the two groups, the Maze Test quotients were 9 points lower for the maladjusted. Karpeles, three years later, tested a larger number of cases, also resident at Randall's Island, and classified the maladjusted by types of offense. Her group included 100 thieves, 72 truants, 43 sex offenders, and 41 called simply "behavior problems." Her control group, of good institutional repute, numbered 185 cases. Their Maze Test quotient was 94, while that of all 256 maladjusted was 86 points, or 8 points lower than the well adjusted, almost the same deficiency as in Poull and Montgomery's previous study (9 points).

Karpeles segregated her cases into two groups, those above and those below 80 TQ (IQ) in the Binet. This was to test my observation that, diagnostically speaking, the Maze Test had its greatest usefulness with high grade cases where the Binet score was inconclusive.

The well-adjusted group of higher intelligence averaged 100.5 TQ in the Maze, and for those who presented behavior problems, the average was 11 TQ points lower, so that social adjustment or its reverse was apparently not closely related to intelligence.

The breakdown of cases according to offenses showed that the thieves' mean Maze score was 92, the truants and sex offenders were about equal with 85 and 86 respectively, and the smaller group with miscellaneous behavior problems (N 41) had the low average of 79 TQ points. Probably the thieves had more initiative and mental alertness than the others, and the last named classification may have included some defectives.

There are other recent studies in which the numbers of cases are less but which are worth citing because of their present-day interest. The results of an investigation in the Children's Annex of the Psychiatric Division of the Johns Hopkins University Hospital were kindly communicated to me, prior to publication (Conners and Eisenberg, 1963). This study provides a good instance of psychologist-psychiatrist co-operation.

There were two different groups available, one of which consisted of children placed in the Annex while they awaited foster home placement, but otherwise were considered normal; the other consisted of cases kept in residence to undergo treatment on account of frequently evident disturbed behavior. In spite of slightly higher verbal IQ's and chronological age, this latter group scored considerably lower on the Maze than did the "normal" children, notwithstanding the fact that the latter could be classified as underprivileged. The difference between the two groups was significant by the t test standard (p < .001). However, there was no relationship visible between Maze scores and the General Anxiety Scale for Children and with the Children's Manifest Anxiety Scale.

Another extremely interesting investigation has been reported to me by Dr. F. Clement (private communication), from Montreull, France, in 1957. He divided 32 carefully selected feebleminded into two equal groups of different etiology. Those with parents of inferior intelligence but who were themselves free from mental disturbance in early childhood were classed as endogenes; those termed exogenes had normal parents but had been affected by maternal conditions during their mothers' pregnancies or suffered in early infancy from shock or infectious diseases capable of bringing about mental deficiency. Both groups were of equivalent ages and intelligence, each averaging 55 IQ in Binet scores. They were respectively 16 years 2 months and 15 years 11 months in chronological age. M. Clement was interested in discovering whether the Maze when applied in its two general forms, the Original and the Extension Series, would reflect the behavioral differences between the two groups, to which a general intelligence test was not sensitive. It should be remembered that practice effects are supposed to be eliminated as between the Original and Extension Series.

As regards the endogenes this proved to be the case, since they scored 10.9 years in the Original, 10.7 years in the Extension. Nor did the relationship of the two series of tests differ greatly in the exogenes, the averages in the two series being 8 and 8.2 years respectively. However, the levels of Maze performance are seen to be almost 3 years lower in the exogenous group.

As regards qualitative scores, there was again little difference. The endogenes averaged 34.5 points in the Original, 32.4 in the Extension Series. But there was a wider spread among the exogenes whose average Q-score rose to 69 in the Original Series and was 62 points in the Extension.

M. Clement comments on these results. He was apparently impressed particularly by the fact that the endogenes are 15 points superior in the Maze as compared with the Terman-Binet, while the exogenes are at or about the same level in Binet and Maze, a fact that he thinks confirms his view that the endogenous group have better practical intelligence and a better prospect of social rehabilitation.

As for the Q-scores, which he notes were, for the endogenes, not much worse than for normals, they were almost twice as bad in the exogenes group, thus reflecting their observable social inadaptability and their characteristic disturbed behavior. His conclusion reads: "De cet ensemble on peut affirmer (tout au moins en ce qui regarde les debiles), que votre test des labyrinthes est un bien meilleur predicteur de l'intelligence 'utilisable' que les tests verbaux, ou les tests factoriellement purs."

This was indeed a clear-cut demonstration of the fact that groups of individuals, matched for age and of almost exactly the same general intelligence level, differ very much in social adaptability and that the Maze reflects this disparity of achievement. The characterization "utilisable intelligence" seems extremely apt. It is true that within the groups there were very wide deviations in Maze scores, both in test age and in quality of performance. The test age range for the endogenes was from 15 to 7 years (Original) and from 14 to 6½ years (Extension). The Q-scores in the same group ranged from 13 to 62 points (Original) and from 13 to 50 points (Extension). But in the case of the exogenes, the range is from 13 to 5 years in the Original Series, and from 14½ to 4 years in the Extension. As regards Q-scores, the exogenes ranged from 100 to 22 points (Original) and from 100 to 26 points (Extension). Yet these deviations are distributed in such a way that even in a small group of 16 Ss they tend to balance one another.

The question of the relationship of the Maze to social adjustment of various kinds, especially with regard to abnormalities of behavior in mental patients, has been discussed in a previous chapter.

It may well prove to be the case that qualitative scores in the Maze, in so far as they reflect temperamental traits rather than the more intellectual factors of planning capacity, actually cover fairly adequately the tendencies just discussed. The fact that in at least ten different studies, six by the writer and four by independent investigators, the Q-scores do differentiate delinquent from nondelinquent groups, lends support to this view. Possibly the gambler's attitude—based on his belief that since all eventualities cannot be foreseen, he may by initiative, readiness of resource, or even by cunning or mere luck, avoid all the consequential pitfalls— is reflected in the delinquent's Maze test execution. His interpretation of the Maze problem is that all he needs to do is to reach his goal—namely, find his way out of the labyrinth. If this is achieved, it often does not matter to him what evasions or disregard of instructions he employs, since these are not vital to success. He uses only sufficient care to "get by," never stops to consider his margin of safety, and as long as he arrives thinks that it does not matter to anyone else how unconventional his route may have been.

It must be admitted that there is more than a shadow of reason at the back of such attitudes—in other words, the delinquent is not wholly wrong. The individual who is cautious about his every step, who carries planning to such lengths that every detail is provided for, will probably be left far behind in the race. Plodding will certainly get you safely there, but almost as certainly too late. It is because life is such a mixture of certainties with uncertainties that safety cannot be the sole consideration. Not all short cuts are dangerous, so that a judicious mixture of deliberation with swiftness of decision makes up a normal way of life. The fact that we all have a delinquent streak explains why there are so many who get into hot water. As an English authority said with regard to the mental misfits —"the trouble in dealing with the feebleminded is that there are so many of us." This, I'm afraid, also applies to delinquency.

With regard to the qualitative scoring of the Maze, the fact of the wide spread of nonconformist tendencies lies behind the delinquent and nondelinquent overlap. But we must also reckon with resemblances of a more positive nature, with the fact that many delinquents possess worthwhile characteristics. It would be only the inexperienced psychologist who would deny possession of excellent if short-range planning ability to some criminals and delinquents. It may possibly be that the care and foresight that attend the execution of a successful criminal operation are absent in the execution of a Maze Test, where the penalties of failure seem slight or almost nonexistent.

Fortunately for the psychologist who sets up situations in miniature and judges the general reactions of his subjects in accordance with what they do in a test, there is a very strong tendency in the vast majority of people to keep their reactions as consistent as conveniently possible. This provides a basis of clinical psychology— to set up controlled experiments of such a nature and with such a method of observation that what the individual subject does will be characteristic of his everyday reactions, and so will betray what manner of man he is.

In all probability there is no group of cases which constitutes a more increasingly serious social problem than the juvenile delinquents, nor is there a greater need than that for understanding why they act as they do. Apparently all the checks and sanctions that society has devised for this condition are powerless to stem the rising tide of youthful misconduct. At what stage does normal motivation slip over into that complex of behavioral expression that we call delinquency? If ever clinical psychologists expect to be considered authoritative in this field, they must pay more attention to charting the mainsprings of action that give rise to juvenile rebellion and irresponsibility.

One very recent investigation seems to me to offer a new and promising approach to this problem. It has been instituted by Rochelle Kainer (1965) in New York.[1] The investigator wished to examine experimentally two opposing tendencies in early childhood, which she termed immediate and delayed gratification. She reasoned that if in response to increased awards gratification was inhibited or postponed, this would signify the practical exercise of planning and foresight. Since it is claimed that the Porteus Maze examines such non-intellective traits of personality and character, an experiment could be devised that would prove the Test's "construct validity."

The investigator's subjects were 100 kindergarten and first grade children divided into two groups according to their choice of either immediate or delayed enjoyment of candy, those in the "delayed" group receiving double the award. Only those who made consistent choices on two occasions were included. Verbal instructions were given in the simplest terms, and the author states that none of the observed results could be attributed to age or sex differences.

To quote the summary of results:

"The Porteus Maze quantitative performance of children who delayed gratification was significantly higher than that of those who chose immediate gratification.

"These results were interpreted as supporting Porteus' claim that the Maze measures a non-intellective aspect of intelligence, which may be more clearly stated as the ability to use reason to temporarily inhibit action."

It was also noteworthy that the verbal ability of the Delay Group was significantly better than that of the Immediate Group, although this did not entirely account for the superior Maze performance.

---

[1] I am indebted to Mrs. Kainer for communicating to me, in advance of publication, a summary of her doctoral thesis as presented in Teachers' College, Columbia University, 1965.

The investigator believes that the importance of verbal comprehension may possibly explain the significant correlations commonly found between the Maze and standard tests of intelligence. I would suggest, however, that the relationship of verbal ability may have been due to the extreme youth of the subjects, though the correlations referred to are found also with older groups. Undoubtedly, a clear verbal comprehension of the situation is important to the type of choice. In the field of child psychology, Kainer's approach would seem to be extremely promising.

Small (1954) carried out a study having a similar purpose to Kainer's, but his subjects were 162 war veterans hospitalized for somatic, non-psychiatric reasons. He correlated Maze scores with "foresight scales," but these were based on verbal self-judgments rather than on practical choices and did not have, therefore, the validity of overt activities. Nevertheless, Small interpreted his findings in almost identical terms as did Kainer, considering his results as "confirming Porteus's claims that the Mazes measure a personality or non-intellective characteristic of intelligence not encompassed by standard intelligence tests, and could be called foresight."

The most obvious next step is to use the same approach to the study of delinquents whose social foresight is certainly faulty. As they would be older, more experienced individuals, awards of a more general appeal than the gift of candy would be appropriate, such as money. It would be possible to vary the procedure from immediate acceptance to one, two, or three days' delay, the scale of awards varying in proportion to the length of voluntarily postponed gratification. The factor of chance could be later introduced, so that the odds against obtaining the progressively increased awards would also proportionately increase. The matter of risks versus gains could thus be investigated, though this would only apply to monetary situations, whereas willingness to postpone gratification might differ with the type of rewards. For these other types of gratification or fulfilment, the psychologist probably would be reduced to verbally expressed preferences.

Racial and social background, age and sex would, of course, need to be taken into account in such studies.

SUMMARY

The difficulties of measuring social behavior—especially that of juvenile delinquents and adult offenders—are admittedly great.

Hence, the evolution of a system for recognizing or differentiating these individuals apart from their legal classification remains one of the unsolved problems of clinical psychology. There are no reliable stigmata of social degeneration; hence the solution can only be reached through detailed studies of behavior. In the writer's opinion, the psychiatric tendency to regard delinquency as a disease and social offenders as sick individuals is not justified. What are the symptoms and the facts with regard to the course of the illness and its recovery?

There are, however, demonstrable temperamental inadequacies, and this demonstration can be made in the majority of delinquents by the use of a special scoring of Maze Test performance, which takes into account errors in style of execution. These when weighted and summated make up the qualitative score (Q-score). This gives us an objective measure, which can be the subject of research to a much more adequate degree than psychiatrically phrased judgments.

The writer's studies of Q-scores since 1941 are outlined and the fundamental differences between this scoring and the mental age approach are emphasized. These early findings showed that adult criminals had higher weighted error scores than younger offenders, and these in turn differed markedly from nondelinquent groups such as bus-drivers.

Male juvenile delinquents in Hawaii averaged 48 points of Q-score, and this mean was very close to that obtained in three mainland studies. New York cases referred for psychiatric treatment had higher Q-scores than were obtained in Hawaii, though the statement of the investigator as to clear discrimination from normals was too optimistic. A Connecticut study of offenders diagnosed by psychiatrists as delinquent psychopaths did not yield as high a mean Q-score, but still the gulf between this and that of matched nondelinquents remained highly significant.

The fact that there is about a 25 per cent overlap of delinquent and normal individual scores raises the interesting question as to why some social offenders have good scores and some nondelinquents have inferior performances. This suggests that these deviant individuals possibly could provide the key to discovery of the decisive factors. Undoubtedly, such an enquiry would result in the devising of other differential approaches, among them a test of adventurousness or "taking a chance."

The ethnic factor in delinquency was also explored in Hawaii in regard to part-Hawaiians, but the great amount of mixture of ethnic strains renders the results difficult to interpret because of the unequivalence of samples. However, with regard to other local ethnic groups, mean differences become apparent.

One experiment was most illuminating, and concerned the presence among supposedly "normal" research groups of a large percentage of self-admitted but unclassified mild delinquents. The lack of any criteria as regards severity of delinquency is also discussed. Failing this, we must rely on the use of vaguely defined dichotomies, such as well adjusted and maladjusted. Two New York studies proved that the Maze brought to light differences in mean test ages not apparent with other less specific tests.

The most promising modern development is that illustrated by Conners *et al.* in Baltimore in a study that showed that the administration of a stimulant drug to emotionally disturbed children brought about changes in Maze Test level and conduct. A French investigation by Clement also brought to light marked differences in Maze reactions of mentally defective "endogenes" and "exogenes," differentiated also by their social behavior.

CHAPTER SIX

The Maze Test and Sex Differences

Someone rather whimsically has remarked that if a visitor from outer space, who was familiar with only asexual reproduction, were to survey the human scene, the subject of his greatest mystification would be the differentiation of the sexes. The obvious outward physical, physiological, and mental differences would seem to him tremendous, but when confronted with observations of temperament, disposition, habits, attitudes, strengths and weaknesses, predispositions or immunities in health, and records of literary, inventive, scientific, and artistic achievement, he would probably conclude that men and women belonged in two distinct species. And being devoid of sexual experience, only the fact that the two species interbred freely might possibly disturb his theory.

But whimsy aside, it has seemed to me that mental differences associated with sex and their practical implications, though a subject of constant personal interest since men and women as we know them began to inhabit the earth, have not been adequately studied. In short, though a long list of students, ending, we hope, with Kinsey, have published their findings, they seem to me to be centered about sexuality rather than sex psychology. Is it not time to recognize that copulative behavior, at least in most respects, constitutes a very small fraction of what may be called sex behavior, in sum probably not more than we devote to excretion, with certainly no greater sense of urgency? As for the associated pleasure in satisfying the urge, it would not for many people be more evident than in eating. In short, as regards its relation to the survival of the individual, sexuality is minor.

This is by way of introduction to a brief section on the differences that exist between male and female performances in the Maze Test. The evidence I propose to offer is sufficient justification, I hope,

111

for presenting it to the attention of psychologists, but the statistical by-products of investigation are also to my mind very important.

My own interest in the subject dates back to my earliest involvement in psychological research. In 1915, with the approval of the Victorian Education Department, I was engaged in carrying out mental examinations of 1,000 school children between the ages of 5 and 14 years. Actually, the group designated as 5 years of age meant those who were over 5 but had not yet reached age 6, and so forth. The median age would be about a half year older. The tests used were the Stanford Revision of the Binet (Terman, *et al.* 1916) and an early form of the Porteus Maze, described in two journal articles (Porteus, 1915a, 1915b) and in a monograph (Porteus, 1919). This series did not then include any maze designs for adults. The mazes for adults were devised later, applied and reported upon by Porteus and Bassett (1920).

In the earlier work, scores for girls on the Maze, except at two age levels (11 and 12 years), had a somewhat higher correlation with the Binet than had scores for boys. The highest coefficient was .75 for nine-year-old girls (N 77), the lowest .24 for seven-year-old boys (N 63). In mean Maze Test ages the boys excelled the girls at every age level up to and including 11 to 12 years, the advantage being about .5 of a year throughout. But between 12 and 13 years the girls reversed the position and exceeded the boys' mean by .4 year. At 13 years there was very little difference, the girls having 0.1 of a year advantage. Above that age level, although numbers were small, there was a tendency for males to re-establish their superiority. At that time I was inclined to associate this female gain at 12 years with a spurt in physical development that apparently came a little earlier in girls than boys. These results, it should be remembered, applied only to Australian school children. It should be noted that on the Stanford-Binet the boys also held an advantage at each age, except at 10 and 12 years when the girls caught up with but did not exceed the boys.

Two years later the study was repeated with 1,255 cases, using a somewhat modified Maze (Berry and Porteus, 1920). The subjects ranged from 7 to 13 years of age and were attending ordinary (State) elementary schools in Melbourne, Australia. Again, boys were superior at every age level except at 12 years, with the boys in the 14-year age group taking a slight lead. Numbers of cases were approximately the same for both sex groups at 12 years (Ns 95 and 96), so that the difference would be likely to be statistically reliable. Thus this temporary spurt in Maze scores for girls at this age would have supported the notion of female superiority, if this were the only group examined. As we shall see, this conclusion would have proved to be completely unjustified as regards overall comparisons.

A further standardization study (Porteus, 1919) was carried out in an elementary school at Vineland, N. J., but applied to only two age levels, 6 years and 7 years. The results agreed with the already observed trend of male superiority; boys excelled girls at both levels. But the interesting question remained—what differences in Maze performances occur at educational levels above elementary grades?

Two adult tests, as previously mentioned, were devised and applied, along with the XII and XIV Year designs, to 682 high school children from 13 to 19 years of age attending schools in three towns of southern New Jersey (Vineland, Millville, and Bridgeton), the investigators being Porteus and Bassett (1920). The XII year test was used only as a practice performance, but for the other three higher tests a record was kept of number of trials and total times. The number of trials would, of course, reflect the individual quantitative Maze scores. Except at 13 years, where the cases were artificially restricted to bright children, and 18 and 19 years, where there was probably a disproportion of school "leftovers," the numbers of cases were adequate for an investigation of this type.

Considering first the XIV year test, once again the boys at each age level excelled the girls, except at 18 and 19 years, where numbers of cases were diminished. In Adult Test I, the boys took less trials (i.e., entered less blind alleys) at every age level except 14 years, where males were very slightly inferior. In Adult Test II, girls held an advantage at 15 years only, with males ahead at the other six age levels. As far as accuracy is concerned, males took less trials in 18 experimental groups, females in 3 groups.

When speed of performance was concerned rather than accuracy, males were quicker than females in all the 21 age groups compared. Times were recorded separately in the three Maze designs, XIV, Adult I, and Adult II. The effect of greater speed ran counter to expectations. Normally, the quicker the performance, the less accurate it could be expected to be, but there seemed to be little relationship betwteen female speed and accuracy.

One other observation concerned a possible relation in both sexes between maturity and Maze performance. The 19-year-old students left in high school could normally be considered the duller individuals, but the Maze performances do not support this conclusion, at least as regards practical intelligence. Males of this age had the highest rank in accuracy in the XIV year test, in Adult I and Adult II. As regards speed, they were first in Year XIV, first in Adult I, and were second only to the 18-year group in Adult II. Quite apart from scholastic standing, increasing maturity in age is apparently an important factor in male Maze performance.

Females aged 19 years, in comparison with other age groups of the same sex, were first in accuracy in Year XIV, first in Adult I, but last in Adult II. Thus maturity was still an important factor in Maze ability for females but not as important as for males.

In a study of children of varied ethnic origin conducted in Honolulu schools (Porteus and Babcock, 1926), it was found that in six age groups from 9 years to 14 years Japanese males excelled Japanese females at all age levels. Exactly the same situation occurred as between Chinese males and females. In this study the numbers of cases seemed adequate. There were 208 Japanese boys, 198 girls; 200 Chinese boys, 188 girls, divided among six age groups.

In 1953–54, work was undertaken in Honolulu high schools to compare the standardization of the new Extension Maze Series with scores attained on the Original Series. The sexes were evenly divided, 150 of each, and when results were combined, it was found that the two forms of the Maze yielded equivalent scores. But when the cases were subdivided into three groups of 50 cases of each sex and results segregated, the males excelled the females in each subdivision. Thus it was demonstrated that 50 cases per group was a sufficient number to demonstrate sex disparity (Porteus, 1955b).

The complete list of individual studies as shown in Table 1, at the end of this chapter, includes American, Australian, Chinese, Japanese, Chamorros, Carolinian children, and three groups of Australian aboriginals, numbering in all 5,282 males and 5,086 females. In 6 of the 105 comparisons made, females were ahead, in 99 the males held an advantage. There seems to be no doubt that in Maze Test performance males are almost consistently superior.

In many groups the advantage is small, but surely it is significant that in 99 out of 105 instances the differences lie in the same direction. If, as is so often the case in psychological research, experiments had been set up for one age group only, the question of sex differences could have been apparently settled, but incorrectly. Had, for instance, studies been limited to Australian girls and boys aged 12 and 13 years, numbering in all 417 cases, the conclusion would have been drawn that girls were superior to boys in Maze performance, a finding that would have been generally false. This would seem to indicate clearly the hazardous nature of "single-shot research." The whole situation also justifies the extremely sceptical question, amounting almost to heresy, as to whether a theory of probability based on the random tossing of coins applies to results when the obverse and reverse sides of the coin are not identical, but different both in shape and weight distribution. Obviously, if male Maze performance is represented by "heads," that side of the coin is weighted differently. Supposing, for example, that the "heads" are weighted in such a way that this side of the coin is disk shaped, while the "tails" sides are flat, would it not be probable that spinning such a coin a hundred, a thousand, or a million times would result in a very uneven balance of heads versus tails? In other words, a doubting Thomas might suggest that the probability set up by the use of perfectly balanced coins holds only for that kind of situation. If the obverse and reverse sides are unevenly shaped or loaded, prediction can only be based on the spinning or throwing of that kind of coin. If this should result in a ratio of heads to tails of 60–40 instead of 50–50, what becomes of the significance of the Fisher t-test? Unfortunately, we do not know, prior to the experimental evidence, just how much or in what way the coin of sex differences departs from standard.

Except in very rare instances, the time, the opportunity, and the desire to repeat an experiment over 100 times do not occur. The physicist has no such experimental limitations; he can replicate his experiments at will. Fortunately, the present writer because of his preoccupation with the Porteus Maze has been able to repeat his experiments on sex differences in the test, using 210 separate groups, providing 105 separate comparisons of males and females with the results as shown in Table 1 at the end of this chapter. Unfortunately, the SD's were not computed in every case so that it is not possible to calculate what the significance of the studies taken together might have been. If the dice were loaded in favor of the males, as is undoubtedly the case, no t-test formula, in my opinion, could indicate the reliability of the difference unless we know the exact type and amount of loading.

Another principle of research methodology is affected by the results of sex comparisons. It would seem that a problem such as the incidence of sex differences is best attacked in the manner recommended by William A. Hunt for the demonstration of any of a mental test's attributes. I have elsewhere quoted his suggestion for test validation, namely, "wide standardization over all sorts of clinical and structural groups and *the repeated demonstration of reliability and validity throughout this standardization.*" In plain terms, psychologists should repeat their experiments rather than be satisfied to announce on the basis of the *t*-test formula that the obtained differences are significant or otherwise. The reliability of the *t*-test procedure may itself be questionable.

Hunt's recommendation of repeated demonstrations has been adopted for the Maze in the fields of mental diagnosis, psychosurgery, juvenile delinquency, psychopharmacology, racial differences, and now sex differences.

As regards differences associated with race and sex, one warning should be re-emphasized for the satisfaction of the oversensitive. The demonstrated differences are only some of many possible variables, and it is at present quite impossible to summate all of these. On the basis of the facts now available, it would be idle to claim that one race possesses all-round superiority or inferiority, or that one sex has any general advantage over the other. What social psychologists may and should do is to discover and delimit the areas of disparity, instead of accepting an emotionally slanted declaration that there are no significant differences—in short, that all men, women, and ethnically grouped populations are equal. This last conclusion would seem to be a complete negation of scientific endeavor. We must continue by all means in our power to measure the differences as accurately as possible, and attempt to discover all the various factors, environmental or otherwise, that may modify or diminish those inequalities. In some ways the attitude of equalitarians seems to resemble that of a religious sect that teaches that if one denies the reality of painful conditions, these misfortunes disappear. Medical and biochemical measures against disease are certainly not a waste of time, money, and energy, though in some areas they are indecisive. It would be preposterous for psychologists to forsake the paths of experiment because of difficulties in the way of reaching reliable conclusions. Our present uncertainties are merely a challenge to further investigation.

But if we accept the verdict of accumulated experiments in this area—namely, that sex differences are real and significant—then we may proceed to consider causes. We are all ready to admit that changes in environment affect test scores, though probably to minor rather than major degrees, dependent upon individual impressionability. It would certainly be wonderful to find that mental deficiency can be corrected by social and education measures, but such is not the case. Cultural stimulation of primitive groups may have its limitations of effects. However, in regard to the effect of nurtural factors on sex differences, we should give some attention to the question as to whether the environment of males and females is actually the same. In spite of having the same parents, living in the same homes, being exposed to the same training and education, brothers and sisters undergo unequal conventional and other pressures to induce them to act in certain ways. Do the two sexes, in any important sense, live in different worlds?

Specifically, in relation to Maze Test performances, do the kind of toys with which boys play, the physical games they participate in, the opportunities to acquire a better understanding of mechanical devices, encouragement to be more aggressive, plus the granting of more independence than their sisters are allowed—do these together result in the development and exercise of more planning capacity, foresight, and initiative on the part of males? These questions call for further experiment.

It has been shown in various sections of this book that as a class, normal individuals excel, in Maze performance, the socially insufficient, the industrially ineffective, mentally disturbed children, neurotic, psychopathic, or psychotic adults, culturally simple or primitive populations, brain-damaged cases, individuals treated with certain psycho-active drugs, and others suffering from extreme Vitamin B deficiency or a debilitating disease such as hookworm. There is also ample evidence that the somnolent and other persons otherwise temporarily insensitive to environmental changes show various degrees of impairment in Maze scores. Since females have lower performances than males, should we conclude that they suffer even to a minor degree the above-mentioned handicaps?

Since such deficits usually fall well within the normal range of distribution, such a conclusion may not be very significant. Nevertheless, a consistent if slight depression in score may be in general important enough to indicate a disadvantage in competition with males. Female environment, on the whole, may be less stimulating and challenging. It is also important to realize that sex disparities are temperamental rather than mental. In the first place the range of temperamental traits seems to be greater than that of intellectuality. It is a far greater distance from idiocy to genius than from the extremes of caution to utter recklessness, or from the most abject submissiveness to unchecked aggressiveness. Within this narrower range, variation of a temperamental trait on the plus or minus side could be expected to show up more definitely in social behavior. The position could be put in this way: A slight departure from the mean either way could make a relatively larger difference in the Maze score than a similar departure from the mean in mentality. It must be remembered that the survival value of temperamental traits is probably much greater than that of, say, scholastic abilities. Whether a person can recall six digits or seven is of little or no importance in earning a living, but a slight departure from the mean in cautiousness may make him accident-prone, determining possibly whether he will go on living at all.

Some traits are so arranged in a narrow-range continuum that any deficiency may make a difference in test scores. If an individual is temperamentally disturbed when confronted with an unusual or novel task or, on the other hand, is so cocksure that he fails to detect rather obvious traps, this trait will be quickly reflected in his Maze performance. Uneasiness in tackling a new task is probably not as pronounced in males as in females due to the fact that the latter are more accustomed to routine activities. Males undoubtedly have the greater variety of experience.

Pressures are also more insistent in inducing females to play the roles considered to be appropriate to their sex. In the accepted patterns of boyhood the male feels he should be more adventurous, more willing to run risks, and therefore becomes more bored with routine. Thus the girl may feel more at ease when attending to familiar details in a job, the boy in planning a new activity. He knows that he will gain more social approval by showing a willingness to experiment, and whatever success he achieves adds to his self-esteem. The adage "never venture, never have" appeals more to males as an incentive to action.

Then, too, there is little doubt that males are more competitive. This is another form of behavior that is more or less thrust upon them by public approval or its reverse. This is probably the best key to understanding, not only of male superiority in the Maze but of many other activities. The solving of a Maze has in it much of the attraction of a game that appeals more to masculine competitiveness.

Lastly, modern civilization seems to call for the making of more decisions on the part of males. In short, the girl or woman pays in reduced opportunities for the increased shelter, protection, and esteem she enjoys. In several areas of conduct it is apparent to her that she will suffer more from impulsive mistakes; hence the consciousness of greater risk tends to make her irresolute.

It will be remembered that in speed of Maze performance females seem to lag behind at almost every age level at which comparisons have been made. This would seem to contradict the view that impulsivity is a feminine characteristic. Having observed Maze reactions in many thousands of cases, it is my opinion that females tend to be on the whole more cautious and that this prudent approach may easily develop into irresolution. In any case, girls seem to take the task more seriously than boys so that errors loom more largely in consciousness, and this attitude in a test that calls for many quick decisions may actually be a disadvantage.

The fact that these are tentative conclusions calls for more experimental research. Here an admission of inadequacy of the test at its highest levels should be made. The demand for a diagnostic test of rather general application has resulted in adaptation of the task to only mediocre levels. To increase complexity is easy, but as soon as the designs become more complex, the test takes on the character of a specialized puzzle rather than a measure of everyday ability. Several investigators have voiced the belief that there are not enough "high level" mazes to demonstrate differences in ability. Possibly a special set of difficult mazes should be devised for the further exploration of sex differences, but I am of the opinion that entirely new tests of high level planning are needed rather than overweighting the Maze approach.

If sex differences in performance do not have an innate basis but are related to nurtural factors, then we should expect them to be less in evidence at the earlier ages when environmental pressures are less differentiated, and to increase at the ages when they grow more and more important. As far as my results go, this does not seem to be the case. They are well marked in the younger groups, with a tendency at or about 12 years to diminish or even to be reversed. At that age apparently the advantage swings once more in favor of males, even when education level is held constant. Evidently we need better and more relevant observation of the behavior of very young children in different environments so as to discover and interpret the facts of the matter. Studies of comparative aggressiveness and competitiveness are certainly in order. In a social climate such as the Australid is nurtured in, the strict regulation of the distribution of food and women reduces competition to a minimum. Such important questions as sex competitiveness will not, therefore, be settled in one but in a large number of racial and other environments, with the emphasis on trends that can be validated only on the basis of replication of experiments. This will have the effect of postponing conclusions and slowing up the speed with which we reach certainty. Here is an area of investigation demanding the cooperation of the psychologist and the anthropologist.

What mankind needs is not more scepticism but more proof, and this applies to chronic believers and unbelievers alike. Belief and disbelief may both be unreasonable; the inquiring spirit never is. But even this statement requires supplementing. We must always remember that human existence is an ongoing operation. In Sir Charles Sherrington's (1933) phrasing, "Science, nobly, declines as proof anything but complete proof; but common sense, pressed for time, accepts and acts on acceptance."

In considering the question of sex differences in Maze performance, data on primitive peoples should be interesting. Unfortunately, the body of facts is scanty but nevertheless points consistently in the same direction, as do results with nonprimitives.

Thus, although comparative figures for Australian aboriginal women refer to small groups, the differences are so pronounced that they are probably reliable. In 1929, I tested 11 women whose average test age was 8.22 years, somewhat above the mean for females of the Central India urban Bhil. The mean for Australian males tested by me in the district of Kimberly, N.W. Australia, was 10.48. Piddington and Piddington (1932) tested 14 women at LaGrange in the same Kimberley district and found their mean to be 8.6, a score inferior to that of males by 1.88 years (Porteus, 1933). Porteus and Gregor (1963) in their recent Central Australian investigations found the Maze level of 12 women to be 9.67 years by the Original Maze, 9.88 years by the Extension, and 10.04 in the Supplement, all lower than the male averages of 10.4, 10.89, and 11.0 years, respectively.

The paucity of numbers of women examined is due to the fact that the investigator had to leave their examination until the end of his stay for fear that his *rapport* with the men would be affected. Had the test been first applied to women and children, it would have been regarded as being unworthy of the attention and interest of fully initiated males. Among the primitive Australids a close distinction is drawn between men's and women's "business," and any invasion of the other's province is not usually attempted. The doings of the white examiner are, of course, fully discussed in the native camps, and this testing of women might have been considered an encouragement of female intrusion into what could be regarded as an occupation appropriate only to males (see Chapter 9). Possibly an aversion to competing with men may have been one factor in the women's inferior performance. Feminine roles are very rigidly defined in Australid society, affecting food gathering, hunting, and most particularly, ceremonial observances related to intiation, which are kept most carefully secret from females. In spite of this, women, as is usual elsewhere, manage to exert considerable influence, more effective than is openly recognized. Both Gregor and I sensed a certain uneasiness on the part of female subjects when introduced to the tests. In any case, their examination was the last piece of research attempted.

This matter of appropriate sex roles was also much in evidence among the Kalahari Bushmen in South Africa. On one occasion, men who had been examined asked the writer to give them some test blanks of Mazes to take home to their "werft" or village, not so that they could apply them to their female relatives but "to show our women how clever we are." In other words, the Mazes constituted a man's game, in which his prowess was to be admired but not copied. Conventional sex attitudes may have affected women's scores, but male advantages are too widespread and well marked to be thus wholly accounted for.

Sex differences in Maze performance are well attested in non-Australid primitive groups. In Indore State, Central India, P. C. Ray and U. Bose examined rural and urban Bhil, the former inhabiting villages in the jungles of Dhar, Manda, and neighboring districts, the latter consisting of soldiers with their families living in cantonments, housing a light infantry regiment of the Indore State army (Ray, 1953). This regiment has been in existence 100 years and its men are therefore well acculturated. The investigators reported results by sexes: Urban males (N 29) scored 8.36 years, urban females

(N 50) 7.63 years, the difference being significant at the .1 per cent level. The rural Bhil males (N 50) averaged 7.44, the rural Bhil females (N 54) 6.97 years. The difference between urban and rural groups is attributed by the author to the cultural advantages of the former.

Another comparison was made for a primitive group, the people of Alor (Du Bois, 1944), but only in terms of mental age means. The test age for males (N 26) was given by Du Bois as 12.8 years, whereas females (N 22) averaged 9.43 years, a considerable disparity.

Sex differences have also been reckoned for the people of Saipan (Joseph and Murray, 1951). These investigators tested the Chamorros and the Carolinians, two Micronesian peoples, the former descendants of the indigenous inhabitants of the Marianas, the latter immigrants (known locally as Kanakas) from the Caroline group. Male and female Chamorros, to the total number of 50 of each sex, were divided into four age groups, 5–7, 8–10, 11–13, and 14–17 years of age, and were tested by the Porteus Maze. In each of the four age groups males were ahead, the differences being small in the case of the younger children but much increased with the 14–17 year age group.

The Carolinians, 50 of each sex, divided into the same age groups, gave a similar picture of male superiority, with the 14–17 group again showing the greatest disparity (2 years 9 months) in test age.

In considering primitive groups as compared with groups of higher cultural standing, it is apparent that while the sex differences are less for younger children, as the primitives grow older the gap between the sexes widens. This fact suggests that the masculine and feminine roles in many features of daily living are more differentiated the further one goes down the cultural scale. But one must beware of considering that the equalization of opportunity would be a very potent influence in Maze performance, and that all that must be done is to wipe out cultural advantages in the sexes and the Maze differences would disappear.

Unfortunately for those who would attach such great weight to environmental factors, the rest of the facts will not fit the theory. There is, for example, the 3½-year difference in mean Maze scores between the South African Bushmen and unculturated Australids, and surely no one who knows both environments would maintain that the Australids of Central Australia have an environmental advantage over the Bushmen. Mixed blood in the case of the latter may have been a factor (see Chapter 10). Furthermore, the male Carolinians do not compare culturally with, say, the Japanese males attending Honolulu high schools, yet there is only a very slight difference in their mean Maze scores. Nor could the advantage possessed by the Japanese of about one year over the Arunta males of Central Australia be considered proportionate to environmental advantage, which is so much greater for the Japanese.

The data on Maze Test sex differences so far presented, as expressed in test ages, clearly demonstrated male advantages, but when we consider the qualitative scores, the situation becomes very differently balanced. Although the two measures, quantitative and qualitative, are derived from the one test performance, it should be recognized that as regards the assessment of human personality they are utilizing two very different approaches. The former test age procedure is based on a definite prohibition against entering blind alleys, the slightest infringement being registered as a failure, involving a penalty of a half year deducted from the final score. The only leniency that is allowed is a specified number of additional trials, each starting from the same initial point. In other words, the scoring method is essentially "pass or fail." Success, therefore, depends first on the exercise of forethought in order to predetermine or envisage the right course, and, secondly, prudence in carrying out the plan. Since these operations require time for prehearsal, there is no speed factor used in scoring unless for a special experiment.

In the qualitative procedure, the subject's effort is not interrupted because of disregard of certain instructions, except in the very rare gross error of cutting across into another segment of the maze instead of tracing the course around. In other words, there is no intervention by the examiner after the initial verbal instructions except in this and one other particular situation. S may cross or touch lines, cut corners, and make as irregular or wavy line tracing of the maze as he wishes; only as regards frequent early liftings of the pencil from the paper is the maze-threading interrupted to repeat the instruction. This happens only after five liftings in any single test, or a total of ten liftings in three successive tests. This relaxation of the rules was intended to avoid too heavy an imposition of penalties on certain subjects who misunderstand the prohibition and "sketch" the course with many liftings of the pencil.

Since it was desirable to limit the maximum error score to 100, "lifted pencils" might quickly push the individual's errors to the allowable limit and thus continuance of the testing would be arbitrarily ended.

Obviously, the qualitative score reflects care in execution more than planning, and thus the two obtained measures are not very significantly related. This is shown by low correlations, mainly around .3, with the highest recorded being .46 and the lowest between .1 and .2. The qualitative score is so named because of its reference to the quality of work that is expended on a task, but since it is a quantitative summation of faults in execution, "qualitative" and "quantitative" should not be used as mutually exclusive terms. They merely indicate differences in scoring emphasis. As far as the planning feature is concerned, we have seen that females are excelled by males.

However, because traits such as neatness or tidiness, attention to detail, obedience to rules, and respect for test structuring all enter into qualitative performance and also affect conduct, the ordinary expectation would be that females would exceed males. But in this respect the picture is by no means clear. With normal subjects, no clear-cut advantages for either sex are at once apparent. As a matter of fact, the sex differences have been overshadowed by the disparity that exists between delinquent and nondelinquent performances. Delinquent girls' Q-scores usually exceed—i.e., are worse than—those of delinquent boys. Their test age scores are also inferior to those of nondelinquents but to a much less marked extent.

In the earliest Q-score study (Porteus, 1942), 100 normal boys had a weighted error score of 21.77, about 3 points better than that of 100 normal girls (24.7 points).[1] This was just about the same sex disparity shown by equal numbers of delinquents, the mean score of boys being 49.35, of girls 52.9. As noted in the above-mentioned publication, girls were more careful and neater in execution, crossing fewer lines and having less wavy or irregular overall records, but disobeying the "lift pencil" instruction more frequently. Delinquent girls also cut fewer corners, crossed less lines, and made less wavy line records, but again had many more lift pencils than boys, showing themselves more unmindful in obeying this specific instruction. They also made more errors in the first third of each

---

[1] Attention should again be directed to the fact that a lower Q-score indicates less qualitative errors and is therefore the better performance.

test design, possibly indicating greater impulsivity in beginning a new task. In attempting to set up a "critical score" that would differentiate 80 per cent of delinquent performances from non-delinquent, it was found necessary to make the cutoff 29 points for boys and 32 for girls, the same difference that existed between the sex means.

Three years later a further study of qualitative scores was reported (Porteus, 1945). In one Honolulu high school (McKinley), where 100 students equally divided by sexes were examined, the Q-score mean was better for males, 15.4 as against 23.1 for females. At Kalakaua Intermediate School, males (N 48) again held a slight advantage over females (N 52), 22.6 *versus* 23.7. But at Washington Intermediate High School, female students did considerably better than boys, the comparative figures being 19.6 (N 50) as against 25.5 (N 50).

Fifty delinquent males scored 48.4, while the same number of delinquent females had the much higher error score of 62.3. Because of the fact that a large proportion of juvenile delinquents are part-Hawaiian, it was decided to compare boys and girls of this ethnic group who were in attendance at Kamehameha Schools, an excellent high school, admission to which was at that time highly selective, with the emphasis on good moral and educational records. The boys (N 31) had the excellent error score of only 13.7 points, the lowest recorded up to that date, while the girls (N 25) scored 15.8, only about one quarter that of delinquent girls, the critical ratio of the difference being over 9.

One other sex difference was recorded. Workers, male and female, at a pineapple cannery were classified by their supervisors as satisfactory and unsatisfactory, mainly on account of work habits. The male "satisfactory" groups (N 25) scored only 14.3 error points, the females so classified (N 33) scored 21.5. With regard to those termed "unsatisfactory," males (N 25) scored 37.3 points, females (N 16) scored 41.6. Thus, in these two earliest qualitative score investigations, males held the balance of advantage, but it was not so marked as in the case of test ages.

This change of position as regards Q-scores is further exemplified in a very recent study (Porteus, 1961). The groups examined consisted of Japanese, Chinese, and part-Hawaiians in attendance at intermediate high schools in Honolulu. Once again males of all three groups were superior to females in test ages, with a somewhat greater disparity for the part-Hawaiian groups. But with regard to Q-scores, the Japanese females (N 198) had a somewhat marked advantage over the males (N 183), the scores being 23.8 error points as against 29.4. In the Chinese group, however, the males had an advantage of less than a point, with a reversed situation apparent for the part-Hawaiians where females had the better position also by one point. It was noteworthy that the Chinese as a group excelled the Japanese in quality of execution and were still further ahead of the part-Hawaiians.

These ethnic Q-score means reflect the current situation as regards delinquency in Honolulu, which has changed markedly in recent years. In 1920 the ratio of delinquency to population was extremely favorable to the Japanese, the figures being Japanese 0.58, Chinese 2.2, Portuguese 3.1, Hawaiians 5.0 (Porteus and Babcock, 1926). Owing to the extreme sensitivity of certain population groups, government agencies were discouraged from publishing this type of statistics. However, evidence from other sources indicates that Japanese males are no longer distinguished by such outstandingly excellent records, though the position of girls is still very good. I believe that the leaders of the Japanese community are well aware of the socially unhealthy trend shown by Japanese boys and are concerned with its correction. The sex incidence of delinquency for the other ethnic groups seems to remain fairly constant, but Japanese family discipline appears to be considerably relaxed. The Q-score seems to be sensitive to this change, and this points to the greater influence of nurtural factors on quality of Maze performance than on test age scoring. In individual instances, Maze Test solutions may be well planned as regards avoidance of blind alleys but still be inferior as regards neatness and care in execution.

At the time of the standardization of the Extension Series (Porteus, 1955b), qualitative scores were also calculated. Again, though in test ages males in three groups, (each of 50 subjects) excelled, females in two of the groups had better weighted error records in the Original (Vineland Revision) and in the Extension Series. Thus it seems clear that the test age and qualitative scores examine different sets of attributes. In the former, males are undoubtedly superior, but in the latter, advantages are divided.

The third form of the Maze, called the Supplement Series (Porteus, 1959a), which, if applied subsequently to the other two forms, yields average scores equivalent to the Extension Series, was devised so as to eliminate practice effects if it was necessary to repeat the test series three times in succession. In its standardization, 508 high school cases in the ninth grade were tested—249 males and 259 females. The demonstration of male superiority—a now monotonous story—was again evident in both the Extension and Supplement Series, but females made better average showings by 2 and 4 points of Q-scores than did males. Generally speaking, the number of weighted errors rose with the lengthening of the time necessary to complete the two series. This did not affect at all the test age performance, so does not seem to be related to mental fatigue. All that we can say is that in a longer sustained task the tendency is to be less careful about details of performance and that this lowering of self-standards of execution is slightly more apparent in males.

In summing up the sex differences in qualitative scores, we find that we have listed 20 studies. In 50 per cent, males had better Q-score averages than females. In the other half of the experiments, the advantage was held by the females. This is, of course, exactly what could be expected if chance selection determined the differences. In relation not to Q-scores but Maze Test age, the case stands entirely differently. In 98 group comparisons, including sixteen drawn from simpler cultural or primitive populations, the advantage of males is apparent. It is true that the sex differences seem to be larger for some of the more primitive groups, and some consideration has been given to the view that the environment of males is different to that of females. But when comparisons are confined only to males, the environmental argument fails to hold up, since the differences in male mean scores are in most cases greater than the sex differences reported. We can only say, in paraphrasing the poet, that environment works in mysterious ways, its wonders to perform.

At the end of the chapter will be found (Table 1) an extensive array of the results of all the sex comparisons that have been made of sex differences in Maze Test ages, followed by a shorter list of Q-score comparisons. To return briefly to the question of the reliability of the *t*-test, we determined to calculate *t*-tests for 18 of the studies in which provision of SD's enabled us to apply the formula. These are listed in order of *t*-test significance as follows:

Hermannsburg Australids	p<.001
Urban Bhil (India)	p<.02
Rural Bhil (India)	p<.02
10-year Japanese (Hawaii)	p<.02
14-year Chinese (Hawaii)	p<.065
Hawaii H. S. students	p<.065
Hawaii H. S. students	p<.074
10-year Chinese (Hawaii)	p<.14
9-year Chinese (Hawaii)	p<.16
11-year Chinese (Hawaii)	p<.16
12-year Chinese (Hawaii)	p<.20
14-year Japanese (Hawaii)	p<.24
12-year Japanese (Hawaii)	p<.26
13-year Japanese (Hawaii)	p<.28
9-year Japanese (Hawaii)	p<.34
13-year Chinese (Hawaii)	p<.46
Hawaii H. S. students	p<.50
11-year Japanese (Hawaii)	p<.50

The above array can only be described as showing a most bewildering disparity among *t*-test significances. Yet all apply to the same subject of investigation, each group was examined by the same examiner, and each dealt with individuals in the same age groups, attending the same schools, and all results are pointing toward the same fact of male superiority in the Maze Test. Yet only four out of the eighteen studies reflect sex differences that reach the level of *t*-test significance commonly accepted by most investigators (p<.02). All the other studies would have justified the conclusion that male superiority was not proved in spite of the fart thr' ?9 out of 105 examinations indicate that thi: is one of the best attested sex differences.

The trouble is that the formula pays no attention to agreeme it among replicated investigations. If it should be claimed that sampling is at fault, how does one proceed further in equating samples? For example, 11-year Chinese and 11-year Japanese are attending the same schools and are probably of the same educational and social grade, yet the significance of one comparison is p<.16, of the other p<.5. Such a disparity surely justifies the sign "Beware of the *t*-test" to protect the unwary student—a warning commonly used to advertise the danger from an untrustworthy canine.

Table 1

Tables of Maze Test Sex Differences

No.	Group	Age	Males		Females			Diff.	Investigator
			N	Mean	N	Mean			
				Years		Years			
1	Australian Elementary School Children, 5–14 years	5.5	16	7.27	16	6.63	M	.64	Porteus, 1916
2		6.5	43	7.92	28	7.54	M	.38	
3		7.5	63	8.57	63	7.98	M	.59	
4		8.5	76	8.95	76	8.39	M	.56	
5		9.5	63	9.41	77	8.86	M	.55	
6		10.5	49	9.94	70	9.76	M	.18	
7		11.5	60	10.82	50	10.1	M	.72	
8		12.5	66	10.9	61	11.3	F	.4	
9		13.5	56	11.97	42	12.07	F	.1	
10		14.5	13	11.79	12	11.67	M	.12	
11	Australian Elementary School Children, 6–13 years	6.5	64	7.15	64	6.91	M	.24	Porteus, 1918
12		7.5	75	7.62	75	7.44	M	.18	
13		8.5	78	8.66	67	8.32	M	.34	
14		9.5	86	9.92	79	9.14	M	.78	
15		10.5	75	10.29	91	10.01	M	.28	
16		11.5	94	11.15	84	10.81	M	.54	
17		12.5	95	11.88	96	12.16	F	.28	
18		13.5	56	12.2	76	12.11	M	.09	
19	American Elementary School Children	6.5	52	7.32	46	6.53	M	.79	Foote, 1919
20		7.5	45	7.96	55	7.3	M	.66	
21	American High School Students, 13–19 years.	13.5	23	Trials 4.39	22	Trials 6.36	M	1.97	Porteus & Bassett, 1920

No.	Group	Age	Males N	Males Mean	Females N	Females Mean		Diff.	Investigator
22	XIV Year Maze Test-Accuracy	14.5	60	4.38	65	5.30	M	.92	
23		15.5	85	3.84	79	4.94	M	1.1	
24		16.5	65	3.20	60	5.01	M	1.81	
25		17.5	59	3.79	53	4.47	M	.68	
26		18.5	25	4.35	31	4.12	F	.23	
27		19.5	14	2.78	16	2.62	F	.16	
28	American High School Students, 13–19 years.	13.5	24	4.04	22	4.54	M	.50	Porteus & Bassett, 1920
	Adult Maze I-Accuracy								
29		14.5	62	4.67	64	4.58	M	.09	
30		15.5	86	3.68	80	3.98	M	.30	
31		16.5	65	3.49	61	4.80	M	1.31	
32		17.5	39	3.15	53	3.56	M	.41	
33		18.5	25	3.60	31	4.33	M	.73	
34		19.5	14	2.50	17	2.94	M	.44	
35	American High School Students, 13–19 years.	13.5	23	4.21	22	6.04	M	1.83	Porteus & Bassett, 1920
	Adult Maze II-Accuracy								
36		14.5	62	5.19	67	6.64	M	.45	
37		15.5	85	6.18	78	5.35	F	.83	
38		16.5	67	4.64	61	6.73	M	2.09	
39		17.5	60	3.83	52	5.40	M	1.57	
40		18.5	25	3.64	30	5.80	M	2.26	
41		19.5	14	3.21	17	7.29	M	4.08	
42	American High School Students, 13–19 years.	13.5	23	Seconds 87	22	Seconds 136	M	49	Porteus & Bassett, 1920
	XIV Year Maze Test-Speed								
43		14.5	59	90	68	130	M	40	
44		15.5	83	88	79	136	M	48	
45		16.5	66	81	61	118	M	37	
46		17.5	58	82	54	115	M	23	
47		18.5	25	79	31	113	M	34	

No.	Group	Age	N		N				Reference
48		19.5	14	71	15	123	M	52	Porteus & Bassett, 1920
49	American High School Students, 13–19 years. Adult Maze I-Speed	13.5	23	101	22	141	M	24	
50		14.5	62	115	66	133	M	18	
51		15.5	83	88	80	121	M	41	
52		16.5	67	93	61	127	M	34	
53		17.5	59	68	53	118	M	50	
54		18.5	25	82	31	101	M	19	
55		19.5	14	68	17	75	M	7	
56	American High School Students, 13–19 years. Adult Maze II-Speed	13.5	23	157	22	228	M	71	Porteus & Bassett, 1920
57		14.5	62	167	67	201	M	34	
58		15.5	82	180	78	209	M	29	
59		16.5	66	154	61	229	M	75	
60		17.5	58	151	53	203	M	52	
61		18.5	25	118	29	220	M	102	
62		19.5	14	120	16	199	M	79	
63	Chinese Elementary School Children, 9–14 years.	9.5	33	Years 10.21	29	Years 9.43	M	.78	Porteus & Babcock, 1926
64		10.5	27	10.5	32	9.58	M	.92	
65		11.5	35	10.8	31	9.95	M	1.30	
66		12.5	37	11.84	35	10.61	M	1.23	
67		13.5	32	11.92	30	11.53	M	.39	
68		14.5	36	12.9	31	11.95	M	.95	
69	Japanese Elementary School Children, 9–14 years.	9.5	39	10.22	29	9.76	M	.46	Porteus & Babcock, 1926
70		10.5	27	11.44	34	10.21	M	1.23	
71		11.5	37	12.03	33	11.74	M	.29	
72		12.5	36	12.4	39	11.8	M	.60	
73		13.5	27	12.77	27	12.17	M	.60	
74		14.5	42	13.35	36	12.85	M	.50	

No.	Group	Age	Males		Females			Diff.	Investigator
			N	Mean	N	Mean			
75	Honolulu High School Students, 14–17 years.		50	15.26	50	14.66	M	.60	Porteus, 1955
76	Mixed ethnic groups—Original Maze		50	15.69	50	15.33	M	.36	
77			50	15.73	50	15.26	M	.47	
78	Honolulu High School Students, 14–17 years.		50	15.4	50	14.66	M	.74	Porteus, 1955
79	Mixed ethnic groups—Extension Series		50	15.82	50	15.33	M	.49	
80			50	16.07	50	15.26	M	.81	
	Intermediate High School Students, 14–17 years. Mixed ethnic groups.								
81	Extension Series		249	15.73	259	15.48	M	.25	Porteus, 1959
82	Supplement Series		249	15.66	259	15.55	M	.11	
83	Japanese Tenth Grade Students—Extension Series		183	15.80	198	15.54	M	.26	Porteus, 1961
84	Chinese		42	15.99	58	15.66	M	.33	Porteus, 1961
85	Part-Hawaiian		99	15.38	82	14.74	M	.64	
86	Chamorros	5–7	9	7.0	8	6.75	M	.25	Joseph & Murray, 1951
87		8–10	13	9.66	16	9.17	M	.49	
88		11–13	14	13.6	14	12.0	M	1.6	
89		14–17	14	14.6	12	13.5	M	1.1	
90	Carolinians	5–7	7	7.5	8	7.17	M	.33	Joseph & Murray, 1951
91		8–10	17	11.33	15	9.25	M	2.08	
92		11–13	14	13.75	16	13.0	M	.75	
93		14–17	12	15.66	11	15.33	M	.33	
94	Australids (Kimberley)—Original Maze		65	10.48	11	8.22	M	2.26	Porteus, 1929

#					TQ			
95	C. Australia—Original Maze	24	10.52	14	8.6	M	1.92	Piddington, 1931
96		50	10.4	12	9.67	M	.73	Gregor, 1962
97	Central India, Urban Bhil	29	8.36	50	7.63	M	.73	Ray, 1953
98	Central India, Rural Bhil	50	7.44	54	6.97	M	.47	Bose, 1953
99	Central Australia— Extension Maze	50	10.89	12	9.88	M	1.01	Gregor, 1962
100	Supplement	50	11.0	12	10.04	M	.96	
101	Island of Alor	26	12.8	22	9.43	M	3.37	Du Bois, 1944
102	Ainu (Children)	9	105.9	17	100.9	M	5	Stewart, 1934
103	Ainu (Adults)	51	93	16	87	M	6	
104	Formosans	23	101.5	9	81.3	M	20.2	
105	Negritos (Luzon)	27	60	20	46.3	M	13.7	

QUALITATIVE SCORES

Group	Males		Females			Diff.	Investigator
	N	Mean Points	N	Mean Points			
Normals	100	21.8	100	24.7	M	2.9	Porteus, 1942
Delinquents	100	49.4	100	52.9	M	3.5	
McKinley High School, 10th Grade	50	15.4	50	23.1	M	7.7	Porteus, 1943
Kalakaua Interm. High School	48	22.6	52	23.7	M	1.1	
Washington Interm. High School	50	25.5	50	19.6	F	5.9	
Delinquents	50	48.4	50	62.3	M	13.9	
Hawaiians—Kamehameha School	32	13.7	25	15.8	M	2.1	
Satisfactory Cannery Workers	25	14.3	33	21.5	M	7.2	
Unsatisfactory Cannery Workers	25	37.3	16	41.6	M	4.3	
Honolulu High Schools Original Series	50	22.3	50	27.5	M	5.2	Porteus, 1955
	50	23.3	50	22.7	F	.6	
	50	24.1	50	23.3	F	.8	
Honolulu High Schools Extension Series	50	23.8	50	24.5	M	.7	
	50	25.4	59	22.3	F	3.1	
	50	24.1	50	22.9	F	1.2	
Honolulu Interm. High Schools Extension Series	249	31.1	259	28.9	F	2.2	Porteus, 1959
Supplement Series	249	31.9	259	27.9	F	4.0	
Tenth Grade Students—Extension Series							
Japanese	183	29.4	198	23.8	F	5.6	Kleman, 1959
Chinese	42	20.5	57	19.8	F	.7	
Part-Hawaiian	99	31.2	82	30.2	F	1.0	

SUMMARY

Investigations of sexuality are more common and in their way more thorough than studies in sex psychology. However, in the course of work on the Porteus Maze Test there have been a very large number of group comparisons of the performance of males and females. In the table that accompanies this chapter, 105 such studies are reported and in 99 of them males have higher mean scores than females. These go back to the very earliest applications of the test, but recent researches both with primitive and sophisticated groups are included.

Various types of Mazes have been employed, ranging from an original form of the scale with a ceiling score of 13 years up to the three modern series—Original, Extension, and Supplement. In some of these studies speed of performance was recorded, but in the majority of instances accuracy as represented by test age was the basis of sex comparisons. The data also refer to a wide range of ethnic groups, including Japanese, Chinese, part-Hawaiians, Australids, Indian jungle tribes, Chamorros, Carolinians, Alorese, and two groups of Caucasians, American and Australian.

But the great variety of results, particularly the differences in the means, raises an interesting statistical question. In all comparisons the same test was used. It was administered by a number of different examiners, but in the majority of instances by the writer or by investigators trained by him. Therefore, differences in method of application were reduced to a minimum and can be considered as only very slightly affecting sex performances. The largest differences are found among primitive ethnic groups and in all cases the same examiner tested each sex group. Obviously, the differences justify only one conclusion: Males are superior, although this fact must not be interpreted as proof of general sex superiority.

The possibility that men and women, boys and girls live in different environments with different types of stimulation and conventional pressure patterns is considered. This is probably truer in primitive rather than civilized conditions, but the writer believes that this situation would not account for such a consistent trend. Probably inherent temperamental differences are to a great degree responsible.

This latter view is supported by the fact that when qualitative scores are compared, male superiority is no longer indicated. Feminine care and neatness enter into the picture rather than planning ability and the balance between the sexes is equal. Out of 20 studies, females are ahead in exactly half, just what might be expected if sampling were the decisive factor. But in regard to planning as reflected by avoidance of blind alleys male superiority is overwhelming.

The almost universal method of deciding the reliability of a study in terms of significance of differences is to calculate a Fisher *t*-test. By its means the judgment is made as to whether the findings can be considered conclusive or otherwise. A Fisher *t*-test of 0.01, if I am correct, means that the chances are better than one in a hundred that the real difference is more than zero.

In this instance, the writer does not need to depend on the Fisher *ι*-test to tell him what the probability in one hundred comparisons would be. He has carried out his experiment one hundred times and the result is that in 99 out of 105 studies males were superior, or about 94 chances out of 100.

Eighteen of the studies for which the variability was calculated were used to calculate Fisher *t*-tests and the variety of figures is bewildering. The puzzling feature is to decide which, if any, gives the true picture of probability. They vary from .5, or five chances in a hundred, to .001 or one chance in a thousand. It may be objected that each N represents a different group of subjects and that therefore its *t*-test applies only to it. This, however, would place an absurd limitation on its interpretation.

CHAPTER SEVEN

The Maze Test and Industry

In the attempt to delimit the relevancy of Maze Test scores, its role has been described as the measurement of planfulness and foresight at a common or everyday level. Yet most of its validation has related to conditions or subjects far from ordinary. Its sensitivity has been amply demonstrated for the mentally defective, for psychotics and psychoneurotics, for psychosurgical cases, for the emotionally disturbed, for the socially maladjusted, for the tranquilized, and for the culturally primitive. It has been proved sensitive for the vitamin deficient. But outside of the problems of standardization and sex differences, little attention seems to have been paid to the common man and his Maze responses.

The reason for this preoccupation with research in the field of the abnormal is easily apparent. It is only under extraordinary circumstances that the psychologist has freedom to operate his testing program, since it involves a certain degree of control over his potential subjects. It is no wonder, therefore, that when he can secure the cooperation of appropriate authorities, he is found working in classrooms, in correctional institutions, in hospitals, in homes for the aged or war veterans, in factories, and the like. If these places closed their doors to psychological experimenters, clinical psychology, lacking all means to add to its knowledge, would wither on the vine. Take away the hope of applying results for practical purposes, such as human betterment, then other branches of psychology, the exponents of which like to think of themselves as engaged in basic research, would likewise languish. In other words, applied and experimental psychology cannot drift out of sight of one another. In the long run, the interests of the individual are paramount. If, for example, there were no probabilities of carrying over the knowledge of mice to men, the animal laboratories would be soon reckoned among the luxuries of science. The main difference between applied and other psychologies is that for one class of human effort the practical goals are seen as immediate; in the others, distant or deferred.

Whenever the experimenter focusses on normal run-of-the-mill people, he must employ some indirection of aim. Thus, for the purpose of selecting people for jobs, he attempts to classify them by personality types in an assumed relation to efficiency. He measures individuals' reactions to fatigue, stress, and various kinds of re-enforcements of interest and effort, with the ostensible purpose of making them more competent in their jobs, to the obvious advantage of industry. He can get financial support rather easily for such practical projects, but for predominantly academic pursuits the scientist had better make haste to shelter himself under the wing of a university of repute, where the dollar-and-cents inquisitor rarely intrudes. State and national politicians like to defend the prestige of their institutions of higher learning. They have discovered that a too blatant exhibition of economic yardsticks of value represented by such questions as the reason for teaching a particular subject, or what some gadget is good for, injure prestige. Teachers in general, university as well as elementary instructors, find their security rather firmly rooted in local pride. To change the metaphor, research workers are glad to warm themselves at the same fire.

The attainment of scientific goals as a by-product can be noted in measures undertaken to deal with great national military emergencies. Here, to an unprecedented degree, was offered an opportunity to the psychologists to study great numbers of men in camp who were just a little while previously men in the street. In the latter situation, the psychologist had no authority and hence no chance of rounding up citizens who were going about their private business and then subjecting them to a round of mental examinations. The great advantage enjoyed by the physical scientist is that when he examines his test material microscopically or chemically it cannot answer back, though in certain circumstances, such as radioactive experimentation, the researcher has found by bitter experience that he must guard himself against counteraction through physical contamination.

In a great military enterprise, there is always an overriding need for haste—to classify and select men from the ranks, to utilize short cuts in choosing officer material, and to put to efficient use the almost countless gadgets and "hardware" that human inventiveness has contributed to the art and practice of modern warfare. Which should be considered the by-product, better human understanding or greater military might, needs no decision. The fact remains that the sudden turning of human ploughshares into swords offers the psychologist unusual opportunities to ply his profession while he himself is in uniform. One of the greatest advantages of selective service is the possible appraisal of industrial trainability.

But these opportunities, thanks to nuclear weapons, are now rare and, we hope, are becoming even rarer, since the knowledge that the next world conflagration will literally consume the world has almost universally, with the exception of the Chinese, percolated into human consciousness. Because great drafts of national man power are seldom needed, the contribution of the Maze Test to military purposes other than the elimination from service of the mentally unfit is scanty.

Early reports of work in the general industrial field are related to its most elementary levels—i.e. the abilities of the feebleminded, who, contrary to former belief, are also the feeblehanded. One very early study into the relationship between the Maze and industrial abilities was carried out at the Baldovan Institution in Scotland (Ross, 1921). This investigation demonstrated a correlation between handwork proficiency and the Binet of .60, whereas the Maze correlated .76. It is noteworthy that the combined Maze and Binet scores correlated .81 with industrial efficiency, a very high coefficient.

In those early days another investigation of industrial aptitudes was carried out by the present writer at the Vineland Training School, N. J., with the cooperation of the Educational Director, Mrs. C. E. Nash, and a number of cottage supervisors (Porteus, 1922). We had previously correlated test results with general estimates of industrial efficiency. The r for males was .67 (p.e. .069), for females .75 (p.e. .058). But examination of the ratings for individuals showed considerable disagreement between raters familiar with the subjects' practical abilities. It was, therefore, decided to carry out a more detailed study. This constituted an occupational scale for defectives. Each institutional job carried on by both sexes, from kitchen work for females to truck gardening for males, was graded into ten steps, each according to its difficulty of performance by defectives. Every pupil in the institution of sufficient mentality and physical fitness to do useful work ordinarily was assigned a job as part of his training. Weekly work schedule changes were made by Mrs. Nash on the basis of the supervisors' or instructors' reports.

As a sample of a job analysis of a comparatively responsible occupation, we may cite the rating scale for orchard and vineyard work:

Operation	Rating	Industrial Index Value
Gathering fallen fruit	1	10
Hoeing around trees } Picking gooseberries }	3	30
Picking grapes } Picking raspberries }	4	40
Sorting fruit } Thinning fruit }	5	50
Searching for borers } Picking apples } Spraying small fruit }	6	60
Picking peaches	7	70
Pruning	8	80
Spraying vineyard	9	90
Spraying orchard	10	100

The ratings were assigned by the overseer in charge of the operation. For example, picking hard fruit such as apples required less judgment than picking soft fruit such as peaches, which could bruise more easily with careless handling.

Obviously, less judgment would be called for in spraying vines close to the ground as compared with spraying orchard trees that would be beyond easy reach, an operation that would take more planning and judgment to do a thorough job. Because of the range of independent activities required, this was rated as a high grade occupation, obtaining a maximum index of 100. Ordinarily, ratings of 8 or above indicated industrial ability at or about a normal level unless the work was carried on under constant supervision.

To illustrate a much less responsible job requiring constant presence and supervision by a supervisor, we may cite the institutional low-grade occupation of Pantry and Kitchen Work. The necessity for supervision came about through the relation of these activities to hygiene.

Operation	Ratings	Industrial Index
Emptying and cleaning garbage cans ⎫ Scraping plates ⎬ Washing vegetables ⎭	1	5
Polishing silver	2	10
Cleaning sink ⎱ Care of bread box ⎰	3	15
Preparing berries for table ⎱ Care of ice box ⎰	4	20
Preparing celery ⎱ Preparing lettuce ⎰	5	25
Washing flatware	6	30
Care of coffee urns ⎱ Care of ice cream freezer ⎰	7	35
Care of meat grinder	8	40
Washing handleware	9	45
Washing glassware ⎱ Cutting bread ⎰	10	50

Some of the items listed quite evidently date the activity. The advent of garbage disposal units, dishwashing machines, etc., would nowadays displace hand operations, but I have listed the operations as they were, mainly to make the high correlations later found with a test for planning and prudence more understandable.

It will be noted that the industrial index that serves as weighting differs for the two occupations cited, orchard work earning double the weighting allotted to pantry work. This comparative weight was based on occupational factors such as skill and judgment required, value of the material dealt with, whether or not the use of machinery was involved, and the amount of personal risk to the operator. Operations involving the health or well being of others also had to be more highly rated than their comparative difficulty would suggest.

The correlation of the Maze with industrial ability was naturally higher for a performance test that reflected practical ability than it would be for a test that was more closely related to academic skills. Thus the Binet correlated .62 for boys, .69 for girls with industrial indices, while the Maze *r*'s were .80 for boys, .81 for girls. These *r*'s agree closely with the results obtained by Ross, as previously cited.

Had more attention been paid by psychologists to the close relationship of Maze scores to industrial efficiency, they would not have been surprised at Jensen's findings with Air Force trainees, which are referred to later. This is one instance of many studies where work with the feebleminded could have paved the way for applications at higher levels. It is the writer's conviction that there are many forgotten experiments from which conclusions might have been drawn or lessons learned, the careful study of which might well have lessened the labors of rediscovery and utilization. In a later chapter I suggest that the study of air flow in relation to boomerang flight might have been helpful to aeronautics.

More than 30 years ago the National Institute of Industrial Psychology in England conducted an investigation on the use of performance tests in vocational guidance (Earle and Milner, 1929). Nine currently well-known tests were used and the results published. As was usual at that time, a great deal of time and effort was expended in working out the intercorrelations of the nine tests, the distribution of scores, and their relationship with Spearman's *g*. These questions no longer demand as much attention from psychologists, the significance of display of columns of intercorrelations between a miscellany of tests of undetermined validity having suffered some decline in esteem. Few research workers now adhere closely to the theory that the worth of a test can be assured by proving its relationship with an array of other tests presumably "good." In the absence of reliable external criteria, the more modern rule, though often as honored in its breach as in its observance, is that each test should stand on its own feet and be crossvalidated through its application to a variety of groups, distinguished by behavioral or cultural differences. We have repeatedly emphasized the importance of sampling of subjects, realizing that test correlations may vary widely according to the samples examined. This variability in correlation coefficients is the basis of our uncertainty, not only as to the amount of *g* but as to what *g* represents. The same hindrance seems to be the nemesis of all factorial research.

Another factor in the gradual disappearance of this type of inquiry is that some of the tests concerned have themselves disappeared from the scene, simply through the toll of time. As examples of this mortality, no one nowadays is particularly concerned with formboards or cube imitation tests except for some specific inquiries.

However, the report in question does give us some information as to the predictive value of tests in relation to proficiency in certain occupations. Five mental measures—Porteus Maze, Cube Construction, Substitution, Dearborn Formboard, Picture Completion—were correlated with instructors' ratings of apprentices, given half way through the course and also with examination results at the end of training. The Maze (with r .44) was fourth at the halfway mark but moved up to an easy first place (r .61) in relation to "passing out" examinations. As the investigators fully realized, such correlations were hardly high enough to justify the making of specific vocational recommendations based on test results.

In the middle of World War II, I received a very interesting communication from a former psychologist, Dr. E. G. Brundage (1943), later commissioned in military service. His communication did not relate to his military experience but to a study upon which he was engaged prior to his induction into the armed forces, and which had a direct relation to the use of the Maze in industrial selection.

Whether as a result of the war or for other causes not known to me, his death was afterwards reported. Brundage, however, was the first to report an occurrence which was rather casually noted as occurring in lobotomy patients several years later (Porteus and Peters, 1947). As I had no further communication with Lieutenant Brundage and this feature of Maze performance, which he called "shatter" effect, has not been fully explored, I have decided to publish most of his letter.

To identify myself, let me say that I am now an interviewing officer with the Office of Naval Officer Procurement under the Bureau of Naval Personnel. The use of the Maze occurred at the Wm. Wrigley Jr. Co. in Chicago, where I was factory employment manager until I was commissioned. Most of my psychological training was in experimental at Columbia, but I took my doctorate at Indiana, where I had some slight contact with Louttit.

The personnel situation at Wrigley's was rather favorable for the profitable use of aptitude tests, since we had fairly large numbers of girls doing the same simple repetitive tasks. I had already worked out fairly satisfactory selection batteries for machine operators and similar occupations, and needed tests to pick inspectors. At Wrigley's, inspecting involves picking up a twenty package box, looking at the top ten packages for any of some fifty defects in appearance, then tilting the box first one way and then the other to see the bottom layer. Inspectors handle about one thousand boxes an hour.

In the experimental battery of twenty tests, I included the Maze without, I confess, any clear idea of what I expected it to test. I deviated from your regular procedure in two ways (I know how it irritates a test author to have his test tampered with): I allowed everyone who had not disqualified himself up to that point to take the Adult I, and I surreptitiously timed each total performance. The latter practice may represent dubious ethics, but it yielded valuable data.

To my surprise, the highest single correlation with criterion was the Maze TQ, with .498. The time score in the Maze was one of the highest, with about .44. When I worked out a multiple correlation between criterion and the twenty tests, I wound up with Porteus TQ, Porteus Time, Placing (of Minnesota Rate of Manipulation), and Number Checking (of Minnesota Test for Clerical Workers). The uncorrected r was about .74. Porteus TQ carried the heaviest regression weight. I am recalling these figures from memory, but they are very close. My sample was 98 girls.

From the behavioral notes I had made while administering the Maze, I classified the subjects into two rough classes: 'rash' and 'not rash'. Using these classes against criterion to obtain a biserial r, the result was .50. I did not throw this into the multiple correlation matrix, since I felt that the rash-not-rash data were already contained in the regular TQ scores.

I do not pretend to be a clinical psychologist, but even to me the behavior manifested while they were performing on the Maze was very illuminating; many of the problems that had arisen in connection with various individuals became much more understandable.

Following this lead, I tried the Maze on a few of our 'statistical problem children', girls who tested well in the aptitude tests for machine operators but who failed on the job and stuck out like sore thumbs on the scatter diagram. What I found seemed to be the most interesting of the Maze results. The high-test, low-performance girls, for the most part, were characterized by 'shattering' on the Maze. They would go along all right until they made their first error, usually at about IX or X. Then they would lose their caution and grip on themselves, lose their personal composure, and start madly tracing around at random. On the other hand, the high performance girls would buckle down and intensify their concentration when such an error occurred. I have, of course, exaggerated the sharpness of the contrast, but on the basis of the dozen or so such cases I had chance to work with before my commission came through, it would seem that you have a test for a sort of psychological 'brittleness' that is very important in certain industrial operations. . .

I was in the process of working out a factor analysis of the inspectors' data when I was commissioned. I had not yet succeeded in rotating the centroid vectors adequately, but it was apparent that the time score on the Maze was very similar to Minnesota Paper Form Board and some of the sub-tests of the MacQuarrie Mechanical Ability. The factorial composition of the TQ was not clear at that stage.

Probably Brundage's experience illustrates better than anything else the value of the Maze as a test of proximate foresight at a comparatively simple industrial level. This was practically the only study with normal subjects (except for standardization purposes) until one very important experiment from the Retesting Unit at Lackland Air Force Base, San Antonio, Tex. Accounts of Lt. Col. Jensen's work and its results were issued at first in a mimeographed copy as a paper presented to the American Association Advancement of Science at their meeting at St. Louis, December 29, 1952. It was entitled "Our Undeveloped Mental Resources" and was based on an earlier mimeographed report from the Air Force Base, dated November 20, 1952. It was not, however, until 1961 that the material appeared in printed form (Jensen, 1961a).

In his AAAS paper, Col. Jensen began with the statement that our nation faces a critical shortage of human talent, and he rightly emphasized the fact that in our search we have neglected those who lacked the opportunity or the motivation—and these hindrances are associatively linked—to equip themselves adequately. "These unstimulated, often unlearned," he said, "constitute a huge reservoir (of human talent)." This should undoubtedly be drawn upon. His experience was that due to a too literate type of military qualifying examination standards, many men who had unsuspected ability were rejected for Air Force training. The tests he referred to were the ACB (AC-1B), or Airman Cluster Battery, and the AFQT, or Air Force Qualification Test. His statement reads:

> Male airmen at L.A.F.B. (Lackland Air Force Base) who fail the AFQT subsequent to failure on the AC-1B, as a group approximate a normal unselected population on the Porteus Maze Test of Intelligence. This is a nonverbal, individually administered test. Clinical judgments as to mental potential are in very close agreement with Porteus ratings—not with AC-1B and AFQT scores. In the clinical situation every individual scoring high on the Porteus test presents qualitative evidence of power to plan ahead, to execute with precision and to adapt readily to tasks of increasing complexity. Once communication is established, they emerge as vital, imaginative personalities, despite what we term cultural (including educational) deficiencies.[1]

Failure was twice as great for men from the South and Deep South states as for the rest of the country. Many were Negroes, and Jensen commented as follows:

> Asked in interview why they failed the group tests, many of them gave answers that add up to lack of motivation to pass, or motivation to fail. This was much more common among Negroes than with Whites and reflects a cultural tendency for the Negro, particularly if he is from the south, to simulate incompetence at tasks imposed by the racial majority to which he does not belong and for which he probably has more hostility than empathy.

In view of this attitude of resistance toward the general testing program, it seems all the more extraordinary that the group did as well as they did in the Maze. No doubt the fact that the test

[1] This experience should be considered in relation to that of Brundage with low level planning. Basic air training is undoubtedly of a much higher industrial class.

was individually applied may help to account for their better showing, but there must also have been a more complete acceptance of the Maze. In spite of indifference or hostility toward mental examinations in general, the test itself must have excited their interest. This appeal is one of the curiosities of testing experience. Chinese illiterates, South African Bushmen, Australian aboriginals, Indian jungle dwellers, Malayan mountain tribes, all regarded the Maze as a worthy challenge to their abilities.

Out of the 634 men failing the group psychological tests, 520 or 80 per cent were retained in training on the basis mainly of Maze performance, while 114 or 18 per cent were recommended for discharge. After interview, those retained were "profiled" in categories for mild or moderate defects, and of these 299 or 57.5 per cent were put down as possessing mild defects, 146 or 28.1 per cent with moderate defects, the most frequent being educational deficiency, 92 per cent falling into this category. The fact that 98.3 per cent of those retained in service completed basic training seemed to Jensen remarkable. "This high rate of survival," he said, "can be credited largely to the fact that most of the defects of those retained in service were educational, and that basic training made few demands on academic skills and attitudes." The same thing is true of the majority of workers in semiskilled jobs throughout the nation who drift into their occupations with a minimum of guidance. Jensen's study, however, proves that very many of those working at unskilled or semiskilled occupations are much more capable than their present level of employment indicates. There is indeed a great reservoir of potential abilities at present untapped under our unsystematic development of industrial personnel.

Col. Jensen sets forth, on the basis of his three tours of military duty, the items he took into account in recommending retention or discharge. First on the list was the Maze Test score, which he termed "a major determinant, though by no means the only one." Among those discharged were 32 classified as mental defectives. Unusually stable personalities accounted for all the "low IQ's" retained in service. The Picture Vocabulary, Reading, and Computation scores were used mainly to determine those who wilfully failed in tests. The above three tests correlated only .12, .09, and .21 with the retention separation criterion as against .37 for the Maze. The Porteus Q-score "was given considerable weight in arriving at decisions and correlated .25 with the criterion." The mean for retained men was 31.7, for the discharged 47.2 error scores, which he notes is typical of nondelinquent and delinquent populations, respectively. Jensen recorded his unwillingness to recommend for retention in service men with delinquent histories or who "made a high Q-score and clearly evidenced rebelliousness or escapism in the clinical examination." Those with high Q-scores he terms "non-conformity-minded," and remarks: "Generally as measured by the Porteus Q-score and supported by clinical judgment, LAFB male basic airmen who fail the group psychological tests are not as conformity-minded as delinquents. We consider their non-conformity as a major factor in failure on the group tests. They choose to ignore instructions and are unwilling to expend the energy necessary for creditable performance. . . . The whites of this group are more inclined to non-conformity than are the negroes" (Jensen, 1952). Under the circumstances of nonmilitary employment, this nonconformity might constitute a serious handicap. Once they are inducted into military service, the discipline may have a salutary effect on such cases.

From the above it is quite evident that the Porteus Maze with its two scorings, test age and qualitative error, played an important part in the selection of trainees. There remains the all-important question as to the comparative success in training of 520 men retained in service in spite of inferior IQ's below 80 in the group psychological testing. This, of course, has a direct bearing on the further question as to the comparative ability of tests to differentiate men by industrial competence as apart from character or intelligence.

Jensen reported that he was able to follow careers of 329 of the retested airmen to the end of their basic training by October 1, 1952. The group represents those surviving after a further weeding out for low mental ability. Of 3,090 men who *passed* the group test and who were thus given the opportunity for adjustment afforded by basic training, 98.3 per cent were reassigned. The comparative percentage of men who *failed* the group tests but succeeded on the individual test and were reassigned after basic training was 96.1 per cent. This means in effect that the individual tests (predominantly the Maze) salvaged 316 men who would otherwise have been discharged as being of too low mental ability but nevertheless succeeded in basic training—a considerable conservation of man power. Many of them trained in sixty consecutive air flights in

company with others selected on the basis of group test performance.

Ratings by technical instructors were given on 141 "retested"
airmen who trained along with 3,090 airmen who had passed the
group tests. The percentages of the two groups who were rated
and promoted were 82 per cent for those who passed the group
tests, 71.5 per cent for those who failed but who were retested
and passed the individual tests. Examination of the records showed
the reasons for failure during basic training stemmed mainly from
"social ineptness and inability to handle personal emotional problems."

This simply illustrates the rather obvious fact that there is no
single test, or group of tests, which tells the whole story with regard
to the personalities of individuals. Success in the Air Force group
tests does not merely reflect educational competency or experience.
The length of the examination period demands from the examinee
sustained attention, resistance to fatigue, and desire to do well
even in an uninteresting task, all qualities useful in military service.
One of the drawbacks of the Maze—corrected since 1955—was
that it was a short, closely observed individual effort, requiring a
relatively short period of concentration on the task in hand. Many
individuals, under the obviously interested attention of the examiner, show at their best in a brief effort, but fail to stand up against
less closely watched but more sustained tasks. Recognition of this
observable tendency actuated the writer to say at one time that
failure in the Maze is more significant than success. There are now
three Maze Series, so that the longer time of application is likely
to penalize the "sprinter," the individual who does well in a short
intensive burst of effort, but lacks staying power.

The main thesis of this book is that the range of relevant abilities that the psychological examiner tests must be wide and that
the loss of psychologists' interest in mental testing that has become
latterly apparent is, we believe, due very largely to demonstration
that reliance on a too narrow test approach is unwise. If the definition of intelligence as ability to respond to a wide range of stimuli
is accepted, then the inadequacy of the conventionally limited test
battery becomes at once apparent. The hope of evolving a very
rapid assessment of human worth is a vain one. The plan of attack
represented by the Air Force group tests amounts merely to a
temporal extension of an already inadequate approach. In the

words of Scripture, the psychologists' practice constitutes "a bed too short whereon a man may stretch himself." From this point of view, the devising, premature publicizing, and popular accept-ance and misinterpretation of the intelligence quotient (IQ) is one of the greatest disservices to clinical psychology that could have been rendered.

Because of the importance to this nation of Jensen's findings reached 12 years ago and their even more critical timeliness today, I cannot forbear quoting part of his summing up of the situation even though it is somewhat outside this book's field of reference.

> I postulate that outstanding mental ability is undiscovered and undeveloped at every IQ level of our population except, possibly, at the lowest extreme. It is concealed by lack of academic skills and unwillingness to perform on the intelligence test. It is retarded by lack of stimulation and opportunity for schooling. It is blocked by emotional turmoil arising from group and family conflicts.
>
> The most readily available source of this hidden potential is the American Negro, some 15½ million in total number. To develop their potentials we will have to breach the barrier of mutual distrust and lack of understanding that separate the races. . . To save these resources we must utilize them. They will not remain unexploited as oil in a reservoir or capped well.

I should like to add this brief comment. Is it not possible that the present enthusiasm for the bestowing of civil rights is mis-placed? I cannot see that political equality is a complete panacea for human ills nor that it will provide the stimulation of which Jensen speaks. In my opinion, that stimulus must come more from within than without. The mere opening of the schoolhouse or the university doors to all comers will work no miracles of educational advancement. Along with the mere removal of obvious barriers to a free flow of talent must exist an internal pressure to force the precious fluid to rise to the surface. May I suggest that the real problem is not only the Negro versus the white man but also the Negro versus his own group's lack of initiative, self-confidence, devotion to educational achievement, courage, and his super-sensi-tivity—all traits in which he must aim at change within his racial group just as earnestly as he urges a change in white attitudes and behavior.

With all the privileges that the white race enjoys, they have not resulted and cannot result in ironing out inequalities in talent and social effectiveness that exist among whites themselves. Social anthropologists never fail to belabor the idea that racial differences are mainly cultural, and somewhat triumphantly point to the obvious progress of ethnic groups when opportunities are provided. I should like to see more emphasis placed on the unassailable fact that culture is man-made and that its springs lie within. We can bestow freedom. What is not in our gift is the ability to use it wisely. After this brief excursion into the troubled waters of civil rights, we can return to our more immediate interest, the matter of the discovery of talent.

The fact that institutions for the mentally subnormal provide exceptional opportunities for experimental work on the interpretation of mental tests has been commented upon elsewhere in this volume. Summarily stated, no other situation is as advantageous for the setting up of external criteria of performance for the validation of tests. Their populations are usually stable. Partial self-help or self-support is the main purpose of their training programs. In this process, rating of abilities outside the ordinary scholastic field is possible, and such criteria are as badly needed as they are hard to come by. Moreover, these judgments are possibly more reliable, since the product of many years' acquaintance with subjects is condensed into the ratings. One drawback is that in some instances the level of education or ability of raters is not very high. Every such institution should have a department of research, so that part of the in-service training given to attendants might include familiarity with the application of rating scales.

One other drawback is inherent in the institutional setting itself. After rating scales of behavior have been arranged and applied, how do we know that the results will accord with behavior outside the institution? Similar questions apply in many other situations, where experiments are being made in a controlled environment. Captive animals, routinely conditioned, may react quite differently under natural circumstances. Predictions of behavior based on individual adjustment to army life, to mental institutions, to correctional facilities often fail when the routine regulatory measures no longer operate. Many individuals do not know how to use their freedom wisely. Every parole officer is fully aware of the pitfalls of behavior prediction.

A recent study that bears the title "The Porteus Maze Test and the Appraisal of Retarded Adults" illustrates both the advantages and drawbacks of institutional research (Tobias and Gorelick,

1962). The authors begin by quoting a timely warning from Wechsler (1959) that "an IQ alone, however accurately determined, is often insufficient for a definitive classification" (of mentally deficient persons). Taking a WAIS IQ of 70 as the dividing line between mental deficiency and social sufficiency, Wechsler points out that many individuals with a much lower level of intelligence adjust well, while others above that IQ point are definitely defective in behavior. This diagnostic caution is one that has been voiced by me for 50 years. To my mind it is not only the inadequacy of the tests that is to blame for uncertain classification, but also the failure to define intelligence. Provided that this definition is stated in terms of response to environmental demands, it must cover the mentally defective. If we cannot at present rely on a test-quotient definition of socially inadequate intelligence, it follows that the term intelligence quotient is a misnomer. One glaring defect in the diagnostic procedure is its failure to take account of foresight or planfulness, but I do not believe that this is the only inadequacy in the testing program.

These comments are not intended to detract from the merits of the Tobias-Gorelick investigation. The distinction that they make between work in a sheltered workshop setting *versus* outside competitive employment is very important. The authors rightly term this employment "a crucial measure of social adequacy." Sixteen individuals with a minimum of a year's training in the Sheltered Workshop were matched as regards Wechsler IQ's with an equal number of persons of similar training. But the crucial distinction was that the first-named group had gained and held outside employment for more than six months, while the second group had failed to do so in spite of equal "intelligence."

The mean Maze score of the employed group was 10.8 years, while the unemployed averaged only 6.8, or 4 years lower. This seems to prove conclusively that whatever the Maze-tested mental or personality functions happen to be, they should not be left out of account in any diagnostic appraisal. The two mean test quotients are respectively 86 for the employed, 53 for the unemployed, and a disparity of 33 points is surely significant.

In fact, the difference may be too striking to be real. The research should be replicated, if possible, with larger numbers. Over and over again the effect of restrictive or unrepresentative sampling has been noted in this book. Moreover, even if this difference between the test verdicts is confirmed, it emphatically does not indicate general superiority of the Maze over the Wechsler. The question must always be considered as applying to restricted samples. The Tobias-Gorelick study proves that for the purpose of predicting the employability of mentally deficient persons, the Maze has pragmatic validity. For general employability at higher levels the case stands altogether differently.

The rest of the implications of this study seem to be well supported by the evidence. The Maze does not have as close a relation with verbal measures as it does with nonverbal, but the latter correlations are highest when the test in question involves a high degree of attentiveness, such as the Knox Cube Test; other measures, such as the Purdue Pegboard, also have a closer relationship with earnings and productivity in a sheltered setting. Obviously, this last consideration has only a slight bearing on the general usefulness of specific tests, unless their value can be demonstrated in delinquency, psychosurgery, drug therapy, differences in primitive mentality, sex differences, and the whole gamut of test applications. There is no expectation that in these varied situations Mazes correlations will be uniformly high.

For experimental purposes, perhaps one of the values of the study under review is its clear demonstration that when groups of subjects are considered in relation to some specific criterion, such as for example industrial employability, the fact that subjects all fall into a general classification of mental deficiency has little relevancy.

This particular situation serves to illustrate in striking fashion the influence of selective sampling. Supposing, for example, someone desired to show the relationship between the Maze and the WAIS. If he correlated the scores of the unemployed group, he would find that their mean was at the Wechsler medium level of 65 IQ, but their mean in the Porteus Maze was only 53 points, with a possibly similar range of distribution. Under those circumstances, the relationship between the two measures would not be close. But if he chose the employed group for study, the correlation between the two tests could be expected to be quite high, since he would be comparing mentally retarded cases who possess relatively high levels of industrial ability with individuals who have relatively high Maze Test scores. The question would then arise as to which of the obtained correlations represents the relationship between the two tests. Neither r could be interpreted without reference to the basis of selection.

Possibly factor analysts, who base their findings of factor loadings on a matrix of correlations, should pay more attention to the selection basis of their population samples. Over 30 years ago I pointed out this matter to Spearman, citing the different range of correlation coefficients obtaining among cases who were all feebleminded, but otherwise segregated differently according to age, industrial efficiency, mental disturbance, etc. He had thought that the *g* loading would be the same for tests applied to the whole body of the mentally defective. After study of the array of varying correlations shown to him, he at once agreed that selection was the crucial consideration and that it would be necessary to work with many different samples. In other words, the *g* loading of a certain test might be a certain figure for fifteen-year-old, mentally defective Negresses, and something very different for twelve-year-old Negro boys who test within the normal range of intelligence, and something else again with Japanese high school students mixed as regards sex.

It is now becoming more widely recognized that a generally high level of correlations with other tests is far from being an index of goodness or value of a specific test. The reverse may even be true as was implied in a review of the Maze written 11 years ago in a British journal (Buros, 1953).

It is amazing that a test devised in 1914 should be gaining in popularity in 1953. Although originally intended as a measure of general intelligence, the Maze has been little used for this purpose; its reliability was too low to make it practical as a clinical instrument, and it did not correlate highly enough with other accepted measures of intellectual functions. But exactly its relatively low correlations with other tests have been the sources of the Maze's revival. It is suggested that the Maze measures some aspects of mental apparatus not covered by other techniques.

Leaving on one side the reviewer's wholly incorrect statement that the Maze is unreliable, or "intended as a measure of general intelligence" and the equally unfounded implication that it has suffered from suspended animation, the suggestion that the test reflects a different type of brain function from other mental measures is decidedly interesting. Helper *et al.* (1963) in discussing the fact that deficits appear after chlorpromazine medication in the Maze and a paired-associates learning task, but not in other tests, suggest that one possibility is that chlorpromazine impairs the maintenance of active attention to novel and significant tasks. These writers further cite the work of Mirsky and Rosvold (1960), who suggest that the midbrain reticular formation is related to this type of alertness.

Some of the above experiences have been mentioned elsewhere in this volume but are so important that they merit the emphasis of repetition.

SUMMARY

Psychologists in their preoccupation with the subnormal and the abnormal are likely to be insufficiently informed as to what is ordinary or normal in behavior. This is due to the difficulty they experience in making wide range investigations of their fellow citizens over whom they can exercise no control. Only in national emergencies, which occasion the calling of many thousands of men into military service, do psychologists have opportunities to test their standards of normalcy. Without such information, applied and experimental psychology tend to drift apart. The sudden turning of ploughshares into swords brings about a change of conditions. Since this so seldom occurs, we are forced to fall back on experience with the nonnormal. Particularly is this the case with the validation of methods and approaches in industrial psychology.

Early efforts to rate industrial ability are cited to indicate that efforts to set up criteria of practical ability have not been fruitless, but such attempts were soon forgotten. The demonstration by Brundage of "shatter effects" in the Maze performance was one such instance.

However, necessity imposed by a national crisis did turn attention to the practical problem of classifying ordinary, run-of-the-mill men with regard to their suitability for basic Air Force training. This development has been described by Lt. Col. Milton Jensen (1952, 1961a, 1961b).

The frequency of failure in a six-hour examination of recruits with the consequence of tremendous loss or misemployment of man power prompted Jensen to apply performance tests, particularly the Porteus Maze Test, and reclassify men for service on the basis of satisfactory scores. The Maze Q-scores were also given consideration as well as the test age.

Evidently due to differences in subject motivation and appeal of the two types of examinations, men retained in service on the new basis did almost as well in training as those who succeeded in the far more educationally exacting Air Force test battery. Follow-up experience with trainees admitted to flight instruction showed that while 82 per cent of the men who passed the latter examination were rated as satisfactory by their instructors, 71 per cent of those who failed the group test but succeeded in the Maze and several other performance tests also were satisfactory. The Porteus Maze, according to Jensen, was "a major determinant" in this retention of men in service.

The potential value of institutions for the mentally retarded as centers for setting up criteria for industrial selections is again emphasized, and in this situation a recent study by Tobias and Gorelick is cited as showing the advisability of using performance tests in the assessment of ability at simple levels. For cases in a "Sheltered Workshop" environment, Wechsler-Bellevue equivalence of score for employable individuals and unemployable trainees was in marked contrast to a four-year difference in the Maze.

The absolute necessity for replication of crucial experiments is illustrated by the above results with two industrial groups of mental defectives. Dependent on which group was selected for study, two diametrically opposed conclusions as to the relationship of Wechsler-Bellevue with the Porteus Maze would be reached. If samples cannot be equated, replication is the only resource.

CHAPTER EIGHT

Australid Mentality: Early Studies

One of the most difficult problems that has confronted psychologists, particularly in the past third of a century, has been the question of the reality and significance of racial differences. Probably its very complexity provides the reason why so little work has been done on the subject. But the march of events, especially the emergence of strong national trends and newly assumed responsibilities on the part of native peoples in such organizations as the United Nations have given this question tremendously added significance. But a mere proclamation of international unity or racial equality does not alter the facts of nature and may even increase their importance. The determination, or otherwise, that many racial differences are inherent constitutes a keener challenge to scientific investigation. The general acceptance of democratic principles, including rights to self-government and equality under domestic and international law, has had the effect of sharpening rather than of blunting scientific interest in individual differences. Equal rights under the law do not ensure equal ability to make the best use of opportunities granted by law, particularly in regard to private property, or even the right to vote, which under some circumstances is withheld or canceled. The abuse of freedom is as much a matter for concern as its preservation. We may be born equally free, but no one believes we are born equally wise. Human inequality is one of the most stubborn facts in nature. Thus the growing concern with the welfare of various primitive racial groups, so-called, demands planned inquiry to determine the connotation of *primitive*. Plainly stated, the problem is to discover in what ways and to what degrees primitive peoples differ from the rest of us. Their welfare may be vitally affected by the discovery as to how deep those differences go, and whether they can be partially or wholly erased through social, educational, and even political better-ment.

The difficulty lies not only in the collection and analysis of the facts and their scientific interpretation, but also the definition of the terms used. If, for example, we wish to consider differences in intelligence, we are at once faced with the necessity of making plain what we consider intelligence to be. Obviously, we should try to agree, at least, on its operational definition. Simply stated, the problem must be defined in terms of what intelligence does. This question cannot presently be disposed of, but is at least partially dealt with throughout this whole volume.

Another great drawback to sober investigation is the fact that strong emotional feelings that are related to the question at once become evident when the differences are interpreted in terms of the superiority or inferiority of whole groups of mankind. So sweeping have past generalizations been, and so invidious are their moral, educational, and even political implications, that many well-mean-ing individuals have felt themselves driven to deny that the term "race" has any definable meaning, or that, if there are racial differences between divisions or classifications of mankind, they are of any practical importance. This is a most egregious begging of the question. Some people can be deluded into thinking that once social equality has been achieved, all else follows, especially in the sense of obliterating the significance of mental differences. This is merely a matter of faith or hope. Such a theory has never been adequately supported by facts, and certainly provides no adequate reason for dropping or postponing investigations of race. Yet this was the most obvious implication of a recent article in *Current Anthropology* (Comas, 1961) under the provocative title "Scientific Racism Again?," which held that because some of the evidence for racial differences is faulty or incomplete, the whole investigation was unscientific and should be dropped from academic or other consideration. This attitude could lead to a negation of all frank inquiry into subjects where prejudices, either for or against, are involved.

As regards the word "race," the truth is obvious that in the history of man there has been so much admixture of blood that racial boundaries are in many instances indistinct or confused. But as regards our present inquiry there would probably be a minimum of dispute over the statement that the Australian aborigines, anthropologically speaking, present the most obvious example of a separate or distinct race.

Whether they are to be regarded strictly as an ethnic unit is open to question. Two anthropologists, Tindale of South Australia and Birdsell of California, believe that on the basis of physical measurements and archeological evidence three different types of Australids, including the Tasmanoid, can be recognized. This may well be the case, but it must be remembered that at the present time opportunities for studying the physical anthropology of the natives of Tasmania are non-existent, and are rapidly diminishing to a zero point for the mainland Australids. Moreover, archeological deposits of a nomadic and thinly scattered people are necessarily scanty. In addition, the existing evidence for the theory has not yet, to my knowledge, been scientifically presented. Hence, it seems premature to speak of Murrayan, Tasmanoid, or other types of Australian aboriginal people. Undoubtedly, both in the northwest and northern parts of the continent, there has been some admixture with Malays and Papuans, nor is it possible to doubt there are racial affinities between the extinct Tasmanians and the continental aboriginal inhabitants. Nevertheless, the contribution of alien blood strains seems to have made a minor impress on the great mass of Australids. What evidence that we do possess seems to indicate strongly that these people represent an ethnic group that is substantially distinct from all others, having had minimum contact over many centuries with their most immediate geographical neighbors.

In sum, there are some wide local variations, both physical and social, but basically their physical and mental characteristics are so different from those of other peoples that the Australids can be truly considered a distinct race. The cultural patterns throughout their continent are also in general so alike that the theory of long separation from other racial influences is fully supported. Naturally, in an area so huge, with means of travel and communication limited to walking and talking, centuries of lack of contact have resulted in variations in cultural devices, languages, beliefs, and social practices. Nevertheless, in spite of micro-evolution, the degree of aboriginal essential unity is extraordinary.

My own interest in these primitive[1] people extends back to child-

---

[1]My use of the term "primitive" as applied to Australids is relative; it does not overlook the fact that in many directions their social organization is very complex and quite the reverse of simple. But in the sense of the tremendous gap that must be

hood days in Australia. My first contact with "the blacks," as they were called, was at about the age of eight years when I was living with my parents in a very small township called Mooroopna, in the north-central portion of the State of Victoria. This region is situated within the Goulburn River valley, now one of the most fertile and prosperous districts in Australia. The river at Mooroopna made a three-mile bend between this village and the now thriving town of Shepparton. In flood time the river overflowed and obliterated the bend so that road communications were cut off until the flood subsided. The almost virgin state of the country 70 years ago was indicated by the wild life that was still to be seen at such times. Opossums, huge lace lizards or iguanas, venomous snakes, and small kangaroos could be seen floating on brushwood being swept downstream, while waterfowl of various kinds were plentiful.

Though the drainage system of the Murray River into which the Goulburn empties was elsewhere probably well suited to habitation by aborigines, native depopulation in the Goulburn valley had evidently proceeded rapidly, so that the appearance in Mooroopna of a small horde of aborigines, the men carrying spears and shields and accompanied by women and children and a pack of half-starved dogs, was quite an exciting, almost disturbing event. Probably they had wandered south from the Murray River but whence they came or whither they went no one seemed to care. We children needed no warnings to keep out of their way, and in a couple of days the visitors disappeared, no doubt much to the local police trooper's and our parents' relief. Thus, even in those days, the appearance of the original owners of the continent was a rare phenomenon. In this case they posed no real threat to persons or property. In other parts of Victoria wandering blacks did constitute an early pioneering hazard. In East Gippsland, shepherds in lonely places and an occasional prospector had been speared to death. One white woman near Bairnsdale had been tomahawked and left for dead by a notorious aboriginal disturber of the peace, but these were isolated incidents.

---

bridged between their way of life and that of civilized peoples they are decidedly primitive. The difficulty that is being experienced in bridging this gap by those who favor assimilation of whites and aboriginals in Australia is proof of this primitiveness. There is no hard core of nationalism to combat, not even any crowding of white population into areas now occupied by natives, yet the status of the Australids in the Australian scene is inchoate or even undetermined. Efforts to incorporate the remnants of this people into full citizenship are at present tentative and experimental.

Some ten years later, my interest in aborigines was further stimulated through the fact that for several months I was a junior teacher in a school at Healesville, about 30 miles east of Melbourne. Several miles away was the mission station of Coranderrk. To give added interest to local carnivals or other social events, blacks from the mission were brought in to give exhibitions of boomerang and spear-throwing, or fire-making with wooden drills, etc. The aborigines also had a football team (Australian rules) that journeyed here and there to play matches against neighboring clubs. As a youth, I had the rather memorable experience of playing against them at Ringwood, now a thriving outer suburb of Melbourne, 15 miles distant.

What impressed us as their opponents was not the aborigines' barefoot skill in making long drop kicks, nor their speed and agility in the game, which were considerable, but rather the fact that the team of 20 players had at least 5 player-captains, all greybeards, who issued vociferous commands to the younger men. This was my first experience with the Australian system of "old man government," which I was to meet many years later in my studies of aboriginal life in Central and Northwest Australia. None of the younger (and better) football players seemed to resent the dominance of their tribal elders, though one showed a flare of temper when a white man, making a dash for the ball, shouted, "Out of my way, blackfellow!" The native immediately turned on his opponent with raised fists and the fierce question, "Who you calling blackfellow?" The Ringwood player was so astonished that he forgot to take up the challenge, perhaps to his advantage, as some of the aborigines were good pugilists and perfectly capable of handling themselves in a fight. Usually, however, they were very good-tempered.[2]

One other personal experience served to show me that the aboriginal sense of humor was at about the same level as that of the average white rural population. About 1916, I visited the native mission station at Lake Tyers, Victoria, for the purpose of obtaining aboriginal head measurements for use by Professor R. J. A. Berry and myself at Melbourne University. I also decided to apply some

---

[2] The Australian game is played on an oval, usually about 180 yards long, and is, next to ice hockey, probably the fastest and most continuously exciting of all ball games. Crowds of up to 100,000 attending matches in the southern cities of Australia yell themselves hoarse every Saturday of the season in support of their favorite teams.

mental tests to children. Seeing some natives amusing themselves by throwing boomerangs in the compound in front of the school building where I was testing, I went outside and attempted to throw one of these implements. I used such unnecessary force that the boomerang circled back behind me and broke a window of the mission church on the far side of the building, opposite to the direction in which I had thrown.

This extraordinary mishap caused such amusement that for several days I could view at any time the whole adult population assembled, while each individual in turn imitated me hurling an imaginary boomerang, thereafter leading his audience back to the church to examine the damaged window. Thence they emerged shrieking with mirth while another native took his place as demonstrator. The humor of the situation lost nothing by repetition until I became the only person who was tired of the performance. Evidently it was ridiculous in that my level of ability was so far below that of the most incompetent thrower in the settlement that I could not have achieved a more unlikely spot for the missile to land. Even the children could not regard me seriously thereafter, and I soon gave up the attempt to examine them. Evidently they considered that such a stupid person as I needed a mental examiner far more than the individuals whose intelligence measurement I was concerned with.

From the white point of view, my purposes seemed equally absurd. At that time any attempt to assess the intelligence of the "blackfellow" was regarded as utter foolishness. They weren't supposed to possess any. Full-blood aborigines were a fast disappearing remnant, whose intelligence was commonly reputed to be little if anything above that of the brutes. Many early settlers in Australia regarded them much as the pioneers of South Africa looked upon the Bushmen—vermin to be got rid of as soon as possible. By 1916, they posed no acute social problem and were considered unworthy of any attention other than curiosity. Only to explorers, lost or perishing in the bush, or to dim-witted wandering anthropologists was their existence of any interest. White owners of land and herds of cattle were not above exploiting their services but with few exceptions showed no concern for their welfare.

My first real opportunity to inquire into the mentality of children with aboriginal blood occurred about 1915 when I was invited by the government of South Australia to visit Adelaide to report on the training facilities afforded the mentally deficient inmates of the Home for Feebleminded at Minda. Because of my expressed interest in aborigines, I was later taken for a couple of days' visit to the Mission Station at Point McLeay, reached by a wood-burning launch that plied Lake Coorong at the mouth of the Murray River. Forty-seven years later I was able to revisit the spot and there observed a plaque on an obelisk commemorating the establishment of the mission and school by the Rev. George Taplin in 1860, 102 years previously.

The results of this early study were reported briefly in Chapter 2, and they need not be repeated here. However, the question of deterioration in scholastic ability of aboriginal children with age, especially at or about the pubertal level, does crop up from time to time in discussions of primitive mentality (Porteus, 1917, p. 37ff). At my second visit to Point McLeay in 1962, I again inquired as to the educational progress of pupils and was told by the principal of the school that only eight per cent reached the fifth grade, though very occasionally a really bright child finished all elementary grades. By this time no aboriginal full-bloods were in attendance. The teachers attributed their retardation to lack of educational ability rather than failing interest. I suggested that lack of regular attendance and parental approval of early dropping out from classes might be responsible, but I was told that this was not the case. While the child attended school, clothes and food were issued more generously, so that parental pressure caused many of the pupils to remain at school even after progress had apparently ceased.

This matter would not be of importance except for the fact that Ashley Montagu, one of the chief proponents of the mental equality of races, has several times (1937, 1945, 1961) quoted the Rev. John Mathew, who stated in his book *Eaglehawk and Crow: A Study of the Australian Aborigines* that the Ramahyuck school for aboriginal children in East Gippsland, Victoria, "stood for three consecutive years the highest of all the state schools of the colony in examination results, obtaining *one hundred per cent of marks*" (Mathew, 1899, p. 78).

As a clergyman with strong missionary interests, Mathew evidently accepted without proper inquiry this completely dubious evidence as to the mental attainments of aboriginal pupils; otherwise he would not have made such a statement.

In 1899, schools attended by native children were few and far between, were run by missions, and were certainly not attended by older children. Because of 50 years of aboriginal contacts with whites, probably many of the pupils were half-castes. About 1935, I inquired into this matter at the Victorian Education Department in Melbourne and was informed that aboriginal and white schools were never officially compared. Pupils at the former educational facilities were not given ordinary school examinations, but were set special tests thought by inspectors to be suited to the pupils' mentality. Schools at that period were never graded by children's examination marks but on the percentage of pupils promoted to the next higher grade. In the case of aboriginal pupils, such promotions were automatic when approved by the inspector.

My informant was a senior officer of the Department who had been for many years directly concerned with the supervision of other school inspectors. His statement to me was that these men were naturally most sympathetic as regards the earnest efforts of mission school teachers to push their pupils along. He also suggested that it would be doubtful if Ramahyuck school had more than a few scholars above the fourth grade. Taking such things into account, the State Educational Department paid little attention to inspectors' reports on these special schools, and certainly would not credit Ramahyuck School with being ahead of any white school, let alone all schools in the State. Unfortunately for Montagu's case, he neglected to quote the whole of Mathew's paragraph bearing on the subject, which sums up the negative as well as the positive aspects of native mentality:

For a people so low in the scale of civilization the Australians exhibit powers of mind anything but despicable. They are very keen observers, of quick understanding, intelligent, frequently cunning, but, as might be expected, neither close, nor deep, nor independent thinkers. In schools, it has often been observed that aboriginal children learn quite as easily and rapidly as children of European parents. In fact, the aboriginal school at Ramahyuck, in Victoria, stood for three consecutive years the highest of all the state schools of the colony in examination results, obtaining *one hundred per cent of marks*. While among Europeans the range of mental development seems almost unbounded, with the blacks its limit is soon attained. An inherent aversion to application is generally an impassable barrier to the progress of an aboriginal's education; in addition to which there is usually the absence of sufficient inducement to severe mental exertion. Unless in the case of those who are so situated that they cannot help attending school, most natives who have been taken in hand to be taught have at best learned to read words of one or two syllables and to write their own names in a very clumsy manner.

This summary, it will be seen, does not differ materially from the experience of present-day educators.

Professor A. P. Elkin, leading authority on the aborigines, has always been convinced of their practical intelligence and has been consistently hopeful of their final industrial and political ability. He was at one time inclined to discount my belief that on the basis of test results, full-blooded Australids as a group were incapable of adaptation to western civilization. This present volume examines still further Maze test performances in which some presumably full-bloods attained high scores. But my previous statement of biologically determined inferiority was not based on Maze tests and was not intended as a blanket denigration of the capacity of a whole people. No one could have been more impressed than I with the wide range of ability uncovered by the tests, and I was quick to call attention to the almost perfect score attained by a Luritcha native, who had hardly seen a white man and to whom not only paper and pencil but also printed maze designs were completely novel. Like Professor Elkin, I have met with really gifted individuals who were, within the limits of their prescientific status, clear and quick in thinking, while with regard to the aborigines as a whole, I have never ceased to be astonished at their remarkable adjustments to and partial mastery of their own environment. If they had shown an equal facility in dealing with all the problems of a civilized environment, then I would regard them as being greatly superior in intelligence to myself.

The work reported in this book will provide evidence of a wide range of endowment as measured by the Maze Test. However, the Maze is far from being a general intelligence test. Indeed, I am very sceptical that there is at present any such thing. There are essential facets or factors of intelligence not yet measurable, and many of these factors are not directly intellectual. These unmeasured aspects of intelligence may account for Professor Elkin's (1961) disappointment at Australid adjustments as recently voiced by him in discussing their achievements: "Moreover, I cannot at this date, nearly 30 years later, point to any full-blood Aborigine who has adopted our civilization. Individuals have proved successful in some of our technical and artistic skills, but they have not adopted our values in the spheres of space, time and property." Undoubtedly, it is the acceptance of such values that marks the civilized attitude. Like myself, Professor Elkin will no doubt be surprised that in individual cases the Maze does adequately reflect technical and artistic skills. It is the other values that psychological tests seem to miss. But in contrast to Ashley Montagu, it is the success that many natives achieve in the Maze Test that astonishes me, not their comparative failures. Montagu[3] and his sociological colleagues cannot have it both ways. They cannot continue to downgrade the tests, or term them "culture-bound," and at the same time view occasional high individual or group achievements as evidence of racial equality.

In an article published in *Mankind Quarterly* (Porteus, 1962), I have tried to summarize as graphically as I can the tremendous handicaps that Australia's indigenous people have had to face throughout the many centuries of their isolated existence. The article is entitled "The Will to Live" and expresses the highest tribute I can pay to their environmental adaptability when I record the fact that they are still our living contemporaries. That fact alone speaks volumes.

The following considerations must be held in mind in any appraisal of the aboriginal way of life. The first is that the continent, with approximately the same land mass as the United States, not only was populated in the most favorably situated regions of the continent, but also was everywhere covered by a thin sprinkling of native tribes. This means that Australids wandered over and subsisted in more than a million square miles of land that the white man, with all the resources of civilization behind him, has so far found impossible to occupy with any assured degree of permanence.

Native population was indeed always scanty, with generous estimates in Captain Cook's day of a total of only 300,000, about the same as the great navigator's estimate of the number living in that most favored region on earth, the Hawaiian Islands. It must have been of great interest to Cook to have discovered, within a brief period of time, a group of Pacific islands where sustenance was so easy and population so dense, and a continent as wide, as outwardly alluring, and yet as relatively empty. One of the reasons for this seemingly general but sparse Australid dispersal was that the area in which a native was born remains "his country," to which he is bound by traditional cultural ties, and he covets none other.

---

[3] Montagu in his latest exposition characterizes my contributions as "two books which constitute monuments to the method by which intelligence tests should not be cross-culturally administered and the erroneous inferences which should not be drawn from them." Unfortunately, he offers no suggestions whatsoever as to how such tests should be administered or interpreted.

With the building of railway lines and establishment of government and mission stations, the blacks have tended to foregather wherever supplementary food has been made available by whites. Unless tribal organizations and ideas have completely disappeared, a native who changes his habitat knows the boundaries of his own home country and will revisit it whenever possible.

This absence of competition for living space, though it has condemned most of the aborigines to an uneven struggle for existence, had the effect of diminishing tribal warfare to such an extent that its absence brought about a remarkable stability of population. It was the advent of the white man, and his interference with native freedom of movement, his extinction of wild life, his introduction of diseases such as measles, trachoma, the common cold, tuberculosis, and venereal infections, that were responsible for a reduction of full-blood population from 300,000 in Cook's day to probably one-tenth of that number at the present time.

What, then, is the nature of the interior, once covered with a thin mesh of aboriginal life? This area probably includes about four-fifths of the entire continent, extending 1,500 miles west from the mouth of the Murray River; thence, except for a thin coastal strip of country, another 1,600 miles from Fremantle to Broome, along another 2,000 miles of littoral to eastern Queensland. This region contains, after a hundred years of white discovery and attempted exploitation, probably about one per cent of the whole Australian white population. The gulf that exists between aboriginal and white philosophies of living can be judged by the fact that 40 per cent of the white immigrants live in two cities, Sydney and Melbourne.

Another rather revealing circumstance is that the vast interior of the continent, known as "the inland," is almost completely unknown to most Australians. This is due mainly to the difficulties of travel, with one single rail route extending 1,000 miles north from Adelaide to Alice Springs and a further equal distance by road from there to Darwin. This is the main and only practicable line of communication through the center. Only in the last 25 years has there developed any marked tourist interest in visiting Central Australia. One magazine, named *Walkabout* (after the aboriginal habit of temporary wanderings), now devotes considerable attention to this region. Central Australia was suddenly found to be, if one of the emptiest, one of the most scenically interesting of all desert regions on earth. Further to the south a single track of the East-West railway links Western Australia to the rest of the Commonwealth.

The area west of the line to Alice Springs, extending in three directions from Alice Springs to the sea, is bounded by two oceans, the Southern and the Indian. Considering its latitude, it remains an area where man has surprisingly left only the faintest trace of occupancy. If the plane from Adelaide north to Alice Springs made a forced landing, what would its passengers ordinarily find?

In the first place, not a drop of running water—no creeks, rivers, or fresh water lakes—the only moisture soakages from occasional artesian bores sunk, possibly, to a mile underground. Except within a hundred miles south from Alice Springs, there would be no eminence of land worth calling a mountain, only low ranges of hills that rise from the desert, march with the railway line, then sink again into the red sand. Here would be a tantalizing reminder that possibly once in ten years water might flow—the evidence, thin double lines of straggling eucalypts, between which lie the swirls and eddies of sand that mark a dry streambed. If not for these lines on the weather-beaten face of the desert, the general slope of land would be indeterminable.

In between are areas dotted here and there by the grey-green mulga trees, mostly dying or dead. In more favorable spots may be seen an occasional desert oak or surprisingly verdant small trees such as the currajong. These and the hardy ghost gums with their snow-white trunks are the only trees of any stature. Perhaps the most consistent desert-defier is the ill-regarded spinifex grass, growing in clumps defended by thin spikes like knitting needles. Throw in residual hills of broken rock and rubble, the worn stumps of one-time mountain ranges, with great stretches of "gibber," pavements of shiny tessellated stones planed flat by wind erosion, a deep carpet of red dust, and a thousand shifting sand hills, and you have the typical Australian inland.

Except for the grim riven bastions of the Central Australian mountains, the land is featureless and well nigh lifeless. What game there is hides in the folds and thickets and broken gullies and is stalked by aboriginal hunters, who outwait in patient immobility the kangaroo or wallaby, suspicious of the scarcely moving human shadow. What vegetable food is to be found must be scavenged by the women, who scour 20 square miles of country for a single family meal. All the space that would be needed to display, if collected together, single specimens of every item of native diet, both animal and vegetable, would take up less than a few acres. Add to the threat of starvation and death from thirst the searing burden of a sun that drives the summer temperature up to 120 degrees in the shade, where there is any, and more than 160 degrees in the open, and you have a terrifying outlook. Deep fissures in the rocks here and there provide stores of water concealed from the sun but not from the animals and birds caught in the crevices, and whose bodies make a blanket of green scum that slows evaporation to a minimum.

Nor is the winter season any more clement. On the central tableland, with an altitude of 2,000 feet, the winter days are warm and cloudless, the night clear and cold, with temperature so low that our waterbags were frozen stiff with frost. The naked aborigines, along with their dogs, sleep between small fires and do not stir until the sun warms them. A nomadic people cannot take time to make even semipermanent shelters. Occasionally, in an infrequent wet spell, they will set up bush shelters, and in the extreme north where the mosquitoes are ravenous, they build round huts covered with paper bark within which a smoke smudge can be lit. Thus it is their wandering habits rather than lack of skill or knowledge that prevent housebuilding. Since it is important for readers to realize the shifts to which the Australids were put in order to continue survival, I would like to quote from the article already cited.

This is what you see over most of the dead heart of Australia. From the air the orange escarpments, the grim red-pinnacled ridges, look like the bones of prehistoric monsters uncovered from the sand. Here is a land whose past is well nigh indecipherable except in the simplest outline. What its future may be no man can say. Perhaps the restless genius of mankind may conquer this loneliness, but what material resources can be drawn upon to this end are at present hidden, except from the wildest essays of imagination. Years ago, my travelling companion, Robert Croll, wrote: "Life took one look at this land and went away."

As to the mountains, they also, like the dry rivers, seem to have been arranged with no set plan, and proceed at cross purposes as though geographical direction had no meaning. They may be carelessly thrown down like handfuls of domes and cupolas as at Mount Olga, or intruded as a hugh brown monolith like Ayres Rock, rising dramatically from the desert. Where they are collected and ranked in ramparts, casual defences against featurelessness, they are either outflanked by open plains or gashed by narrow chasms through which streambeds like the Finke River or Jay Creek make their way with a fine disregard of terrain. Geologists say that these erstwhile rivers are more ancient than the mountains and determined their own courses long before the ridges crumpled and rose about them. Twice a day the mountains glow with color, when the sun is at its rising and setting, for then a patina of beauty is cast over red fissures and brown pinnacles.

But beauty cannot dull the edge of hunger, nor grant any surcease from the bitter struggle to survive that faces man, beast and plant in this region of earth, surely one of the most inhospitable outside the frozen latitudes. No single article of vegetable food, with the exception of an edible nut from Queensland, the macadamia, now cultivated in Hawaii, has been added to the white man's larder. There are several fruits, but none of them would appeal to any but the semi-starved; no cultivatable cereals, no green things worth eating, no milk-bearing animals, nothing that could serve as a beast of burden. As for the dingo, or wild dog, in the dry winters and the extreme heat of summer an aboriginal could outlast a dog, let alone a team dragging a sledge. Nature has set her face against concentration of life—plant, animal or human.

For meat the natives must rely upon euros or bush kangaroos, plus wallabies of smaller size and kangaroo rats, emus, wild cats and the dingo. But these are so sparsely scattered that hunting makes excessive demands on tireless tracking, patient stalking and unfailing knowledge of these creatures' ways of life. Skill with a weapon, whether spear or hunting boomerang—a curved throwing-stick which does *not* return—is commonplace, the hunters having been trained in their use since childhood.

The Dutch navigators of the early seventeenth century were apparently quite satisfied from their seaward observation that this vast segment of the continent, bounded by the north and northwest coasts, was not worth any colonizing effort. Carstenszoon, master of the *Para*, who sailed into the Gulf of Carpentaria in 1623, reported:

"In our judgement this is the dryest and barrenest region that could be found in the world. And even the men are more miserable than any I have seen in my time."

Nor did that buccaneer-navigator, Dampier, modify Carstenszoon's judgment of the people. He wrote:

The inhabitants of this country are the miserablest people in the world. The Hodmadods (Hottentots?) of Monomatape, though a nasty people, yet for wealth are gentlemen to these, who have no houses and skin garments, sheep, poultry and fruits of the earth, eggs, etc. as the Hodmadods have; and setting aside their human shape, they differ little from brutes . . . They have no houses but lie in the open air without covering, the earth being their bed and heaven their canopy. They live in companies, twenty or thirty men, women and children together.

In view of such harsh pronouncements, it is little wonder that the Australids are still regarded as "the lowest on earth" and that it will take long to raise them in contemporary esteem.

Since animal species also show rather remarkable ability to adjust to their environment, the mere fact that the Australids are surviving could hardly be cited as proof of their intelligence except for one important consideration. Human survival involves not only food and water but also tribal organization; provision for young or less active members; the transmission of human skills, systems of thought, and experience; social regulations to govern marriage, food distribution, and other human relationships; and, most specifically, mental exercise through the handing down of legends, ceremonies, ideas, history—in short, all the things that we cherish and practise, and that animals do not. This entails not merely survival, but survival as humans. All these things are provided for in the Australid way of life. To this extent, therefore, Australid co-existence with ourselves may be accepted as an indication of basic intelligence. The testing of that intelligence meets with the same but enhanced difficulties that hamper the measurement of the ability of people of our own kind. Persistence, prudence, planning capacity, foresight, consistency of purpose, ability to set up and abide by self-standards of behavior are inadequately measured by present-day psychology. In as far as the Maze Test seeks to amend these deficits, its results are important. We are indeed fortunate to be able to record in some detail two major investigations of aboriginal mentality, widely separated in time, which give an opportunity to examine the consistency or reliability of the findings.

In 1929, at the invitation of the Australian National Research Council, I traveled through Northwest Australia for several months and then visited Central Australia. Groups of natives were seen and examined at two Catholic missions at Beagle Bay and Lombadina, northeast of Broome. We then traveled 700 miles overland from Broome to Wyndham through the Kimberley district, allowing me opportunities to test aborigines at a Government feeding station at Moola Boola, with branches at Violet Valley and Turkey Creek. In Central Australia the work was carried out at the Finke River Mission at Hermannsburg among the Arunta, or Aranda as they are now called. While there, I was fortunate enough to come into contact with a group of Luritcha, a name given to a complex of tribes living to the southwest of the Krichauff range of mountains. By some means these people had learned that food was being distributed at Hermannsburg and had journeyed in from about 200 miles distant. The group numbered 38 persons—men, women and children—who were completely naked and had had no previous contact with whites, with the possible exception of Dr. Roheim, a social anthropologist, who had a few weeks previously conducted an expedition into their country. Several Luritcha who had been in the Mission for a couple of years provided the means of communication between the Arunta and the visitors, who possessed a common sign language but spoke completely different aboriginal dialects, unintelligible to each other. Outwardly, at least, this group of visitors fitted very well the description penned by Dampier, more than 250 years previously, of the aborigines he saw on Australia's northwest coast.

Dr. Kenneth Fry, a medical man with psychological interests, had visited Hermannsburg a short time previous to my visit and had tested some 25 of the men by the Porteus Maze. However, I was not certain as to how carefully he had followed directions for application and scoring of the tests and hence I did not feel able to use his results; nor, because of practice effects, was I able to re-apply the Maze to his cases. I was therefore limited to 25 full-blood adult males. At that time I did not use the adult test in the series. With this fact in mind, the records of this study have been examined and rescored so as to bring them as closely in line as possible with recently applied procedures. We have used a ceiling of 15 years in the rescoring; in addition, the rule with regard to inverting any successful test that followed a failure in the test immediately previous had not previously always been applied. This change in procedure would in some cases lower the final score but would help to counterbalance the effect of not applying the adult test, which would prevent some individuals from gaining additional credit.

The reasons for not applying the adult tests were due mainly to my lack of experience with the Maze as a measure of primitive ability. As previously mentioned, my earlier efforts had been confined to testing younger children, mostly half-castes, and older subjects had shown a decline in performance. The expectation was that adults would show a further loss in interest and efficiency. My testing schedule was crowded and I knew that the time to be devoted to examining each individual would be short. Only later did I discover that the Maze was very acceptable and that other tests in the "battery" were of little value. It was impossible then to obtain supplies of adult designs, since I was 6,000 miles away from my home base and I was already overloaded with much testing and measuring equipment that later proved to be scarcely suitable for application, the results having very limited value.

In order to make better comparisons with scores recently obtained in Central Australia, the records have been grouped by districts. I have combined results of all the cases examined at Beagle Bay Mission and its subsidiary station, Lombadina, both situated on or near the coast between Broome and Derby. These natives were of the Nyul-Nyul and Baadi tribes. They live about 800 miles from Alice Springs.

This was the country that had been partially explored in 1838, 91 years before my visit, by Wickham and Stokes (1846), who discovered the Fitzroy River. Misjudging the normal volume of this stream, 20 miles wide in "the Wet" or monsoonal season and a chain of deep waterholes or lagoons in the dry months, Stokes was most enthusiastic over finding a "navigable" river leading into the interior. He wrote: "Doubt, disappointment, difficulty, danger, all, all were unheeded or forgotten in the one proud thought that for us was reserved an enterprise, the ultimate results of which might in some future year affect the interest of a great portion of the world."

This expansive mood seems characteristic of the early Australian visitors to these regions, including not only explorers but those who embarked on more prosaic mining ventures or established cattle stations. They were all incurable optimists, imbued with the confident belief that the personal fortunes of pioneers would grow and prosper in step with the development of the tremendous future of the country. Stokes, for example, in naming Beagle Bay in memory of the ship in which Darwin collected many scientific facts basic to the theory of evolution, spoke of its voyage when "so much was done for the extension of our maritime knowledge." His imagination roved far ahead, visualizing this as a populous region with coastwise shipping carrying its products to a waiting world.

As I saw it almost a hundred years later, it was little different from its condition when first visited. It still remained an almost interminable plain, with scarcely perceptible sandy rises, clothed, or rather choked, with a blanket of low trees, locally known as *pindan*. In 80 miles there was not a single habitation, outside the mission stations of Beagle Bay and Lombadina, where, under the wing of the Pallottine Brothers, the natives were gathered. Our truck ground along the single trace that cut through the pindan from Broome. It was barely passable in the winter season but quite impassable for weeks in "the Wet," when the whole region was a sweltering swamp alive with all kinds of reptilian life.

Here aboriginal sustenance was easy compared with living conditions in Central Australia. The Mission workers, with mistaken but heroic zeal, had already proved to the natives how the latter could make the best of two worlds. They could live for a time on the white man's flour, tea, sugar, and meat in exchange for temporary acceptance of his moral and religious tutelage. As soon as they wanted a change, they stripped off everything, including clothes and religion, and went on the "walkabout," returning to their ancestral modes of life until they again hankered after "the flesh-pots of Egypt."

As originally planned, my project included a comparison of natives from the Northwest and those living in Central Australia. It had been suggested by sociologists and others that there should be a close relation between mentality of peoples and their physical environment, the theory being that the more repressive the living conditions, the more depressed the mental levels would be. It was suggested that the struggle for survival, if acute, would leave less time for developing the arts, industries, psychic life, and social organization, and that this general cultural lag would react unfavorably on mental development. It would be a doctrine with rather comforting implications, if improvement of economic, industrial, and social status would eventually bring about greatly improved status as regards mentality. Such optimism rested mainly on provision of better and freer education. With moral and religious instruction added to the program, it was assumed that the uplift would surely be completely effective. These were noble objectives, and missionaries, colonial administrators, and teachers devoted their lives and talents to the cause of native betterment. But success has never been any better than partial. The most indefatigable efforts, backed by the most unselfish example, seem to reach a disappointing limit. The law of diminishing returns reacted very quickly. One essential consideration was overlooked. This plan of attempted equalizing does not work as regards individual application. In spite of educational and social advantages, the dull person remains ineffective. Why should we expect to make it work with ethnic groups?

Another trouble with the theory was, and is, that it is held most enthusiastically by those who are themselves furthest removed from actual contact with such human problems. In frank talk with missionaries, administrators, and teachers, one soon uncovered misgivings, doubts, and occasionally feelings of downright frustration. Only loyalty to the cause, high courage, and the conviction that to give up was an admission of personal failure or cowardice kept these people at their task.

These, rather than arm-chair philosophers and scientific dreamers, are the real heroes of the cause of racial uplift. Some among the so-called leaders of thought showed serious misconceptions. For example, John Dewey (1902) sums up the Australids' environment as being "upon the whole benign, without intense or violent unfavorable exhibitions of natural forces (save in alternations of flood and drought in some portions), not made dangerous by beasts of prey, and with a sufficient supply of food to maintain small groups in a good state of nutrition though not abundant enough to do this without continual change of abode." This is a gross understatement.

It is true that the Australids are not subject to attack by savage carnivores, though venomous snakes are indeed a danger, but to call aboriginal living conditions "benign" for at least three-quarters of the interior of Australia is just about as inept a description as I can imagine. The very fact that in the continent's most temperate regions a nomadic habit for the natives was unavoidable speaks volumes to the contrary. However, the Northwest coastal regions, in spite of hurricanes, floods, seasonal droughts, and summer shade temperatures ranging to 120 degrees, do not, at least close by the infrequent rivers (one each to about 300 miles of coast), present real sparsity of food supplies. The profusion of bird life near Beagle Bay was astonishing. In a half-mile's early morning walk, my companion C. S. Childs and I counted 50 different species of land and sea birds. In a single bend of the river near Fitzroy Crossing, wallabies and kangaroos were driven past a moving picture camera by five aborigines and myself in incredible droves, numbering in all at least several thousands. Yet 10 miles on either side of the river's chain of waterholes the land was empty, while to the south one of the most inhospitable regions in the world stretched for 1,500 miles. Enough has been written of the Central Australian region to point the contrast between its general aridity and the seasonal fertility of the Northwest or Kimberley region.

It seemed obvious to me at the time that I was offered a unique opportunity to test the theory of the overriding importance of physical environment on mentality by examining two groups of people of the same race, but dwelling in the most diverse conditions as regards the struggle for existence. Testing should then provide conclusive evidence of the tenability of the theory. That seemed to me to be an entirely reasonable plan of research, but results were received with indifference and in some quarters with criticism and downright rejection.

Some of the arguments brought forward were curious. One was that an adverse environment might be stimulating rather than repressive and that therefore environment remained a decisive factor in influencing mental development. Incongruity lay in the fact that this view was suggested by some of the same individuals who had held that intelligence must be *lowered* by adverse environmental circumstances.

However, the weight of criticism was directed toward the significance of the tests applied for the purpose of assessing mentality, the chief being that it was ridiculous to take tests evolved by white psychologists in civilization and attempt to apply them to Australian aborigines. How could such people be expected to show interest and capacity in measures that are entirely alien to their culture? Fortunately, it proved impossible to prejudge how alien a testing device might be and whether its novelty would, or would not, hinder its acceptance. Nor was it possible, I found, to anticipate interest or motivation in relation to the apparent nature of a test. To a people who use a sign or gesture language, I assumed that Thurstone's test of sorting drawings of hands into left and right, according to positions of thumb and fingers, would fit in with familiar aboriginal cultural behavior, while tracing with a pencil through a printed maze would be of more doubtful acceptance.

My preconceived ideas as to which tests would work were soon abandoned or modified. Our aboriginal subjects, for example, were not at all interested in building color designs. These were not their colors nor their designs. The Thurstone Hand Test, described above, they regarded as childishly simple and not worth serious attention. They saw no point in hastily fitting wooden insets into a formboard. Shaping the spur of a spear thrower so as to fit into the shaft of a spear was a far different matter. As a matter of courtesy, they would repeat numerals after me but did not know nor care whether they were in the right order or not. They could not see any necessity for hurrying over any task, and so all my tests scored on speed were worthless.

Since my experience with the Maze Test had been limited to

half-caste children, I was very dubious as to how adult men with little contacts with whites would react to the Maze. To my surprise and satisfaction, I found that the test met with almost universal acceptance. Only one individual out of many examined showed any unwillingness to continue work on the problem and he was suffering from a very painful toothache. Even yet, after many applications of the test among a good sampling of primitive people in East Asia, Africa, Australia, and America, I am still at a loss to account for this undoubted interest in a pencil-and-paper maze. This opinion as to the acceptability of the test has been confirmed by every worker in the field, the subjects of study including Ainu, Formosans, Senoi, Sakai, Ghurkas, Tamils, Bajou, South African Bushmen, Shangaans, Mchopi, Amaxosa, Wakaranga, Ndau, Bathonga, Navaho, Saipanese, and the Australid tribes reported in this volume. All these subjects evidently regarded the test as a worthwhile challenge to adult effort, far removed from "baby plays," as the test was contemptuously referred to by some anthropologists 33 years ago.

As regards the Australians, my status among them was high through being regarded in the light of an intertribal messenger. At Beagle Bay I showed the old men (with appropriate secrecy) pictures of the sacred objects called by the Aranda (Arunta) *tjurunga,* or churinga (Spencer's spelling), and they entrusted me with some of their own *minburi* to show other tribes. When under cover of darkness I exhibited these to the Luritcha and Arunta elders, they were accepted as credentials of a high order, so that despite my evident and hopeless ignorance of native lore, I became a person of importance whose wishes would be honored. This acceptance may well have helped my testing program in Australia but would not account for the attitude of primitive subjects elsewhere.

The degree of contact with whites, particularly school experience, has been frequently cited as a factor affecting test performance. This would seem to be true for groups but does not seem to apply individually. Subjects with absolutely no educational background achieved excellent scores, while some with schooling showed inferior performance. In other words, just as we should expect, education does not cancel out individual differences in Maze Test ability. As to other conditions, particularly those that affect the keenness of the struggle for existence, the comparison of the Northwest and Central Australians is most significant.

One other mental measure was satisfactory as far as acceptance by the aborigines was concerned. This was a memory test founded on the tapping of xylophone keys in a certain order. Four metal tubes of different lengths were suspended within a wooden frame so that when struck with a mallet four musical tones were produced, varying according to the length of the metal tubes. The examiner tapped these in order, then required the subject to imitate the same performance. The test varies in difficulty from the simplest sequence of tubes 1, 2, 3, 4 to more complex sequences, as 1, 4, 2, 3, 4, 1. The number of correct repeats is converted into a test age scoring. My 1929 notes read: "This was one test (of a specialized memory type) in which there was no lack of attention displayed by the aborigines." This was the only other test in which the aborigines appeared reasonably motivated toward success and might provide a measure of ability underlying school learning potentialities. The fact of the comparatively poor results achieved by aborigines was important.

Of individuals from Northwest tribes, whose locations ranged from Beagle Bay to Wyndham connected by 700 miles of very rough track, we examined 60 cases and found their average auditory-visual test span to be only 7.32 years. In the Central Australian group, about 700 miles south by compass course, the average for 40 cases was 8.35 years. In other words, though both scores were low, the group living in the less favorable environment scored about a year above the group that inhabited an area much better watered and well stocked with native food.

With regard to the Maze Test the gap in performance was much wider. The northwestern sample (rescored) numbered 67 and their average Maze was 10.42 years. The central group, of whom 5 were Luritcha and 20 Arunta, averaged 12.17 years, a difference in favor of the central natives of 1.75 years in test score. As to white supervision, the Arunta had been under somewhat longer tutelage. The Beagle Bay Mission (Catholic) had been established in 1890, the Finke River Mission (Lutheran) about 14 years earlier. The Lutheran policy toward native ideas and customs was rather more restrictive, with the missionaries doing their utmost to discourage circumcision and subincision, and ceremonies that tended to keep alive aboriginal religious beliefs and pagan practices. The Catholic Brothers had a somewhat more permissive or possibly indifferent attitude, though they bitterly opposed any practices that seemed to run contrary to mission teaching. However, in both cases, as soon as natives were beyond observation, there were ceremonial happenings to which the authorities would have given no countenance. My impression was that the Catholics were aware of what went on but were not too much concerned, provided their native flock accepted church discipline and attended mission religious exercises, particularly the Mass; the Protestants played a more active role in opposing all non-Christian activities. In the Beagle Bay area my party came under criticism because we induced the natives to stage an old-time "cobba-cobba," or dance, in which women took part. Though there was nothing at all unseemly in any of the scenes we photographed, the Brothers felt that this was somewhat subversive to their civilizing efforts. If it happened outside the mission, they took no notice. Actually, we were caught between two fires in a dispute between the mission and the local constable of police, who lived near the mission but was quite independent of its control. Antagonism between government officials and religious authorities occasionally was much in evidence.

Moola Boola with its branch station at Violet Valley was a Government cattle station set up under official control with the avowed purpose of discouraging the natives from spearing cattle belonging to neighboring white station owners. It was thought that if the aborigines owned cattle of their own, which they were allowed to slaughter under supervision, they would leave other people's property alone. However, Governmental herds were not infrequently raided by bush natives from country further north who were no respecters of either the persons or belongings of more civilized aborigines. Even quite close to the station the natives continued their own traditional ceremonies but kept them hidden from the white manager and his staff. As a "messenger," I was privileged to see and photograph some of these.

The rest of my subjects were gathered in Wyndham, some of them being inmates of the local jail, incarcerated for a variety of offences from tribal murder downward. These prisoners worked on the roads of Wyndham under armed guards. They regarded my visit as a welcome change and seemed delighted to meet a white man who respected rather than held in contempt their cherished ideas. Again, I had no complaint with regard to their interest, not to say absorption, in the task of maze-threading. I was also able to examine the crew of the mission lugger, which came from Forrest River to collect supplies at Wyndham.

The greater familiarity with whites resultant in living on a mission station was reflected in a difference in score between the Beagle Bay-Lombadina groups and an almost equal group of non-mission natives. This amounted to about three-fourths of a year of test age in favor of the former.

As far as the Maze Test can be regarded as a measure of adaptability, evidence for which is presented elsewhere, these results should effectively dispose of the idea that improved living conditions, bringing about a relaxation of the struggle for existence, are mainly responsible for better intelligence scores. Our evidence clearly points in the opposite direction.

The results of this work have been summarized, with the reminder that they are not strictly comparable with the most recent findings because of several varying conditions, the first being a difference in the test application. As previously mentioned, the Maze Series used in 1929 did not include the Adult design so that the ceiling of the series was 15 years instead of 17 years as at present. Another difference was that in my earlier work the rule with regard to inverting a test design and reapplying it whenever the test immediately prior had been failed was not consistently followed. In some cases, the effect of the rule would have to be a lowering of their score to the amount of at least half a year or more. Nine cases among the Beagle Bay-Lombadina, or Northwest mission natives, would have been affected. The same number (9) of the nonmission natives would also have had lower scores.

On the other hand, 21 cases among the mission aborigines would have had the opportunity to increase their scores had the ceiling of the test been increased to 17 years. Twelve of the nonmission subjects might have increased their scores. In other words, the application of the inversion rule would have tended to decrease scores, but the use of the Adult test would have raised them. To some extent one variation in procedure would have offset the other, but the net result would be to depress slightly the 1929 performance in comparison with our latest results.

Another variation was that more forepractice was given in 1962, a fact that again would tend to improve performance. However, as will be seen later, these variations in procedure did not, especially for "bush" natives (i.e., those who were not too closely identified with mission life), have very much effect on the mean scores.

The only early psychometric investigation other than my own 1929 work was carried out at MacDonald Downs station about 200 miles from Yuendumu, the site of Dr. Gregor's study described in the next chapter. This was done about a year subsequent to my Hermannsburg visit and was carried out by Fry and Pulleine (1931), two medical men who wrote to me with regard to testing procedures. They reported their efforts in these terms:

> The Porteus mazes have proved to be the most interesting of the normal tests, and therefore the one which presents the best prospects of success, but the "normally prepared" mind is not being tested, and the task is abnormally hard for the native. While watching a native at work on these problems one can almost feel the intensity of the mental strain involved. . . . Tests with the mazes "caught on" more successfully than any other performance test. The maze for five years was used to explain the nature of the problem, stated in terms of a cattle yard and an animal trying to escape. The subject was given a pencil and a copy of the six-year maze for a trial, and he was sometimes helped in this. No more help was given after this, except to indicate the starting point and the final point of exit.

This, it will be seen by reference to the next chapter, followed almost exactly along the lines adopted by Gregor in his investigation. From the detailed records supplied by Fry and Pulleine, I have calculated the means for 11 males and 7 females to be 10.1 and 8.5 years respectively.

SUMMARY

In spite of the complexities of the general problem of racial differences in mentality, the Maze Test has been the means of contributing important, if not crucial evidence on the subject. The most promising point of attack has been through the study of primitive peoples, the chief difficulties being the definition of race, the extensive travel involved in making contact with subjects in faraway places, and finally the choice of tests that would be acceptable to primitive subjects and so might adequately reflect their intelligence.

The Australian aborigines, or Australids as we term them, offer an example of a division of mankind, who by reason of long and almost complete geographical isolation have physically, socially, and possibly mentally developed so much along their own evolutionary lines that most competent anthropologists would agree in regarding them as a separate race.

The difficulties in the way of making direct contact with them are so obvious that this may explain why so little work has been done. As an acceptable psychological measure, the Porteus Maze, much to the surprise of its author, proved in all ways the most suitable. The proof of the significance of its results are presented throughout this volume.

A brief sketch of the writer's first experiences with "the blacks," as the aborigines are called in Australia, forms the background of comparative studies, the first of which was an examination of half-caste children at Point McLeay, South Australia, where at the same time opinions of teachers as to their school aptitudes were gathered.

But before dealing with the consideration of major studies in this field, a verbal picture of the Australids' physical environment in the interior of their continent is presented. The purpose was to show that its natural inhospitality, not to say hostility to human occupancy, is in itself proof of their remarkable adaptive ability necessary to ensure survival—a proof of a more general type of intelligence than can be obtained from test reactions. In material culture, however, the Australid today does not look very differently from how he was described by the first white explorers.

The writer's seven-month study of these people in 1929 is summarized and its difficulties outlined. It was planned to visit and contrast the tested intelligence of two groups—the first, members of a group of tribes inhabiting a fairly well-watered region abundantly stocked with native game; the second, the Arunta (Aranda) tribe living in Central Australia. The time was near the end of a ten-year drought when the natives were putting up the grimmest of struggles to survive. My expectation was one commonly held by social psychologists and sociologists that the more repressive conditions would depress the level of Arunta test scores below those of aboriginals living in a far more favorable environment. To the writer's surprise, the reverse was the case.

Received by the elders of the tribe as playing the role of an intertribal messenger, the writer initiated testing procedures. Only two measures, a xylophone test of memory sequences and the Porteus Maze, were received with any marked degree of aboriginal interest. The Central Australians did surprisingly well in the Maze, averaging about a year in advance of the composite group of tribes in the Kimberley district. A suggestion by some critical reviewers was that a repressive environment could make excessive demands on mental alertness for survival, and therefore might have a stimulating effect. This might well be the case, but the curious feature was that the suggestion came from sociologists who had supported quite the opposite argument.

Though the natives accepted the xylophone memory-sequence device, the scores of both groups were so low as to suggest that inferior rote memory might be one of the factors in the poor scholastic achievement of these people. The inner resistance of aborigines to white instruction in missions and government stations was another probable factor in low educational achievement.

CHAPTER NINE

Australid Mentality: Recent Studies

The work previously described was done mainly during the Australian winter season from April to September, 1929, these being the months when travel and work are most tolerable in the continent's interior. The first part of the period was spent in the extreme Northwest where by September the weather has become humid and the coming of the monsoons threatens. July and August are very agreeable months in Central Australia (which the monsoons rarely reach), with October becoming hot in the day with cool nights. The rest of the year is extremely unfavorable as regards working conditions.

In 1961 I was fortunate enough to get into touch with James Gregor, who took a position as assistant professor in the Philosophy Department of the University of Hawaii. His doctorate was earned in philosophy of science, but he had determined to devote some time to becoming familiar with experimental work in the Maze Test as part of the data of science. After a series of demonstrations by me, Dr. Gregor undertook the testing of a group of 25 male juvenile delinquents, using the Vineland or Original version of the Maze, followed by the application of the Extension and the Extension Supplement Series. These were then scored both for test age and qualitative application. He also supervised the testing of 25 delinquent girls by a graduate student. In this way he became familiar with the Maze Test, having at least as much experience with the test as the ordinary psychological examiner possesses. I had no hesitation in accepting his help in augmenting the data on Australid mentality, more particularly their Maze performance.

In June 1962, after I had revisited Central Australia to make all possible arrangements for Dr. Gregor's entry to aboriginal stations under control of the Commonwealth Department of Native Affairs, and had also journeyed to the Finke River Mission at Hermannsburg where I had worked 33 years previously, he flew from Honolulu to Alice Springs. With the necessary official sanction, he was first located at Yuendumu, 180 miles northwest of Alice Springs, at a Government station near which groups of aborigines, mainly belonging to the Wailbri (Walbiri) [1] and Pintubi tribes, had congregated. This settlement, now under the control of the Native Affairs Department, Welfare Branch, includes a school, dispensary, store room, and residences for the white staff. Under its present official control, it had been established about ten years previously, but many of the natives had been at the station for a much shorter period. Another settlement had been set up at a place called Papunyah and in order to obtain subjects with very brief white contacts, Dr. Gregor visited this settlement for a period of several days. For the most part, his examinations were carried out at Yuendumu.

The question as to whether the people at Yuendumu are representative of the natives of Central Australia is of interest. Their way of life is typical of present-day conditions in Central Australia, namely, residence with their families at the station, interspersed with bush excursions, which the natives call "walkabouts." Fortunately, the food resources of the Yuendumu aborigines and their immediate neighbors have been carefully studied for many years by Dr. T. D. Campbell and his associates at the University of Adelaide, South Australia. As early as 1939, Campbell published several articles relating to the dental conditions to be found there, and these supply valuable information, particularly as to dietary resources. At that time, the natives at the settlement were receiving Government rations of flour, tea, and sugar, and some individuals supplemented these through more or less temporary employment at various Central Australian cattle or sheep stations. Hence, a rather mild degree of white acculturation had taken place. Except for this, the natives were typically aboriginal. The important feature is that as regards adaptability to environment, these natives subsist in an arid and frequently desert region, typical of most of the Australian interior. As Campbell put it, "most of the field research locations lie

---

[1] As will be easily realized, the spelling of Australid names is very confused. The tribe made famous by Spencer and Gillen is called variously Arunta, Aranda, and Aranta. Locally the Yuendumu natives are called Wailbri, though anthropologists seem to prefer Walbiri. Spencer's churinga has become "tjurunga," and so on.

in territory well within the range of desert climate." According to Prescott (1936), in this whole area "the soil moisture throughout the year is maintained below the wilting point of plants." A very large area is occupied by sand hills. Hence, Campbell summed up the situation as regards the natives as follows:

"Whatever may have been their origin, even if their material culture does stand low in the evolutionary scale, this arid environment is so limited in its food productivity that it allows for nothing else but a wandering life, an ever-moving search in quest of food, thus making these people typical nomads—food-gatherers and food hunters in the fullest sense of the words." Their diet includes "anything at all that is safely edible," and this covers many things that by white standards would be entirely unwelcome and even repulsive to nonaboriginal palates.

No more than the briefest listing of sustenance items is needed here, since these conditions have been described by many writers. Permanent water rather than food governs concentration of humans. Temporary pools found in rock fissures are, of course, dependent on rainfall that is most uncertain as to distribution and amount. In good seasons—alas, too infrequent—the face of the country changes, and with it the keenness of the struggle for existence. As I have elsewhere pointed out, it is the periodic occurrence of tragic emergencies rather than the ordinary run of events that determines the survival of isolated communities in the Australian interior.

My first visit to "the Centre" coincided with dry conditions for 10 years and severe drought for 5. Rationing at Hermannsburg was restricted because of the excessive strain on mission resources, and new arrivals were fed and then encouraged to "go bush" and attempt to live on the country. The harsh living conditions allowed for little margin above starvation point. Before the drought, the mission itself, with its hundreds of square miles of land and several thousand head of stock, looked prosperous on paper. The location had been finally selected after a couple of years of unsuccessful effort at another desert location. With mountains nearby and the Finke River flowing through the property, the site was considered most favorable. But the river did not always flow and it took almost two years of unceasing struggle for the missionaries to travel north from near Adelaide with their sheep and cattle through the wilderness to reach the new site. The story of this grim trek with its terrific hardships is feelingly told by Pastor P. A. Scherer (1963) in a book giving an account of the Mission's 89 years.

This country was kind to neither natives nor white pioneers, and at the time of my arrival at Hermannsburg, the drought seemed never-ending. Horses and cattle had died in hundreds, the camels that carried drinking water to the Mission from springs in the mountains were weak, gaunt, and famished, while the crows, which in the beginning had waxed fat on carrion, were either dead or had migrated.

Elsewhere I have told of my contact with groups of natives, men, women, and children, scouring the bush for food, collecting beetles, grubs, lizards, ants—anything that moved. Some of the men and older boys were literally running from rock to rock, searching under clumps of dry spinifex grass or under logs. Meanwhile the best hunters in the group roved far afield, lying by the hour near some hidden spring or soakage in the hope of spearing a kangaroo or other game. Those who have seen this country in good seasons can have no idea how grim such a struggle for mere existence can be, nor how necessary to survival is a social organization that enforces sharing of food to the last scrap of sustenance. Here is the final demonstration of how vital social foresight must be. This, in brief, is the background against which Australid performance of the Maze Test must be viewed.

But Campbell's (1938) expedition to Cockatoo Creek situated about 15 miles from Yuendumu followed after good rains, so that neither men nor animals were short of water. The position of soaks where shallow wells could be sunk was a matter of tribal tradition, and these were favored over deep but constricted rock holes that were usually fouled by carrion—mainly the bodies of drowned reptiles, birds, etc. Obviously, the most reliable of these water sources were those well hidden in the hills or gullies. How well preserved is this traditional knowledge was proved to me by a personal experience on a short expedition. Old men, who had themselves not visited the spot since boyhood, were able to map out on the sand the location of a soak in Palm Valley so accurately that our camel boy was able to locate this hidden source, which covered only a few square yards of damp soil.

As to food, the "corms" or bulbs of nut grass (called *yelka*), grass seed, which is only in seasonal supply, and seeds of some acacias are carefully collected and ground on flat rocks. Large yams similar in bulk to a child's football and smaller ones the size of a potato are relished, as are also the fleshy leaves and stems of *munyeroo* (a yellow-flowered succulent), but, except where the soil is unusually moist, such juicy vegetable foods are almost non-existent. Species of fruits, hopefully called native figs, peaches, plums, and solanum make good reading but are of negligible eating value. Their names convey some fleeting resemblances to their counterparts in civilized orchards. Not a single one of them would be worth cultivating.

Only in seasons of abundance is any discrimination of taste indulged, especially in flesh foods. Normally the whole of a kangaroo, including the intestines, is roughly cleaned, then partially cooked and devoured. The five-foot goanna or lace lizard is favored because of its fat, and when a spiny echidna[2] is captured, its flesh is prized for the same reason. Large snakes are also eaten but are rarely obtainable, while the bustard or wild turkey is enjoyed even by whites. The emu, the brolga, or "native companion," and the cockatoo make tough eating, but unless in the grip of starvation, the aborigines would rather not indulge in dingo meat. However, it is eaten on occasion. Bones are frequently broken up and the marrow enjoyed. When food is scarce, the bony fragments may be chewed and ingested.

As luxuries, honey from the small native bee is enjoyed, and, in the spring, the native will crush the flowers of the native *hakea* or honeysuckle in their mouths. The honey ant, fed by other workers until its abdomen is distended to a half inch in diameter, is also highly prized, but the labor involved in digging down perhaps six feet to reach the bottom of the nest where the living honey pots are found is considerable. Nevertheless, when the honey-gorged ants are unearthed, the bitten-off abdomens, distended with honey, provide the digger with a rare delicacy. Witchetty grubs, as long as three inches, when roasted are said to be delicious. Both honey ants and grubs, being difficult to transport, are not subject as strictly to the rules of tribal food distribution and are frequently devoured on the spot as soon as discovered. A sweet white exudation from the leaves of a couple of eucalyptus species called manna gums is also gathered and enjoyed.

In order to show the extreme variability in food supplies, we can cite an account given by a participant of a 12-day walkabout or

---

[2] One of Australia's two monotremes. The other is the well-known platypus.

foraging trip as recorded by Dr. Campbell and his associates.
The aboriginal party consisted of five men and six women and the
informant was an intelligent native named Tim. An unusual mid-
summer rain had made sustenance very much easier. Four donkeys
upon which the women rode part of the time and which served to
carry extra food were used. This circumstance, combined with the
fact that flour, tea, sugar, and tobacco were also carried by the
party, showed that this was a very modern aboriginal expedition.
In other respects it was an ordinary "walkabout," the journey as
planned being from one known water supply, either rock hole,
soakage, or spring, to another. When the desired spot was reached,
the women made the camp while the men hunted.

The latter process was much easier than in former times through
the fact that the aboriginal party owned dogs capable of catching
and pulling down a large kangaroo. It is noteworthy that one entry
in the account reads: "Women went to collect yams. Also their dogs
caught a kangaroo." These dogs are in many cases part-greyhound
and part-dingo, which are more effective as hunting companions
than the half-domesticated pure dingo. The whole trip took about
three weeks, and detailed account of 12 days showed the total catch
to have been:

13 kangaroos	Many yams (collected in 6 days)
11 goannas	Native gooseberries
2 echidnas	2 pints honey
1 large carpet snake	Honey from corkwood tree
1 native cat	

Since some of the kangaroos and at least one goanna were noted
as "large," meat supplies were plentiful. Goannas, especially the
tails, are considered excellent food, as are also echidnas, but these
last are very small. When the flour for making "damper" gave out
on the sixth or seventh day, yams were substituted, and this may
account for the fact that not until the fifth day was the search for
yams in spinifex country begun. At the end of the "walkabout," the
party returned to Yuendumu.

It has been mentioned elsewhere that the sites of ceremonial
centers may have helped to conserve animal life, but undoubtedly
the issuing of rations at aboriginal stations was a more important
factor in wild-life preservation. As long as the native population can
obtain civilized provender, they are not likely to exert themselves
to search for native foods. Meat rationing in Government feeding

stations is restricted, only canned meat being available in small quantities. The desire for more animal food is doubtless a main incentive for walkabouts.

Enough information has been presented to give a picture of native living conditions at the present time. This outline indicates considerable changes through white settlement and influence, but the basic patterns of behavior characteristic of "bush" living are still followed in the vicinity of Yuendumu. At Hermannsburg, after more than three-quarters of a century of white tutelage, the pendulum has swung much further in the direction of more civilized practices. Native education there has been a much more potent factor in change than at Yuendumu. This detailed statement has been thought necessary in order to indicate that acculturation to white standards has only just begun, so that if assimilation with whites is important to native mental status, the subjects of Dr. Gregor's investigation have not been much affected. The Yuendumu population can be considered typical of those to be found in the major part of the continent's interior. These people would not differ materially as regards their general way of life from the men of the Kimberley district examined by me in 1929. Another point of immediate importance concerns the way in which the mental examiner and his novel devices were accepted by the people he was studying. In this respect, I have thought it best to use Dr. Gregor's field notes (with a minimum of editing) as written at the time and forwarded to me from Central Australia. Not only is the material most interesting, but the methods of approach may prove to be worth studying by future investigators of the problem. At any rate, it disposes of the question of interest and motivation on the part of primitive subjects in the Maze Test.

Dr. Gregor's account of the means of attaining rapport and encouraging his subjects is most interesting. In spite of this permissive approach, I would consider it impossible to engender interest if the test had not had a natural appeal. This conclusion is based on experience in trying other tests, which by *a priori* judgment I deemed very suitable for appraising primitive mentality. As noted in Chapter 8, I am quite at a loss to explain why the Maze should have this special appeal. It is certainly not characteristic of the bush Australid to resist fatigue in a task unless he considers it inherently interesting. Blackwood (1927) has noted this difficulty in applying tests to other primitive people. "Anyone," she remarks, "who has tried to persuade a member of any primitive group to continue doing something after he is wearied of it, will realize the importance of adjusting the time limits of a mental test with the utmost care." Hence, the persistence of effort reported by Gregor is the more extraordinary. He points out that to work through all three series of the Maze—Original, Extension, and Supplement—without a rest or change between, certainly invites fatigue in both subject and examiner. Yet, even when the subject was working at a painfully slow rate, he was unwilling to give up his efforts to solve the problem. Dr. Gregor's notes on field procedures and natives' reactions follow:

Testing Procedure and Aboriginal Reaction

"After establishing preliminary rapport, the technique employed varied with different circumstances (when a subject was selected on the settlement, permission was obtained from his immediate supervisor), the native then accepted the fact that he was to come with me 'to do something.' Upon being told to sit at the table with me, most Ss evinced reactions ranging from embarrassment to curiosity. Fear and suspicion were allayed by the offer of a cigarette and, if possible, small talk in pidgin. After I had tested several mature males on the settlement, word had gotten around that the 'American doctor' was playing games with the 'fellows,' so there was little apprehension evidenced by Ss. Most of the Ss thereafter seemed eager to participate. In only two cases out of the approximately 60 Ss examined did they give evidence of unwillingness. I did not attempt to force them into the test situation. When S was approached at his own camp site, I found him more relaxed. *Rapport* was best established by the offer of a cigarette. Generally we were then the subject of considerable attention and the Ss seemed to enjoy the prestige of being selected for the 'game.' Several Ss requested that I join them at their camp site to 'play the game.' The practice maze was introduced. The rat became a *maloo* (Wailbri-Pintubi for small kangaroo) and the cheese became 'tucker' (food), which all the natives around the settlement fully understood, even if they understood nothing more in English. I pointed from the kangaroo to the tucker and indicated with the blunt end of a pencil the way the kangaroo would go to get the tucker. At each incorrect turn, I said 'no tucker, no good' and shook my head vigorously, making a face showing disapproval. Each correct passage was identified as 'good, good' with a smile of approval. At the last possible choice point in my demonstration, I generally pointed in the wrong direction and waited for the subject to indicate any comprehension. In many if not most cases, S shook his head to show that that would be the wrong way. I then turned into the right way and generally we both said 'good, good' and then 'tucker.' Where there were sufficient practice tests, I did the V year test practice myself in pencil. Almost all Ss without exception realized that they were not to cross lines even though I had not conveyed that information to them orally. Whenever during the subsequent testing S crossed a line, he almost invariably gave a sign of dismay and retraced his course to avoid crossing the line. The same was true whenever a corner was cut even though I had not, of course, indicated that corners could not or should not be cut. Almost without exception S either made a sign of acknowledging error or retraced his steps. The only admonition I could not convey either by example or pidgin was 'no lift pencil.' However, in some cases, I was convinced that the subject realized he was not to lift his pencil. When he aped my tracing of the first practice maze (whenever I had enough practice tests to do one with the pencil), he held the pencil to the paper and looked under, around and over his hand (which obstructed a clear view). In the Vineland Revision I noted if S realized when he had made an error—and only then was I thoroughly convinced he knew what was expected. In all recorded tests the subjects gave such signs, either minor irritation with themselves, a guffaw, dismay or sitting back and expecting me to remove the test in which they realized they had failed. Failure was always attended by S's awareness. The Maze is self-corrective in that sense—S is necessarily aware of his error and the administrator merely removes the test. Almost every S without exception realized he was not to back out of the blind turn. In two or three cases S had to be stopped and 'no good' repeated, with his attention directed toward where he had backed out of an incorrect turn. It was never necessary to repeat such a demonstration. S was generally fully aware of what was expected after I had undertaken the practice maze, which is why it is essential that practice mazes be available in the testing of non-English speaking subjects. I did employ alternatives—the blunt end of the pencil and in some cases erasing practice mazes—but the ideal method is to trace the first maze so that directions can be delivered by demonstration.

"Upon completion of the Vineland Revision, I immediately commenced the Extension. I found this was an advantage because most subjects were pleased with their beginning success on the simple mazes after having failed the more difficult mazes of the upper levels of the Revision. The Supplement was begun immediately upon completion of the Extension. If the subject showed any fatigue, I gave him a cigarette, lit it and stretched myself. (The subject generally did likewise.) After a brief rest, I indicated the maze that I had placed before him and in no case did the subject fail to immediately take up his pencil—without any appearance of tedium or annoyance—and begin again. In the majority of cases the subject did not show signs of fatigue and in many gave evidence of wanting to continue. Most showed determination and those that could speak some English said, 'I win this time. This one he proper [3] good,'—or the equivalent. At Yuendumu the natives used 'I go bush' (with attendant laughter) to indicate an error, and 'That one proper good' to indicate success. At Papunya it was 'no good' or 'wrong one' to register awareness of failure and 'I win' to announce success. There were variations of course: 'Kangaroo no tucker' and 'Fence' for failure to notice a blocked passage, and 'Good, tucker' 'Number one' for success. Not a single recorded performance was perfunctory. One subject took over 25 minutes on one single maze (a XII or a XIV on the Revision, I believe). In some cases the three series took three hours to complete, in others all three were completed in less than an hour. In some cases S was evidently disappointed that the 'game' was over. Occasionally, individuals who had observed almost the entire test asked to be tested themselves. In most cases, observers dispersed after about 15 minutes of testing and I was left alone with the subject. When I selected a subject on the settlement and brought him to a table I had prepared for testing, he was almost always alone. Occasionally, some natives were attracted and on several occasions I had to good-naturedly stop them from assisting the subject. In a number of cases the testee, upon completion, suggested to me that I 'play the game' with a friend of his to see if 'him, too, proper smart.' On these occasions the earlier subject generally watched with evident satisfaction whenever his comrade fell into a maze trap. There was always

---

[3] At the time of my visit to Central Australia in 1929, a favorite pidgin English word was *properly*. For example, an actual rather than a classificatory system parent was distinguished by the statement: "He my *properly* father." Possibly with further white contact, the natives use *proper*.

good-natured banter, with which I liberally partook. There was a light tap on the head and a 'what's the matter, you' for a failure, at which the subject generally roared with real mirth. Sometimes there was a chuck under the elbow. When the subject succeeded, there was a 'hey, you proper smart, number one,' and so forth. The Ss were generally so deeply engrossed in their task that they neither looked up for passing planes, trucks or fighting dogs. (When trucks pass, the natives generally stop what they are doing until the truck is out of sight.) One subject did not look up when I took his photo with a flash camera! The flash generally startles the natives (as it often does Europeans who are familiar with it), but in this particular case the aborigine did not even take notice. In all cases Ss seemed to enjoy the experience. I think the prevailing conditions had a great deal to do with the willingnesss of Ss to undertake the testing. The aborigines are provided weekly rations so that hunting is no longer necessary. Most of the men sit around their camps and either play cards or loll. The opportunity to undertake a 'game' that was challenging, made them the object of attention, and was rewarding (I generally gave each testee several cigarettes upon completion of the three series) appealed to them.

"When the three series were completed, I had the testee repeat Year XI of the Revision, and in most cases Year XI of the Extension and Supplement as well.

"I was astonished at the rapidity with which the subjects understood what was intended. There was absolutely no difficulty in conveying my intentions, particularly in the cases where I could execute, with pencil, the V year practice maze. The subject then did the V, with aid if necessary, and then did the VI without any assistance. The only place where there was some difficulty was in Year VIII of the Vineland Revision, where the exit is not marked. On some occasions I was not convinced S knew what was intended, so thereafter I asked 'You see no fence?' or 'Where kangaroo get out?' Where S knew no English at all, I had him complete Year VIII of the Revision and when and if he failed, I pointed to the exit and observed his expression. I could generally tell whether the information was new to him because he showed evident 'insight,' a new appreciation of the test demand. In many cases it was evident that he knew where he should have gone but had simply failed. This became evident when he indicated clearly that he realized when he had made an error, either by an 'awww' or good-humored pique. If there were observers, they would wait until he made an error and then laughed with glee or shouted 'wrong' or 'bushed' or its equivalent in Wailbri-Pintubi. When Ss understood some English, the answers to 'where fence' and 'where no fence' were given with the appropriate gestures, pointing to the exit with a finger or the pencil.

"In at least three cases, Ss showed some discomfort and I inquired through gesture, pidgin, and signs what was wrong. The Ss pointed to the cause of their discomfort and I shooed them off into the bush. They had evidently been so involved in the testing that they didn't want to take the time to ease their respective bladders!

"There was no difficulty making the transition from the X year to the XI year maze, which I thought might happen because of the changed form.

"The only injunction it was impossible to follow was that S and the examiner be alone. It was possible in only half the test sessions. But in most cases audience interest lagged after a brief period, though in any event the presence of observers seemed to please S. Rarely were the observers close enough to profit by the observation. My hands and S's hands generally obscured the test itself. The audience simply wanted to observe my antics; I occasionally whistled, sometimes clapped my subject on the back—this seemed to spur him on and amused his fellows. I became a 'character' in the Wailbri and Pintubi camp—the men rarely failed to greet me after the first day either in Yuendumu or Papunya. When I was away from Yuendumu many of the natives asked for me, approaching the white staff members specifically for this purpose. When I returned many of them inquired if there would be more games. At Papunya I never sat at a native camp without (after once having given some tests) showing my 'wares' to the occupant, pointing to him and the sample maze. If he nodded yes, I knew that he had either observed some of the testing or the others had spoken of the 'game.' If he did not give evidence of agreement and simply appeared mystified by what I intended, I sat down and showed him the practice maze with the 'kangaroo.' In no case did a prospective subject refuse at this point or give any evidence of disinterest or annoyance. There were one or two cases where a prospective S refused to go with me to the dispensary where I had set up a table for testing (much more comfortable than squatting in a 'wurlie'), but I suspect it was because they either thought I intended to put them to work, or was going to commit them to the nursing Sister's care.

"The Maze lends itself to mime demonstration and easy comprehension to an astonishing degree. Most of the instructions suggested for the testing of English-speaking subjects are apparently self-evident after careful demonstration. Demonstration by the examiner using the practice maze V satisfied all the requirements of mime testing. The maze itself seems intrinsically interesting to the aborigines. Practically all the white staff commented on the length of time each S spent on the testing. Some told me that they had misgivings when they heard I was to do pencil-and-paper testing. They thought the natives possessed too brief an attention span for such procedures."

The most important question as to the validity of Gregor's results is posed by the second last paragraph of the above account of his testing procedures, wherein he states that he found it was possible for the examiner and subject to be alone "in only half the test sessions." It is impossible to assess how much advantage was gained by the onlookers, who undoubtedly took the test later. Even though the period of observation was brief, and the view of the test partially obstructed. it would be quite beyond an examiner to decide how that observation would affect onlookers' later performances. This would not operate in remembering specific traps—though that might be occasionally possible—but could affect the general attitude or mental set toward the test. Observation of others' mistakes would naturally lead to the judgment that success calls for extraordinary caution and preconsideration. In ensuring interest of subjects, putting them at ease in a novel situation by giving the examination an air of cooperative effort, Dr. Gregor may have leaned so far backward as to lessen the validity of his results. It must be remembered that in every face-to-face situation, involving individuals, white or otherwise, and an examiner, the subject may be ill-at-ease, distrustful of his ability, and concerned with his general showing. If it were possible in any way to compensate for or sweep aside all these temperamental feelings, the test result would not be representative of an individual's ordinary behavior.

In my earlier experience with the test, I at first allowed two or more aborigines to be present but soon discontinued this practice as I found that errors made in the presence of others could be a cause of embarrassment. When other natives were present, they were given no opportunity to observe the actual threading of the Maze, their attention being taken up with physical and psychophysical measures applied by my assistant. All cases previously examined by Dr. Fry were excluded from tabulation of the results (see Porteus, 1931, pp. 304, 308).

After the first couple of subjects, I found no difficulties in individual examinations. Dr. Gregor, I believe, may have underestimated the familiarizing effects of native camp gossip. After the second half-day of testing, every aboriginal I examined seemed quite familiar with what he was required to do and set to work with a minimum of demonstration. I did not have the opportunity to give as much forepractice as Gregor used, which undoubtedly made the whole test more difficult for some of my cases. My *rapport* with the natives was probably closer than his, as I came with the status of an intertribal messenger bearing churinga from other regions and was assigned by the old men to an equivalent subsection and allotted a totem. My tribal brothers were sometimes mystified at my refusal to help them solve a difficulty in the Maze, but soon accepted the situation. I encountered no other difficulties.

The above discussion should not be interpreted in any way as reflecting criticism of Gregor's approach, but is intended to illustrate the complexities encountered by any investigator of primitive mentality. His easy relations with his Australid subjects may, in individual cases, have resulted in a better demonstration of their ability than did my own approach, but on the whole may help to account for his somewhat higher means of Maze performance.

It will be apparent that the 1962 testing program was considerably extended beyond the 1929 experiment. Since that earlier time two additional series, called the Extension and Extension Supplement have been standardized in such a way that they should yield scores equivalent to the Original or Vineland Revision Series if given one after another, the succession being immediate. Reference to the figures relating to standardization of the Extension Series (Porteus, 1955b) will show that with 300 Honolulu high school students in the ninth and tenth grades, ranging in age from 14 to 16 years, equivalence of score in the two series was attained. The purpose of this research was to provide two practice-free, or practice-controlled series of tests. It had long been recognized that even though the Original Maze ranged from five to seventeen years with, in all, ten maze designs graded in difficulty, it was still a "thin" test. Not only was it advantageous to discover what would happen in individual cases if the testing could be continued for an additional 20 to 40 minutes, but in certain types of research practice-free forms were necessary. When, for example, the mental effects of brain operations, such as lobotomy, were to be measured, a preoperative test was required. If, as we have seen, the same form of the Maze was applied after operation, changes consequent on the brain injury might be lessened or obscured by improvement through practice. If the second series of tests was made just enough harder as to obliterate differences in scores or obviate the average practice effect of a second application, that factor could, in general, be disregarded. In short, whatever measurable mental changes were noted they could be ascribed to the operation rather than to increased familiarity with the tests. That was the reason for devising and standardizing the Extension Series (Porteus, 1955), and later the Supplement. But as we all know, frontal lobe operations went out of surgical fashion for the relief of psychotic symptoms and tranquilizing drugs took their place in psychiatric practice. Research in this field also demanded a third Maze Test Series. If we wished to measure the continued effects of ataractic medication, it was necessary to administer a pretranquilizer test plus another Maze Series after the period of treatment; and if we wished to judge the permanence of effect, we needed a third practice-free or practice-controlled form.

Not only was this necessary for psychopharmacological research, but much also could be learned about normal reactions in a long continued task. Would individuals tend to improve, decline, or remain constant as regards the three series of tests involving prudent planning and foresight? This was the reason for applying the three Maze forms to Australids. The clinical value of applying the three series of the Maze has not yet been fully exploited in other experimental situations, but if and when this value is recognized, the Original, Extension, and Extension Supplement tests will be available.

In sampling the mentality of primitive people like the Australids, we thought it would be useful to know whether initial success was a flash in the pan or, conversely, whether consciousness of early mistakes or inferior performance would lead to better adaptations. In short, how well will the individual adjust to a lengthier trial of the traits in question? The resistance to fatigue and sustained interest by Australids was remarkable.

Data of the two investigations conducted by Porteus in 1929 and

Gregor in 1962 are given in Table 2, but before discussing them we may repeat the reminder that the results are not strictly comparable. As previously mentioned, more forepractice in the test was provided in the Gregor study, and allowing other natives to observe part of the testing may have helped to raise the Australid mean.

In reporting the results of the two investigations, it has also been necessary to adopt the same method of scoring. The new data collected by Gregor have been treated as if the adult test had not been applied, so that in both 1929 and 1962 the ceiling score is 15 years. Revision of the former data on these terms has resulted in a mean of 12.17 years for Hermannsburg males examined by Porteus in 1929 and 12.92 years in Gregor's study, an increase of .75 year. As indicated elsewhere, there are good reasons for considering the latest group of full-bloods, mainly Arunta, as not being truly representative of the Australids of Central Australia, and indeed of the continental interior. One hundred years of white contact plus the advantages of mission schooling during childhood and youth have undoubtedly conferred advantages reflected to some degree in Maze scores. Under present conditions industrially competent natives remain as employees of the mission.

On the other hand, the group examined by Gregor at Yuendumu and which included Wailbri and Pintubi, the latter less acculturated, can be assumed to be much more typical of the aboriginal population at large. The expectation that their scores when calculated without the adult test would closely approach the results earlier attained by natives of the northwest or Kimberley district was fully borne out. The 1929 Kimberley mean was 10.48 years (N 65), while the 1962 average (using the same scoring) was 10.4, a difference of only .08 of a year. In comparison with primitive groups in South East Asia, India, Africa, and North America, the mean of Australids can be taken to be about 10.5 years.

When the full Original Maze scale was applied, including the adult test as shown in Table 2, the mean rose to 11 years for the Wailbri-Pintubi group and 14.3 years for the highly selected Hermannsburg cases. This term "selected" applies only to Gregor's Hermannsburg subjects, all the full-blood males available there having been tested. With the addition of the Extension and Supplement Series, the reproach that the Maze is a "thin" test has been completely removed. Working through the three forms may involve solving 24 mazes graded in difficulty up to adult levels and

Table 2

Maze Test Means of Australid Groups

Earlier Studies				1962 Studies*			
Group	N	Mean	SD	Group	N	Mean	SD
Kimberley Males (Porteus, 1929)	65	10.48	2.34	Yuendumu Males (Gregor, 1962)	50	10.40	2.63
LaGrange Bay Males (Piddington, 1932)	24	10.52					
Hermannsburg Males (Porteus, 1929)	23	12.17	1.75	Hermannsburg Males (Gregor, 1962)	25	12.92	1.77
Kimberley Females (Porteus, 1929)	11	8.22		Hermannsburg Females (Gregor, 1962)	12	9.67	2.47
LaGrange Bay Females (Piddington, 1932)	14	8.60					

* Adult test eliminated to make the 1962 series scoring identical with the 1929 series.

in some instances Australid subjects took up to three hours' work and never less than one hour of intensive effort. Altogether this constitutes a severe trial of persistency in a task, of resistance to mental fatigue, and the ability to sustain interest. It was anticipated that this threefold extension of the length and difficulty of the examination, especially of Australids with only brief contacts with whites and with little or no schooling, would demonstrate rapidly deteriorating interest and effort. As will be seen by the scores presented in Table 3, and confirmed by Dr. Gregor's personal observations, this expectation completely failed of fulfilment. Only one group of adolescent males, 15 years of age and older, showed decline in the means from the first throughout the three series.

Table 3

Australid and Delinquent Test Age Means Compared[*]

Group	N	Original Mean	Original SD	Extension Mean	Extension SD	Supplement Mean	Supplement SD
Yuendumu Adult Males	50	11.00	3.34	11.68	3.40	11.52	3.53
Hermannsburg							
Adult Males	25	14.3	2.39	14.90	2.35	14.60	2.89
Adult Females	12	10.0	3.02	11.0	3.54	10.7	3.54
Adolescent Males	18	11.5	2.91	11.14	3.35	10.6	3.35
Honolulu							
Self-admitted Delinquents	61	Not applied		15.5	1.60	15.2	2.11
Detention Home Delinquents	25	13.90	2.99	Not applied			

[*] Complete scores.

In order to assist ready reference and at the same time reduce the number of tables, Table 3 includes the Original, Extension, and Supplement means for both males and females. Unlike the data presented in Table 2, these are complete scores including the adult tests. The sex differences are discussed in an earlier chapter. For purposes of interest, the table also shows what happened when delinquent males were examined in Honolulu. In the group of self-admitted delinquents among high school boys in Honolulu there was a slight drop in the mean for the Supplement Series when compared with the Extension mean.

In each group of Australid adults there was a rise in average score from the Original to the Extension, followed by some decline from the Extension to the Supplement mean, but in each case this last score remained definitely higher than the Original mean. In the case of adolescent males, 15 years or older, we have noted a steady decline from one series to the next. This raises the interesting question as to whether evaporation of interest may be more observable in an adolescent than in a more mature group. For the latter, the fact that they scored better in their third series than in their first seems convincing proof of their willingness to persevere in a task presented by a white examiner, an attribute not previously observed in the Australid temperament.

Cultural aspects resulting in a rather generalized familiarity of Australids, especially males, with designs somewhat similar to the Maze have been pointed out. In an article recently published in *Mankind Quarterly* (Porteus, 1962), it was stated that these people frequently incise designs, usually concentric circles, on their churinga (tjurunga). These patterns include also half-circles, spirals, straight or curved lines, and occasionally tracks of birds, people, or animals. Many of these in simpler form are repeated in the bodily decorations that form an integral part of their sacred ceremonies.

In some other parts of Australia, mazelike patterns are engraved deeply on the trunks of eucalyptus trees, after a portion of the bark has been removed. One such example was illustrated as compared with a simple maze, but a much more striking design is pictured on page 25 of McCarthy's (1938) brochure on native art, the tree having been found in the Dubbo district of New South Wales, about 1,200 miles southeast of Alice Springs. This booklet also presents a most impressive documentation of Australid artistic and designing ability, and should have wide circulation outside Australia. Unfortunately, the illustrations of quadrangular designs common in West and Northwest Australia are too dark to give clear images of the patterns. These are even more similar in appearance to Maze Test designs.

The Mankind Quarterly article cited herein also points out that devising string-figures of quite complex designs calls for planning and prehearsal, much as do Maze Test performances. Making these figures constitutes a common pastime among primitive peoples all over the world, so that they would not have any peculiar relationship with Australid Maze ability. Enough has been said, however, to show that the appearance of a Maze Test would occasion no surprise to a Central Australian adult male; on the other hand, its similiarity to decorative patterns familiar to him on his sacred objects and his most valued tools and weapons would predispose him favorably in considering the Porteus Maze as being worthy of earnest attention. Again and again, the absorption of the Australid in the task of maze-threading has been commented upon, and Gregor has added notable confirmation of these observations.

The high level of performance, particularly of the Finke River (Hermannsburg) group, provides a strong contrast with the scores at the lower end of the Maze "spectrum." The spread of Maze-tested abilities between the Kalahari Bushmen and the Australids appeared to be very great, since the former could attain a mean of only 7.56 years, or nearly 3 years below the Yuendumu performance in 1962, and almost 3 years below the scores of Northwest Australid tribes examined by me in 1929.

SUMMARY

After some months of training in the application of the Maze Test in Honolulu, James Gregor, who had taken his doctorate in philosophy of science and wished to get first-hand experience in the gathering of data on the mentality of primitive people, visited Central Australia in the winter season of 1962. Prior to his arrival there, the writer on his second excursion into this area after 33 years was able to arrange for Dr. Gregor to work at Yuendumu, 180 miles to the northwest of Alice Springs, and also at Hermannsburg, 85 miles west of the same center.

As the Wailbri and Pintubi tribes, mainly around Yuendumu and Papunyah, had never been subjected to psychometric measures, the first question was whether in comparing their results with earlier studies these people could be considered typical of the inhabitants of the Australian interior.

The food resources of the area are described and information drawn from an unpublished report supplied by Professor Campbell of Adelaide University, who in the course of repeated visits had become familiar with the native customs and habitat. Unusually good rains had fallen and the contrast between living conditions then and after prolonged drought were striking. Knowledge of the location of permanent water in hidden places was vital to survival and jealously guarded.

The process of food-gathering was illustrated by Campbell through a detailed account of a modern native "walkabout," showing some effects of contact with whites, but otherwise giving a picture of aboriginal sustenance away from the Yuendumu settlement. The actual testing process and method of introducing the test are set forth from Gregor's field notes, and are reproduced for the benefit of others who may wish to test primitive peoples. Special circumstances with regard to the presence of onlookers and other possible influences on Maze Test scores are discussed.

The effects of expansion of the test series from one to three forms and the lengthening of the testing period to one to three hours are dealt with. Gregor's results are compared with those obtained by the writer 33 years previously in the Kimberley district. After adjustment with regard to changes in methods of application and scoring, the differences in means are very small. The sustained interest and the resistance to fatigue, surprising to all who know the Australid's ordinary reactions, are commented upon. Natives of the Yuendumu region may be regarded as truly representative of Australids.

The surprisingly high levels of Maze performance in comparison with other primitive groups may be in part accounted for by the similarity of the Maze Test to some totemic and decorative designs excised on trees, shields and other implements, sand paintings, and ceremonial patterns on the bodies of performers. This may have facilitated Australid acceptance of the Maze Test.

With regard to the Hermannsburg group, also examined by Dr. Gregor, the excellence of their performance is attributed in part to their long period of white acculturation, but more particularly to the fact that they were a selected group, six of them being successful watercolor artists and the others singled out for mission employment on the basis of other skills.

But in contrast with this high level of test age, the qualitative record of this group was much inferior, only about the level of two groups of delinquents examined in Honolulu, these latter cases being of very mixed ethnic blood.

CHAPTER TEN

The Maze Test and Ethnic Differences

Besides the Australids there is one other extremely sparse aggre-
gation of humans that few anthropologists would hesitate to
designate a distinct race. These are the Bushmen of South Africa.
In one important direction their situation differs from that of the
Australids. Their geographical isolation was self-sought; that of the
Australian aborigines was imposed on them naturally. These latter
may, far back in prehistory, have reached and populated their island
continent because of pressure from stronger peoples, but if so, it was
so many centuries ago, possibly two hundred, that we cannot even
guess at the circumstances.

With regard to the Bushmen, we do know why they are at present
living in the Kalahari and when they made this their last refuge.
They were caught, not between the upper and the nether mill-
stones, but in a whole complex of grindstones, those never-ending
mills of racial pressure that in Africa grind so relentlessly. The
Dutch, and to a lesser extent the British, 300 years ago pressed on
them from the south; the Bantu, Zulus, Matabele, etc., attacked
them from the Northeast, and to the West lay the sea.

The story of their final struggle and retreat into the desert is
written in blood, and those who would know of their fate from the
pen of a gifted writer should read *The Lost World of the Kalahari*
(Van der Post, 1958), which can best be described as an act of
historical contrition on the part of a descendant of some of the men
of the Boer commandos. These carried on a long and ruthless war
of extermination against these little people, whose presence and
untameability posed a threat to colonizing plans.

Only in a "lost world" could the Bushmen conceal themselves, and
when I visited the Kalahari in 1934, a couple of thousand miles of
desert travel brought me into contact with only 25 adult males,

about 50 per cent of whom could be regarded as authentic repre-
sentatives of their race. I visited them in their *werft*, a collection of
huts in the bush veldt, each a half-dome open on one side and
devoid of any thorn bush fence to keep the lions at bay. A tiny fire
burned in front and at the back lay their meager possessions, the
most essential of which were the ostrich eggshells in which their
precious water was stored and hidden. But I soon realized that even
then the race was but a remnant, and that the name Bushmen
signified a way of life rather than a distinct people. But the physical
characteristics of the little folk were unmistakeable—the pepper-
corn hair, the apricot tinge of the skin, the strange foxlike shape of
face with broad forehead and pointed chin, the small but graceful
physique, marred only in older years by that strange steatopygic
bend. They were, however, not the only fugitives in this trackless
wilderness. There they mingled with fleeing remnants of the people
who called themselves Ba-kalahari—the people of the Kalahari—
and some mixture of blood was inevitable. There was, however,
one group of Bushmen that I met with near Khutse Pan in the
Central Kalahari who seemed in the main to be excellent representa-
tives of their race, although there were several of them whose dark
skin color and slightly larger stature suggested that they were not
pure Masarwa, as the Bushmen called themselves.

Like Van der Post, I was intrigued with reports that north of the
desert vast stretches of the Okovango marshes contained hidden
villages of "river Bushmen," and like him, I was paddled or poled
by natives over 120 miles from Maun into the center of the
swamp, our guides in constant fear of attacks by malignant hippos.
We threaded a maze of weedy shallow channels to avoid deep,
hippo-infested water, where makoras (dugout canoes) had often
been torpedoed from below by these resentful monsters. In reading
Van der Post's account, I judged that had my visit been about 20
years later we would have met near the center of the swamp, since
we approached the same goal from opposite directions. Like him,
I too saw only flimsy frameworks of dwellings on the islands of the
marsh and encountered briefly a single Bushman. In my subsequent
journeyings I found Bushmen outside the swamp, but the further
north I went the more apparent was the admixture of blood. Still,
I was extremely gratified to be able to be in contact with people
who still lived in Bushman style—without agriculture, depending
wholly on the things of the veldt for existence. By means of the

Maze, I could make some rather scanty comparisons in mentality of people known as Bushmen, contrasting them with men of another race who lived in similar fashion a matter of 6,000 miles or so across the ocean. Naturally, not only the similarities but the differences in the two environments and ways of life captured my attention. Thus I could repeat, though in different outline, my experiments in comparing mentalities in relation to environmental conditions such as I had carried out in northwest and Central Australia five years previously.

As far as sparsity of population was concerned, this was more marked in Australia, but as regards food supplies, the Bushmen had a decided advantage. Though the Kalahari is called a desert, the central area through which our small party traveled was comparatively well stocked with game. During the heat of the day, the almost indistinguishable sandy rises, covered with scattered thorn bush, seemed empty, but in the early morning and evening game could be seen on the move, mainly in pairs. Each pair had their own accustomed feeding territory, the whole area being patrolled from the air by the vultures. Any unwonted disturbance, such as the sound of shots or fleeing animals, broke up the settled browsing pattern, so that in the first couple of days of hunting, game movements were much in evidence. Apparently, each pair of animals watched its neighbors and any unusual behavior excited the whole population. Once the animals had pinpointed the danger, the area was vacated. Our advent was like casting a stone into a quiet pond, the disturbance spreading out in all directions over possibly a 30 mile radius. I believe that this was the secret of the sudden congregation of vultures at a kill. In contrast, Bushmen hunting caused very little disturbance. The Kalahari thorn-bush vegetation rendered stalking easy, and the use of the poisoned arrow made it possible to wound a single animal without especially disturbing the rest. The Bushmen's problem was then to track and follow the beast until it dropped from the effect of the poison. A few species, such as the springbok, moved about in small herds. The rest were in pairs, especially the lions, and the news that lions were abroad spread like wildfire. That was the bush telegraph in action.

The point is that no comparable concentration of game could be found in the Australid *habitat* except under most exceptional circumstances. Nevertheless, the Australian bush is also patrolled, and

the native habit of putting up smoke signals is a deliberate adver-
tisement of group movements so that the presence of strangers
is immediately evident. The occurrence of surface water, either in
permanent or semipermanent supplies, is one advantage that the
Australid possesses over the Bushmen. Scattered thunderstorms do
fall in the Kalahari, enabling the Bushmen to collect and store the
precious fluid in ostrich egg shells, which are then hidden in the
sand. The sucking up of water, using hollow reeds thrust into damp
sand soakages, is also successfully, but most painfully practised. The
two regions can be summed up by saying that more water falls in
the Kalahari than in Central Australia, but the soil is too absorbent
to hold and store it.

The saving feature in the Kalahari is the presence in season of the
tsama melons, the vines of which cover the ground after the
thunderstorms. Game and Bushmen follow the melon and obtain
both food and drink thereby. No such plant resources are available
to the Australian aborigines. In both regions, ecology and psychology are interdependent. The natives live in groups, the cohesiveness
of which depends on psychic as well as environmental factors.

As the general physical environment of the Australids has already
been delineated, it seems appropriate to devote a little more attention to the nature of the Bushman habitat. In 1934, from Mafeking,
the administrative center for the Bechuanaland Protectorate, we
drove northward 400 miles, paralleling the railway that ends at
Livingstone in Northern Rhodesia. The line skirts but does not enter
the Kalahari, so that a drive of 25 miles from the railway station at
Gaberones was necessary to reach our base at Molepolole. This was
at one time Livingstone's place of residence while he learned the
Sechuana language and formed plans for his earliest expeditions
that carried him up to Lake Ngami, a journey of about 1,000 miles
to the northwest. We had hoped to drive across the desert to reach
the Ghanzi district where Boer farmers had established a small
settlement. After several weeks, we decided to return to Molepolole,
skirt the central Kalahari via Serowe, 300 miles distant, and thence
follow Livingstone's track to the Okovango.

Molepolole was just on the fringe of the desert, a rather pleasant
native town set among the hills, mainly rocky kopjes, noisy with a
crowd of baboons that came down at dawn to raid the pawpaw garden of our host, companion, and guide, John Knobel. He was a well-
educated Boer, who for years had maintained a trading store there.

A single ox-wagon trail led west into the desert, along which our truck ground slowly in low gear, harvesting the seeds of the Bushman grass until our radiator was plugged solidly. This necessitated stops every 15 minutes to try and clear the air flow and to fill up the radiator from which the water had boiled away.

This was not yet Bushman country, but near an ancient river bed—the only noticeable feature in 100 miles—was a Bakalahari village surrounded by a sketchy lion fence of thornbush. Building this fence was more an act of faith than a protective device, since any active lion could have penetrated it. Only when a known man-eater was ranging the district did the natives show any concern. Then the whole male population concentrated on its destruction. The Bushmen, on the other hand, take absolutely no precautions against lions, except, when possible, to keep out of their way. The only trouble reported to us was when a Bushman group living near our camp killed a wounded springbok that the lions had evidently been stalking, and hung some of the meat in a tree close by one of their half-dome huts. The lions had then to be stood off all night by hurling lighted stocks from a central campfire. They were so persistent that the Bushmen were glad to abandon the rest of the carcass to the lions. They admitted freely that by right of prior discovery the lions were the rightful owners of the animal.

We noted that the Bakalahari took better care of their stock than they did of themselves. On our route they had built a stout stockade of crooked posts for a night corral. Here the cattle were guarded by night fires, while the boys and youths tended them all day in their grazing on the veldt. The game, of which there was no scarcity, had its main concentration around a milewide pan, a low depression that might conceivably be one of many craters left by meteors. From here the natives directed us to a Bushman *werft*, or village, 50 miles further on.

The real threat to survival was the absence of surface water, the only temporary pool being a half-mile from our final camp, which was about 150 miles inside the desert. Each Bushman family had its private stock of ostrich egg shells filled with water and buried in the sand. That seemed to me the only long-term foresight used by the Bushmen. The Australids attempt no water storage. It was easier for them to mark down and visit hidden rock holes than to develop any artificial means of storage. The location of some of these supplies was often the carefully cherished secret of the old men, knowledge of which bolstered their tribal authority.

In spite of surface waterlessness, the whole quarter of a million square miles that makes up the Kalahari is very far from being true desert. From Molepolole we followed our amended plan and drove over 800 miles to the Okovango Swamp. The last 100 miles followed the course of the Botletle River fed by the annual overflow of the Okovango into the marshes. When the flood water came down, this area contained one of the greatest concentrations of game in Africa. Why the Bushmen did not desert the desert and move to the forests and swamps of the northern Kalahari was inexplicable unless the reasons were psychological. Outside the desert the Bushmen were the despised serfs of the Bechuana. In their own territory, they were their own men; they were kings of the arid veldt, where only they could survive. Like the Australids, they clung to their own undisputed homeland. As to their reputed subserviency to the Bakalahari—that to them was a cosmic joke. They knew they were the better men. I suspect that was their attitude to these intruding whites. They were always laughing because they had us to laugh at.

Enough has been said to indicate that Australid and the Bushman habitats are extremely different but that survival would seem to have been more easily attainable in South Africa; this, too, in spite of the constant menace of wild beasts, from which the Masarwa appeared to suffer. I wonder, however, whether we were not projecting our own fears on them. The interested reader will find in two earlier books (Porteus, 1931, 1937) a more extended comparison of the Bushman and Australid ways of life.

The inclusion of these pages of bush philosophy in a psychological volume is admittedly unusual, but if we are to attempt any discussion of the relationship of environmental factors to mentality, even a brief psycho-anthropologic survey of the comparative difficulties of survival of the ethnic groups under review is necessary. I have no hesitation at all in affirming that the Bushman way of life, through extremely difficult, is on the whole easier than that of the Australids. Hence, the average differences in Maze performance in favor of the latter lend no support to the theory that Maze-tested intelligence is materially affected by culture and environment rather than by race. The evidence for the significance of results is presented elsewhere throughout this volume. For a most sympathetic appraisal of the old-time Bushmen, their courage and character, reference should be made to Van der Post's almost affectionate account of "the little hunters" in his book. I would add this footnote. The Australids and the Bushmen often laugh, sing, and sometimes dance. Perhaps this may be interpreted not so much as a defiance as a temperamental defence against loneliness, and the best possible insurance of sanity.

The writer is well aware that there are means of assessing racial adaptive behavior other than comparison of Maze Test performances. But it so happens that the last named are objective and can be scored numerically. Much more significant, but impossible to express quantitatively, would be the two peoples' status in material culture, which represent the cumulative results of planning capacity, plus communicated industrial skill. Unfortunately, these two factors cannot, except in most general terms, be separated and appraised.

The Bushman, for example, depends mainly on the bow and arrow for his meat and to a lesser extent on the spear used as a stabbing weapon, or very rarely as an assegai thrown by hand. We do not know the circumstances of the invention of the bow and arrow, but no one, I think, would be bold enough to ascribe its devising to these South African hunters. It would be much safer to regard it as an item of diffusion of ideas or culture. But the habit of dipping the arrow points into deadly poison is dependent on knowledge peculiar to their specific environment. It is the poison that makes the weapon most effective. The Bushmen use a mixture of snake venom, the milky juice of euphorbias and other plants, and the desiccated bodies of the *ngwa* grub in its pupal stage of development. The use of these poisons indicate intimate environmental knowledge and the foresight necessary to apply that knowledge. The use of the poison arrow influences the Bushman way of life more than any other circumstance. The Australid does not use the bow and arrow, but depends on the spear; he does not rely on poison to secure game, and, though the eggs of the emu are about half the size of the ostrich egg, he does not use them or any other receptacle to store water. The question then arises as to any evidence of inventive skill that he displays. In my book (Porteus, 1931) on the Australid, I devoted many pages to demonstrate the long-term planning that enters into many of his social observances, especially the initiation practices that establish on an unassailable basis the authority of the old men of the tribe. This is a social device of extreme survival value in such a region as the interior of Australia, where the emergencies of living are frequent. At present we are concerned more with material culture.

With some slight modifications the material of the next two pages has been taken from a monograph by the present writer and A. J. Gregor (Porteus and Gregor, 1963).

The boomerang, at least the well-known variety which returns to the thrower, is probably an implement original to Australia, although curved throwing sticks have been devised and used elsewhere. However, the returning boomerang is regarded by Australids as being more of a toy than a serious hunting or fighting weapon, though it may occasionally be thrown into a flight of birds with useful results. The hunting and war boomerang is made of much heavier wood, and in fighting its somewhat curving flight makes it hard to ward off with a shield. It does not return to the thrower.

On the other hand, the spear-thrower seems to have claims to being a unique Australian invention. It is cut and shaven thin from a piece of very hard wood, such as mulga, so as to become an implement about thirty inches long and two or more inches wide, slightly convex on one side, concave on the other. The distal end, which is held by the thrower, is narrowed to a "neck" so that it fits easily between the aboriginal's forefinger and thumb. The other end has attached to it a sharp, thorn-like peg, bound in place with kangaroo sinew and embedded in hardened gum or resin. This point projects forward and fits snugly into a hole drilled into the shaft of the spear. The weapon about to be thrown lies along the length of the spear-thrower, or *wommera* (woomera), and is held in position by the thumb and forefinger of the thrower, who grasps the neck of the implement with his other three fingers. The strength of the attachment of the peg or spur is shown by the fact that a *wommera* collected by the writer 35 years ago is still quite serviceable.

The native raises his throwing arm and bends it so that it extends backward behind his shoulder. The added leverage supplied by the throwing stick as applied to the rear end of the missile propels it with such force that its range, when thrown javelin fashion, is increased from less than 50 yards (maximum recorded by Spencer and Gillen, 143 feet) to 120 yards. It has a quite effective range up to 80 yards. I have seen remarkable accuracy in transfixing a target the size of a man at that distance.

The remarkable feature about this implement is that the principle of rear-end propulsion is applied in few other primitive weapons, the chief exceptions being the bow and arrow, the rocket and, possibly, the blowpipe. It finds its most modern application in jet-propelled aircraft. Considering the very long isolation of the Australid race, it is quite possible that the invention of the spear-thrower was prior to, or contemporaneous with that of the bow and arrow. In any case, it deserves high credit as an ingenious device, probably as patentable, had both been invented in modern days, as the bow and arrow. In open forest it is probably quite as effective a weapon as the archer's equipment; in brush it is probably superior. It is rare indeed that the Australid, hunting under ordinary conditions, comes home to camp empty-handed.

In addition, the Australid has displayed economy of inventive effort by attaching to the handle of the spear-thrower a sharp flake of flint or quartzite embedded in hard gum so that it makes a most effective adze, useful for shaping boomerangs, fighting clubs and shields, and for incising various decorative designs on these implements. Thus with this small addition, the Australid has converted a weapon into a tool of comprehensive purposes—his version of turning swords into ploughshares. He has equipped himself with an adze many times more useful than one held in the hand, a tool most helpful to his survival. Of more adventitious value is its employment in fire-making when its edge is sawed back and forth in a groove in a shield made of much lighter material such as the bean-wood tree. This mode of friction ignites the sawdust, which is then fed with grass and blown into flame. On several counts the *wommera* is a plain instance of ingenuity and inventiveness. Thus the relatively good maze scores of the Australids may not be so much out of line with their inventiveness.

With this brief summary of some of the adjustive mechanisms in operation among primitive populations, we may now turn to the evidence of comparative mentalities as reflected in Maze Test scores and presented in Table 4. But before we can properly interpret the

Table 4

Maze Scores: Illiterate Adults

N	Group	Locality	Maze Mean Years	SD	Investigator
50	Rural Bhil	Central India	7.44	1.2	Ray
25	Bushmen	Kalahari, S. Africa	7.56	2.17	Porteus
29	Sakai Jeram	Coastal Malaya	7.88	2.49	Stewart
100	Abor, Upper Padam	N.E. India	8.3	1.25	Chowdhury & De
100	Abor, Lower Padam	N.E. India	8.34	1.61	Chowdhury & De
28	Mchopi	Port. E. Africa	8.34	2.45	Porteus
29	Urban Bhil	Central India	8.36	1.8	Ray
50	Santal	India	8.55	1.79	Chowdhury & De
22	Negrito	Luzon, Philippine Is.	8.86	2.76	Stewart
145	Pasi (Minyong)	Upper Assam, India	8.9	2.24	Chowdhury & De
100	Kanikkar	S. India	9.27	2.19	Ray
25	Shangaans	Port. E. Africa	9.3	2.66	Porteus
36	Bengali	W. Bengal	9.42	2.44	Vicary
59	Santal	N. Bengal	9.52	—	Vicary
27	Pasi (Adi)	Upper Assam, India	9.63	1.63	Chowdhury & De
50	Wailbri	C. Australia	10.4	2.63	Gregor
56	Senoi	Mts., Malaya	10.43	2.73	Stewart
56	Keidja-Nyul	N.W. Australia	10.48	2.34	Porteus
24	Karadjeri	N.W. Australia	10.52	2.6	Piddington
27	Chinese	Peiping, China	10.52	2.67	Stewart
22	Bajou	N. Borneo	10.61	2.56	Stewart
25	Amaxosa	Cape Prov., S.E. Africa	10.78	2.76	Porteus
21	Ghurkas*	Malaya	11.33	2.71	Stewart
50	Chinese Coolies	Peiping, China	11.68	2.74	Stewart
20	Tamils*	Malaya	13.18	2.32	Stewart

* Ghurkas and Tamils were immigrants working on Malayan plantations.

significance of these findings, we must take into consideration several methodological factors. The most important of these is, as previously pointed out, the question of selection, specifically whether the group examined can be regarded as typical of their race. We have previously drawn attention to the high level attained by the Hermannsburg group as compared not only with the Bushmen of the Kalahari or even other Australid tribes. The Arunta group, as we have indicated (see Table 2, Chapter 9), must be considered highly selected by reason of their technical and artistic skills, and this, we believe, accounts for the wide gaps of over 2 years in test age between them and the Wailbri-Pintubi. But these latter are almost 3 years above the level of the Kalahari Bushmen, as are also the tribes hundreds of miles to the North of the Wailbri in the Kimberly district.

Maze Test means that closely approximate the Bushman average were also attained by East Asian groups examined by Dr. Kilton Stewart and reported by me (Porteus, 1937). The Bushman mean (N 25) was 7.56 years, whereas Stewart recorded 8.02 years (N 29) for Sakai Jeram, a coastal tribe in Malaya. That these levels are by no means exceptionally inferior has been shown by P. C. Ray (1953), working in conjunction with U. Chowdhury and R. K. De. They obtained similarly low means for jungle-dwellers in India. These investigators used the Original Maze series, and followed closely my methods of scoring and application. To make these comparisons easier, the data on all illiterate groups are gathered together in the table. The number of cases examined in India alone mount up to over 700, to which I have added Santal and Bengali groups reported upon by Vicary (1938). The only mean score below that of the Bushmen was rural Bhil with 7.44 years. The close approximation of these scores to each other should be noted, the extent of the range throughout the whole table being from 7.44 to 9.63 years, a spread of only 2.19 years.

Degree of acculturation does not seem to be a decisive factor in success in the tests except as between urban and rural Bhil, but there the difference was only .92 of a year. On the other hand, Ray states his belief that the Santals who live near a town and are employed as coalminers are more acculturated than the Kanikkar and the Abor of Lower Padam. Yet the Kanikkar rank second highest in the Maze, above the Santals, while the Adi Pasi, though considered lowest in acculturation by Ray, had the highest group score. He admits that the Kanikkar and Adi Pasi "having no schooling and of decidedly lower acculturation than the urban

Bhil show superiority over the latter and the differences are significant at the 5 per cent level of probability. These findings suggest that differences in native mentality exist." According to our calculations of the data Ray supplies, the *t*-test probability was .02, conventionally rated better than .05.

Even allowing for the fact that the Hermannsburg Arunta were undoubtedly a favorably selected group, their high scores in the Maze are still surprising, being exceeded by four groups only, Carolinian males, 15.8, Chamorros, 14.8 (Joseph and Murray, 1951), and North American Indians over 15 years of age who scored 14.68 in Havighurst's and Hilkevitch's (1944) investigation, while Sparling (1941) reported a Maze Test age for Ontario Indian children over 12 years as being 14.4 years. Stewart's study of Ainu in Northern Japan yielded a mean of 13 years.

In regard to Gregor's latest investigation of aboriginal mentality as set forth in this book, we should consider still further the probability that from the standpoint of intelligence the natives examined at the Finke River Mission should be regarded as highly selected.

The Finke River Mission was established at Hermannsburg, according to Rex Battarbee, in 1877, 87 years ago. Two of its superintendents, Rev. C. T. F. Strehlow and Rev. F. W. Albrecht, were each in charge for very many years. Hence, efforts to influence the thinking and ways of life of the natives there have been consistent and intense for almost a century. Whether or not anthropologists would approve all missionary efforts to discourage certain tribal customs, they would agree that the advancement of the Arunta has been the steady aim of those in charge of the missions. They learned the native language, set up a school, and instructed their charges in their own Arunta (Aranda) tongue. Whatever white acculturation was possible under mission circumstances was accomplished. Six or more of the Hermannsburg group tested by Gregor belonged in the school of Australid artists led by the late Albert Namatjira, who achieved wide acclaim as a watercolor artist both in Australia and elsewhere. His personal story provides the most striking illustration of the fact that a high Maze Test age mean is not necessarily an index of the social adjustment of a group. This has been emphasized in relation to delinquents, whose mean test age is not so inferior, but for whom the qualitative scoring (Q-score) is a better measure of social ineptitude. The data on this point are given in Table 5.

Namatjira's biography (Porteus, 1963) provides an interesting but tragic case history. Credit for launching him on his artistic career belongs to Rex Battarbee, well known Australian painter, who hired Namatjira as camelboy on one of his earliest painting expeditions to Central Australia. At Albert's request, he gave the latter painting materials and some minimum instruction. He later took the native with him on a two months' painting trip. Battarbee (1951) in his book on Australid art tells how dramatic was his discovery of Namatjira's talent. He writes:

> My greatest surprise came after we had been out for two weeks and were painting in Palm Valley. Albert brought along a painting of the Amphitheatre to which I had not even seen him put a brush. I immediately saw his talent. Here was a man, a full-blooded member of a race considered the lowest type in the world, who had in two weeks absorbed my colour sense. I felt that he had done the job so well that he had no need to learn more from me about colour. At that time I well remember writing home to my people saying that this man would become famous as an artist. From then on I simply corrected any faults that occurred in such things as composition.

Battarbee paid tribute to Albert Namatjira's fine qualities quite apart from his artistic abilities. He told of his thorough reliability, his keenness to do a good job, and his ambition and intelligence. He wrote: "His is one of the finest examples of an Australian aboriginal family one could wish to meet." He mentioned particularly the mission's discouragement of long stays by the natives in Alice Springs; "otherwise they might be swallowed up in one of those blackfellows' graveyards, the slum areas of Australian towns and cities." In 1951 it was still true that "Albert never looked back, and the more successful he was, the harder he worked."

T. G. H. Strehlow, son of the early missionary, born at Hermannsburg and speaking the Arunta tongue fluently, summed up Albert as "one of those gifted aborigines who has destroyed the myth of the constitutional incapacity of the Australian native to learn and to apply methods learnt from Europeans. For that reason alone Albert Namatjira will always deserve from us unstinted honor and recognition" (Battarbee, 1951, Foreword).

Unfortunately, later events have proved this judgment to be premature both as regards the generalized adaptability of the race and this particular aboriginal's personal adjustment, the confirmation of this statement being provided by Strehlow himself (1961). The story is recounted in a booklet entitled *Nomads in No-Man's Land*. After full citizenship had been conferred on Namatjira, he celebrated his legal emancipation by becoming openly addicted to alcohol, an example set for him by many white men in Central Australia. After Albert's imprisonment for sharing his liquor with an aboriginal fellow-artist, he seemed reformed, but shortly after died. As Strehlow puts it: "Australia's best-known and most gifted aboriginal son had not been able to bridge successfully the gulf that had always remained between himself and the white Australian community." The tragedy was that Namatjira attempted the almost insuperable task of adjusting himself to two worlds, his own and the white man's, and his failure serves to emphasize the incompatibility of the two divergent philosophies of living. The way of life a group evolves is surely dependent on their temperamental qualities as well as on their mentality. Nevertheless, Namatjira, despite his sad end, provided the main part of a remarkable chapter of Australid achievement in watercolor painting.

The inclusion of native artists in the group examined by Gregor at Hermannsburg would tend to raise the average Maze score considerably. Maze-threading and watercolor painting have at least one thing in common. Each stroke of the brush must be carefully planned, for once committed to paper it cannot be erased or altered. Foresight, mental prehearsal are essential to success in both activities.

Moreover, the fact that some of these scenes are not painted on the spot but are completed without the aid of any preliminary sketches indicates that when this is the case these natives possess a most extraordinary memory for color and form.

The influence of selectivity of the sample can be safely inferred, not only through the inclusion of artists but also by the presence in the group of other individuals, well trained by the mission in various forms of local industry. Some were stockmen (cowboys) employed on the huge area used by the Mission as a cattle run or station; others were mechanics, truckdrivers, a tanner, a ranch foreman, and even two "evangelists," who acted as assistant missionaries, visiting and ministering to aboriginal groups whose work lay at a distance from the main Mission. Actually, full-blood males at Hermannsburg were few, since only those who had special interests or abilities to keep them there remained. Employment in Alice Springs or neighboring cattle ranches [1] draws off most able-bodied males.

---

[1] Called "stations" in Australia, the distinction being that ranches in America rarely extend over millions of acres. A holding in Central Australia of 1,000 square miles would be considered a small "station."

Including the artists, the group available for examination could be expected to rank high in intelligence.

Thus the relation of the test to rather generalized factors that seem to be represented by artistic and technical skills may account in large part for the high scores attained by the aboriginal group at Hermannsburg. There is, however, another scoring of Maze performances that puts aboriginal social responsibility in an entirely different light.

This scoring, which is discussed more fully in the chapter on delinquent Maze performance, pays no attention to entrance or avoidance of blind alleys, which is the basis of the scoring that expresses mental age. The former centers on the executive quality of performance by penalizing the crossing of lines, cutting of corners, general irregularity or "waviness" of lines, and lifting of the pencil from the paper while drawing, following an initial warning that this should not be done. There are also additional penalties assessed against mistakes made at the beginning and end of threading each test design. The higher this qualitative error score, the worse the performance.

Reference to Chapter 5 will show that studies by independent investigators (Wright, 1944; Grajales, 1948; Docter and Winder, 1954; Fooks and Thomas, 1957) have confirmed my findings that delinquent groups had Q-scores rather closely centered around an average of 49 points, the mean obtained by me in similar investigations. Nondelinquent groups average about 25 error points, or about half the delinquent mean.

On the strength of the above findings and the reputed inferior social adjustments of the Arunta group, it was decided to compare the Hermannsburg qualitative scores with those of a group of delinquents, temporarily confined to the Detention Home in Honolulu. These cases may be characterized as incorrigible adolescents with poor social adjustments, not severe enough to warrant their immediate commitment by the Juvenile Court to a training or correctional school. Undoubtedly some of them will eventually be committed as seriously delinquent cases.

The reason for selecting this group for comparative purposes was that Gregor had examined these cases as part of his preparation for work among the Central Australian Australids. One change, however, was made in the qualitative scoring; he found it difficult to get some of his native subjects to understand clearly what was meant by the injunction *not* to lift the pencil, nor could he use any pidgin-English equivalent phrase. So the item was dropped from both scoring categories. Judging by performances, this was tantamount to conferring an advantage on the Arunta group, since the deleted "lift pencils" errors were far more numerous in their case. On the other hand, the prohibition against crossing lines was thoroughly understood, since when this occurred, natives often indicated their realization of error by stopping until prompted to continue with the test or by lifting the pencil and attempting to correct their mistake by redrawing the line.[2] Actually, because of greater familiarity with English, the Arunta group should have had less difficulty in understanding instructions.

The results obtained with mildly delinquent youths in Honolulu can be compared with Arunta qualitative data. The first named consisted of self-admitted delinquents examined in 1959, procedures having already been described in the chapter on juvenile delinquency. Excluding those with minor traffic offences, 49 admitted some difficulties with the police, and to these were added 12 from the records of the Juvenile Crime Prevention Division. Thus the investigators were left with the surprising result that almost one-third of those questioned, who would normally have been classified as nondelinquent, had actually been in trouble. Certainly this strikes a cautionary note for this type of study. Since no definite police action had followed, the group was classified as "self-admitted, mild offenders," and their scores have been added to the comparative figures presented in Table 5. To make fairer comparisons, only those cases, both aboriginals and delinquents, who completed the adult designs are included in this table, the effect being to reduce the means well below ordinary levels. Unfortunately, only the Original Maze was given to the Detention Home group, while the intermediate high school students had been tested by the Extension and Supplement Series.[3]

An examination of the table enables us to make comparisons of these reduced Q-scores of the Yuendumu group and, the Arunta with either of two groups of rather mild delinquents. The Wailbri-Pintubi (Yuendumu), as could be expected from illiterates, make

[2] The same tendency toward self-correction was also noted by Piddington (1932) with Karadjeri natives.

[3] For test age means of the groups of which these individuals are a part, see Table 3, Chapter 9.

Table 5

Australid and Delinquent Q-Score Maze Means*

Group	Original			Extension			Supplement		
	N	Q-Score	SD	N	Q-Score	SD	N	Q-Score	SD
Yuendumu (Adult Males)	26	51.69	23.27	31	54.35	22.31	31	60.23	23.75
Arunta (Adult Males)	23	39.13	19.83	22	39.18	21.18	22	45.59	25.19
Delinquents (Self-admitted)		Not applied		60	31.01	20.96	58	34.34	20.71
Delinquents (Detention Home)	21	35.19	17.34		Not applied				

* Lifted pencils scoring omitted. Only cases who completed whole series to Adult level are included.

the worst showing with a gradual worsening of error scores from 52 to 54 to 60 points, as they proceeded through the Original, Extension, and Supplement Series. The Arunta score is the same in Original and Extension (39 points) but rises to 45 error points in the Supplement. Delinquent means similarly reduced, were 35, 31 and 34 points in the three series without much change due to the lengthening periods of testing. However, it is worth noting that the Arunta group have worse scores than the delinquents in each of the three Q-scores. If these results are at all closely related to social adjustment, as is the case with white subjects, then the prospects of their adaptability to changed conditions under the government assimilation policy are not too good, a little worse in fact than for white delinquents. This policy may provide in Australia a similar outcome as is observable in Africa, where the results of conferring voting privileges on native populations before they understand the issues on which they vote are disappointing. At least there will be no worries about Communist influence over such a pitiful remnant of people.

In summary, it will be seen from these figures that insofar as the Q-score can be accepted as a measure of social adjustment, the chances of adaptation of a full-blooded Australid group, even if selected for superior mentality from the body of men of their race, are somewhat less than those of a group of mild delinquents in the first year of high school in Hawaii. The latter were of mixed ethnic backgrounds, mainly Japanese with, however, a considerable quota of part-Hawaiians, some Portuguese, and a sprinkling of others such as Chinese, whites, etc.

Whatever is conceived to be the basic causes of social maladjustments, the qualitative score in the Maze seems to reflect more adequately than does their test age Australid inability to conform to white regulations or standards of behavior (see Porteus and Gregor, 1963). The warning with regard to the selectivity of the Arunta group should, however, be repeated; the test age mean of 11 years obtained by the Yuendumu natives should be accepted as more representative of the performance of Australids in general, as would also be their Q-scores.

Psychosomatic changes in Maze performance have been demonstrated by O'Shea, Elsom, and Higbe (1942) in cases of induced vitamin-B deficiency, with complete recovery brought about by thiamin feeding. The above results, unobtainable so far with other mental measures, seem to attest the fact that the Porteus Maze can be regarded as uniquely sensitive, psychosomatically speaking.

Another investigation by Waite and Neilsen (1919) should be bracketed with that of O'Shea, Elsom, and Higbe (see Chapter 4) for its possible bearing on the subject of inferior Maze performances on the part of primitive peoples. Waite and Neilson attempted to assess the effects of hookworm infection on North Queensland school children. Dr. Waite, State Director of the International Health Board, divided 340 school children on the basis of microscopic stool examinations and hemoglobin tests into three groups, noninfected, lightly infected, and heavily infected. Nurse Neilson, without knowledge of their classification, applied to pupils the Goddard Revision of the Binet and an early form of the Porteus Maze.[4]

The investigators summarized their findings as follows:

Lightly infected children in our series averaged 5.4 months by Binet and 2.0 months by Porteus lesser mentality than their hookworm-free associates, while the heavily infected children showed by comparison with hookworm-free an average of 19.5 months per Binet and 13.5 months by Porteus. . . . The Porteus test as used tends to score all children higher than the Binet-Simon scale.

They also noted a "uniform slowing down of mental processes" when total times of performance were recorded.

In view of the unequivocal losses associated with vitamin-B deficiency, and also the effects of hookworm, it seems strange that further investigation of Maze performance in malaria, sleeping sickness, extreme malnutrition, and other debilitating conditions has not been undertaken, since this might give us at least a partial explanation of inferior scores of some primitive groups. Here, it would seem, is a fertile field for medicopsychological research.

SUMMARY

In addition to mental examinations of Australids there is one other racial group, the Bushmen of South Africa, whose Maze Test reactions are of great interest. These constitute a sparse remnant of the original population of little hunters who were displaced by invading

---

[4] The article in question gives no information as to the training of the examiner in mental testing.

hordes of Bantu tribes and Dutch and British colonists, and who sought escape from extermination in the Kalahari desert.

The writer describes their habitat and their physical characteristics and sketches briefly their way of life as he saw them in 1934 (Porteus, 1937). The contrast between environment and material culture of Bushmen and Australids is commented upon, with special emphasis on differences in food supplies, water, and ways of life. On the basis of his personal observations, the writer concludes that while both environments are difficult and repressive, the advantages as regards food supplies are heavily on the side of the Bushmen. Conversely, the balance as regards Maze-tested ability is markedly on the side of the Australian aboriginals.

The Bushmen's intimacy with their environmental resources is acknowledged, particularly with regard to the choice of poisons that make wounds from their arrows lethal; but they cannot, of course, be credited with the invention of the bow and arrow, undoubtedly a product of the diffusion of ideas.

The Australid depends on the spear, and his inventiveness finds its main expression in the *wommera*, or spear-thrower, which by the addition at its end of a sharp stone flake he can convert into a most useful adze. He can also use it as a scoop and utilizes its edge for the hard wood component in firemaking. This implement and the boomerang are probably Australid inventions, and this ingenuity is possibly related to comparatively superior Maze Test ability. On the other hand, the Bushman shows better distant foresight in his water-storing. The method of increasing propulsive power of the spear by use of the *wommera* (woomera) is described.

The question of the representativeness of the groups examined in Australia by Gregor is discussed, as is also the degree of acculturation of various primitive people in India as reported in tables of comparative Maze Test scores.

Another important factor was selection as applied to the Arunta group examined by Gregor. Preliminary to the discussion of Q-scores attained by these Australids, the history of a famous Arunta watercolor painter is presented. The inclusion of other artists in Gregor's Hermannsburg group may help to account for their high test ages. Their inferior average in the qualitative scoring, which among whites indicates poor potentiality for social adjustment, is in marked contrast to their good test age scores. Their Q-scores are somewhat worse than delinquent means of cases examined in

Hawaii. This may bode ill for the success of an Australian government's policy of assimilation of the Australid into the white community. By common repute, bush Astralids have made very poor adjustments to white social standards.

Finally, as a possible explanation of the low test performances of many primitive populations, reference is made to two investigations that demonstrate how diet deficiency and debilitating diseases may affect mental development. The writer believes that this would be a most fruitful field for medicopsychological research.

CHAPTER ELEVEN

Unfinished Business

There is one phase of Maze performances which was discovered too late for much to be done about it. This concerned the test's projective features, and remains at a very obvious loose end. As will be seen, this aspect of Maze Test performance has been amply demonstrated, but what remains to be done is to determine the significance of the phenomenon in terms of social or personality values. We believe that the same question as to their meaning applies to many other tests commonly used as projective measures. The situation calls for some preliminary discussion prior to reviewing the work initiated in this direction with the Maze.

One of the most remarkable shifts of interest observable among psychologists pertains to the Rorschach Test. Actually, the past 25 years of clinical psychology have been marked by two decided trends in opposite directions with regard to mental tests. The first has been the decline in approval of the Binet Scale in at least two of its forms, the Stanford Revision and the Terman-Merrill Scale; and in contrast, the second has been the rise in psychological estimation of the Rorschach Test. It is the present writer's considered opinion that neither change in psychological esteem has come about through any notable accession of knowledge established by adequate research. The reasons for the recent additional shift in popularity from Binet to Wechsler are also partly supported by clinical hunches that the earlier test series cannot be relied upon in mental diagnosis as firmly as we were wont to believe. It will be interesting to observe whether the Wechsler-Bellevue Scales are capable of carrying the diagnostic weight now attached to them. Some incidental evidence on this point has been presented earlier in this volume.

As has been shown in the chapter on psychosurgery, faith in the adequacy of any Binet type of approach has been seriously weakened by the failure of these tests to be sensitive to one impressive if indirect criterion, the mental effects of surgically controlled brain damage to the frontal lobes. True, that control was far from perfect, but nevertheless the inability of these highly revered mental measures to reflect adequately results of neurosurgical interventions has been a great disappointment to psychologists. These results will undoubtedly bring about shifts in formerly accepted theories regarding localization of brain function. In addition, the Columbia-Greystone investigations are likely to mark the end of an era of blind trust in some of the chosen instruments of clinical psychology.

Because of the apparent lack of concern by some psychologists with regard to the validity of some of their most esteemed psychometric tools, it is worth while to quote again the summary of the Columbia-Greystone project published by Carney Landis (1949). He summarizes psychological changes after psychosurgery in these terms:

We gave thirty-five different tests before operation; we repeated most of them three weeks after operation and all of them four months after operation. From the thirty-five tests we derived 135 different scores of performance from the tests. Nine times out of ten neither the average nor the variability of the operative group differed significantly from that of the control group. The Wechsler-Bellevue Intelligence Test, either in its entirety or in the analysis of the twelve subtests which make it up, was unchanged. The sorting tests, which indicate the ability to generalize or to abstract, were not significantly changed. Word Association, Time Judgment, Mirror Drawing, Continuous Problem Task, all learning scores, and most memory scores were unaltered. Eight of the ten scales to evaluate personality, based on the Levy Movement Cards, were unchanged. Most of the Rorschach scores were unchanged.

In Chapter 3 of this volume we have already quoted Landis (1951) with regard to the comparative insensitivity of the tests ordinarily used in diagnosis of mental retardation. It should be said, however, that this demonstrated failure to reflect the effects of extensive brain damage does not constitute a general indictment of these tests, though it does emphasize the unwisdom of relying on such tests as sole arbiters of social competence. Obviously, the breach in the diagnostic dike can be partially plugged by including a measure sensitive to brain damage, such as the Maze.

It must also be remembered that Landis and his co-workers considered neither the practice effects in the Maze nor the important factor of the lapse of a sufficient interval of time for the full effects of operation to appear. Smith (1960) has since published his eight-year follow-up study which proves the permanence of the test deficits.

In the above Landis quotation, mention of the Rorschach Test, one of the tools most popular with both psychologists and psychiatrists, is somewhat incidental; but there is abundant evidence of its comparative insensitivity to brain damage. In his study, Landis also observes that: "Personality changes and loss of psychic pain are not regularly reflected by any personality test, including the Rorschach." (Landis, 1949).

Zubin (1949), in the same research conference, said: "An examination of the Rorschach records of the patients subjected to operation indicated that some of the subjects have altered in their personality while others remained unchanged. No definite pattern of changes emerged. Furthermore, the control patients frequently showed the same type of changes observed in the operatee group."

These findings do not differ from the pioneer study of Thelma Hunt (1942), whose report seems cautiously indefinite: "the amount of quantitative change is not generally large and extensive enough to warrant drawing any significant conclusions from them."

Yet surely a much clearer correspondence between Rorschach and personality change might have been confidently expected in patients for whom, according to Mary F. Robinson (1950), the type of lobotomy carried out by Freeman and Watts had "checked the terrific emotional tension characteristic of many preoperative patients." However, as far as reflecting such a marked personality change, the Rorschach proved to be distinctly disappointing. A full discussion of this situation would hardly be appropriate here, but some outstanding observations might be mentioned in more detail in as far as they affect the Maze.

Robinson lists among the *sequelae* of lobotomy, a lack of personality depth, complacency, indifference to the feelings of others, absence of sense of guilt, and a reduction of the sense of self-continuity. Her subjects showed a very definite loss in "planning ability and the maintenance of set and prolonged attention." She was able in her investigation to use as her controls a small group (N 12) of fully recovered former mental patients who had not been operated upon. These tested 13.9 years by the Porteus Maze as against a mean of 10.6 years for lobotomized patients (N 68).

Carney Landis listed the three most commonly affected traits of personality changed by psychosurgery as being vigilance, zeal, and what he calls anguish. The last he described as "apprehensive dread, psychotic affect, psychic pain, intractable pain."[1] Quite obviously a person's style of response is likely to be dominated by the presence of such distressful and emotional preoccupations, and if these are removed by psychosurgery, the patient's personality will be radically changed. "Zeal" we would identify with *initiative,* and the tendency to use vigilance is to my mind the temperamental characteristic that is plainly demonstrated by the Maze Test. The removal of anguish from the patient clears the way for better test performance.

Partridge (1950), an English authority on the subject, wrote a book based on a personal survey of 300 patients. He sums up the commonly observed "personality changes" as inertia, reduced affect, diminished restraint, restricted interest, avoidance of effort and discomfort, and difficulties in conceptual thought. All of these effects of operation would together or singly change markedly the patient's style of behavior.

Landis, Zubin, and Mettler (1950) report that in spite of such a marked difference in characteristic behavior "various projective tests, including the Rorschach, disclosed no regularly appearing change even in those patients who recovered from psychoses."

In her studies of the people of Alor, Dr. Cora Du Bois (1944) gave Rorschach examinations to 57 subjects and submitted them to "blind" analysis by a well-known authority in this field. Unfortunately, there is reason to suspect that these analyses were colored by what the analyst thought was the typical behavior of primitive subjects. For example, primary color reactions were interpreted as expressing "unrestrained impulsiveness. . . . They are suspicious and distrustful, they are so not only toward everything that is unknown and new to them, such as foreigners, for instance, but also among themselves." He uses such terms as indifferent, listless, disliking effort or strain, unrestrained, deceitful, cheating, making no distinction between *mine* and *thine.* This, it must be admitted, is a typical "blind analysis" of character by someone who has had no personal contact with untutored peoples, and is the common view of most white men who have neither the wish nor opportunity to understand primitive man. A typical characterization of a native by his prejudiced exploiter is that he is a lazy, thieving savage.

[1] *Vide, Proceedings Third Research Conference on Psychosurgery,* 1954, p. 83.

As viewed from a highly civilized viewpoint, much of this criticism is probably just, but not only because the primitive group is "capsulated" by its environmental and cultural milieu. Our understanding of primitive ideas is just as capsulated by our environmental conditioning. The savage is necessarily more practical than theoretical, his generalizing ability being restricted because he is still in a prescientific stage of thinking. He has excellent reasons for being distrustful of strangers, especially whites, but is probably not a whit more distrustful of us than we are of him. If the Alorese are like the Australids, they are listless or unwilling to exert themselves on the white man's projects, but are lacking neither in energy nor initiative in pursuing their own purposes. As regards their own cultural belongings, savages make very clear distinctions between "mine and thine." After bitter experience of the white intruders' disrespect for native property rights as regards land, water sources, native game, and even his women, it is no wonder that the aboriginal pays back by spearing cattle and an occasional human.

Civilized observers have sometimes remarked upon aboriginal stupidity in not being lost in wonder at such marvels as the modern airplane and other mechanical inventions. But the white explorer gets lost in the bush and has to be rescued. He cannot read animal tracks or "spoors," nor use a boomerang or spear-thrower, skills that a native child can master. If there were such a thing as an Australid Rorschach expert, should we be surprised if he reversed the judgment so that we rather than the Alorese or Australids "come close to moral insanity?" If this verdict is founded on Rorschach responses, then these latter have been falsely interpreted. It is perhaps idle to compare the sanity of cultural groups, but it is my belief that considering his background of experience, the savage is as sane as we are.

My chief criticism of the Rorschach approach is its limited experimental relationships in interpretations. Reactions to supposedly unstructured inkblots cannot help but be influenced or conditioned by personal experience. Nevertheless, as far as it goes, the Rorschach procedure appears to be a fairly valid approach. The claim has been advanced that this technique is "capable of yielding information about the personality as a whole, the personality organization, and a wide variety of personality traits." According to Wells, it attempts to answer questions as to where the subject looks for his meanings and what meaning does he find. Whether the answers it supplies are true is a matter for much more complete experiment than has yet been provided. In any case, validation supplied by the patient's own ideas as to his personality is inadequate evidence of Rorschach diagnostic verdicts.

It seems to me that the same objection that applies to the Binet type of tests of intelligence has weight with regard to the rationale of the Rorschach, namely, that its view of personality, like that of Binet intelligence, is too restricted. When using a Binet type of test, psychologists are still dogged by the half-truth that the tongue, *par excellence,* is the organ of cleverness. It is true that a general I.Q. of 135 or more cannot possibly be assigned except by dependence on unusual language facility. "Genius" under an I.Q. definition is thus confined to those who deal most effectively with words. In this present day and age, the scientist seems to need much more the understanding of mathematical formulas and their application to technology. Probably all the verbalizing ability he needs is basic English and the practised use of his own kit of technical terms. Therefore, an intelligence test based solely upon verbal ability is not a valid method of measurement for a significantly influential portion of the world's population.

The Rorschach test is similarly invalidated. In the first place, personality expresses itself in action just as much as in perception. In the second, any measurement of personality is further restricted in that the subject's responses are wholly verbal. Just as intelligence is expressed by what a person does as well as by what he says, so is personality. Surely a man reveals his predispositions as much by the way he does a job as by how well he makes a speech, or interprets an inkblot.

The Maze as a projective device may fall short of indicating job efficiency; in other words, the social value to be attached to derived scores is yet to be determined. Briefly described, this Maze approach shows the degree of the subject's tendency to perseverate subconsciously in the execution of a repeated Maze performance. Actually, this tendency to self-consistency is inherent in the theory of mental testing in general. If S can repeat seven digits in order on one examining occasion, we assume that he can do so on the next. If he reacts imaginatively in a certain way to color, form, or movement in a Rorschach inkblot, we assume that his next response to the same material will approach uniformity. This means that he has a deeply engraved way of looking at things, and this may be interpreted clinically. The proof of this last assumption is what we call validation.

As regards the Maze Test, the tendency towards perseveration in executive details was discovered quite by accident. In a study by John Barclay,[2] which was initiated by Dr. Bernard Bloom, chief psychologist at the Hawaii State Hospital at Kaneohe, the same battery of tests that had been used in the Columbia-Greystone projects and had been found sensitive to psychosurgery was replicated.

In looking over this double set of Maze responses, the present writer was struck with the outstanding resemblances between some of the paired performances, notwithstanding the fact that routine administration of chlorpromazine had intervened during the time interval of over a month between the two testings. When the names and other identifying marks were concealed and the designs shuffled, it was found possible to match the two separate performances correctly in 60 per cent of instances. This was done by comparing the type of turns made in threading the Maze and the style of beginning and ending the test design.

While it was found that these similarities in execution extended to every test throughout the whole series of Mazes, it was not necessary for matching purposes to use more than the XI year test. Later still it was discovered that we could match with an even more restricted sample, namely, the lines from the beginning point "S" in the center, up to and including the second opening in the design, together with consideration of similarities in beginning and ending the test.

The experiment was then extended to delinquent boys and girls. It was found that their performances could be individually matched in upwards of 90 per cent of instances and that this was true of nondelinquents in a slightly smaller percentage (Porteus, 1959). Using the records of adult criminals, the same success in matching by two examiners was apparent. Differences in "matching" successes existing between different scorers were due to the fact that in the later work there was a change in emphasis with regard to the importance of endings and the allotment of additional points for general resemblances.

The reason for considering the whole process as projective was the degree to which the adhesion to a set pattern was subconscious.

2 Unpublished paper.

It must be remembered that in the majority of performances S's attention is centered almost wholly on finding his way through the Maze, and that consequently he is somewhat indifferent to the fine points of execution. Questioning as to where he actually began the tracing, whether on the "S" or how much short of it, showed that it had not been impressed on his conscious attention, nor was there any recollection of the type of turn when he changed direction. Moreover, in case we wished to use the same individual for additional experimentation, we had to be careful to keep such questioning at a minimum. Once attention had been directed towards details of performance, the consistency of type of execution increased. The only cases wherein there was evidence of conscious attention to the style of performance were those individuals who made a large number of right-angled turns. The ordinary examinee seemed to be concerned wholly with finding his way out of the Maze and not with how he marked his course.

It is noteworthy that Foulds in England found that careful right angle turns were characteristic of psychoneurotic obsessionals. Reference to quotations from Fould's paper cited in Chapter 4 will show that obsessionals exhibit slow tempo, few gross errors of direction and lifted pencils, with "firm straight lines down the center of the channel and careful, right-angled cornering, with consequently very few crossed lines." Our subsequent work in matching performances of adult criminals in Oahu Prison indicated that this type of response is also more typical of recidivists as compared with infrequent offenders. In one case a two-year interval elapsed before the design for Year XI was repeated, but the second performance was very easily identified as the work of the same individual.

One other justification for regarding perseveration of patterns in successive performances as a phenomenon of subconscious memory is the fact that retention follows the laws of trends similar to those of ordinary conscious memory. If an interval of two months instead of 15 minutes was allowed to elapse between the first and second applications of the two XI year designs, the pattern tended to fade with time, just as is the case with consciously remembered activities. In normal individuals, only about 35 per cent of performances could then be correctly identified, a decline from 90 per cent of correct matchings if the second trial followed after a 15-minute interval. However, when the longer interval was allowed to elapse between re-examinations of delinquents, the fading was much less pronounced than with normals. The percentage correctly matched fell to 70, a decline of 20 per cent, whereas in the nondelinquent group there was the much greater decline of 55 per cent of matchable records. This suggests that subconscious memory operates more strongly in delinquency; in other terms, delinquents are more set in their ways than nondelinquents. As we all know, delinquent conduct is most difficult to correct by precept and example, probably because of this closer adherence to self-established patterns of behavior. The determination of the frequency of occurrence of this phenomenon of subconscious perseveration was established on the basis of attempted matching of 680 pairs of individual performances. These cases consisted of normals, juvenile delinquents, adult criminals, feebleminded, and psychotics; and in some of these groups sexes were segregated. The net result was that approximately ten per cent of these individuals showed so few similarities, according to our system of inspection, that their two separate performances could not be identified as the work of the same person. In other words, there was no recognizable pattern of response. Of the 90 per cent who could be matched, about 60 per cent of them could be paired easily, and 30 per cent with increasing difficulty. The matching process has been previously described (Porteus *et al*, 1960). In the performances of many persons the pattern was repeated so closely that they might just as well have appended their signatures.

But as was pointed out at the time, to demonstrate the phenomenon was one thing, to fit it into a scoring system was another. Judgments of the degree of resemblance of two corresponding turns in a Maze design, or the similarity of the final strokes of the pencil at the exit, are naturally somewhat subjective, though a better agreement of raters could be achieved with the aid of what we called "ground rules" and illustrations of pairings. Various methods of increasing reliability of scoring were suggested, among them I.B.M. scanning (Porteus and Diamond, 1960). Unfortunately, it was not practicable at this stage to utilize this method. Actually, the correlations between three raters' scores ranged from .87 to .94, using the system of scoring paired resemblances. The system of allotting scoring points was as described hereunder, and the process is facilitated by the charts shown in the accompanying Figures. Test designs illustrated are from the Extension Series.

Under this system the highest allotment of points was for the most complete adherence to the structuring of the Maze design. The subject began both performances exactly on or within 1/32 of an inch of the "S" which signifies the starting point in the XI year Maze; he drew as nearly midway between the parallel lines of the design as he could, and made his turns or changes in direction at corners or in passing through openings with almost exact right angles. Examples of meticulosity or perfectionism are rare, but a few cases approach that standard. Facsimile reproductions in the two performances will be achieved more directly in completely right-angled drawing.

When working on the scoring system, we debated long and earnestly the question as to whether an almost exact facsimile performance based, however, on carefully executed curves rather than angles, should not also be allotted equally high points. Such a pair of performances is illustrated in Figures 1 and 2. However, though this swinging around the turns is a quite logical progression, it is less responsive to the structure of the design than is a right-angled performance, and therefore earns a slightly lower total score.

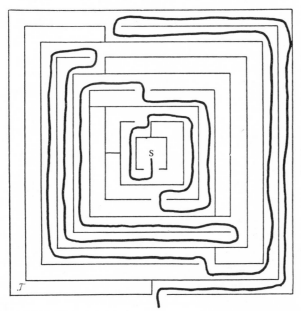

Fig. 1. First Performance Year XI (Non-delinquent girl)

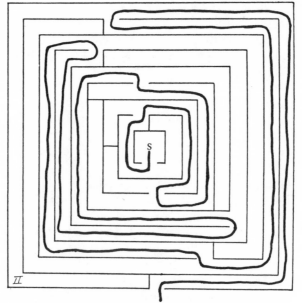

FIG. 2. Second Performance Year XI (Non-delinquent girl)

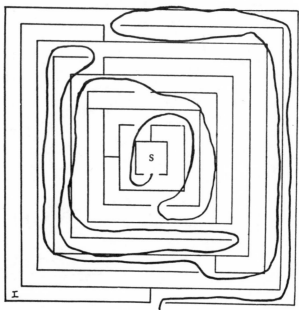

FIG. 3. First Performance Year XI (Delinquent girl)

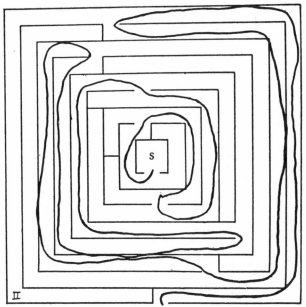

Fig. 4. Second Performance Year XI (Delinquent girl)

Exact or nearly exact right-angle turns are allotted 4 points for each pair. Exactly similar or near similar surves earn 3½ points.

It should be noted that regularity is not the sole feature in matchability as may be discovered from examination of Figures 3 and 4, which show the paired performances of a delinquent girl, the similarity of pattern being easily apparent. Scored in detail (up to the second opening), these have been allotted points according to the system set forth in an article by Porteus, Barclay, Culver, and Kleman (1960).

The points allotted to paired resemblances in performance were called at one time "Consistency-Flexibility" (C-F) scores. Later on we theorized that the extremes of scoring represented deviant individuals. At the low end were those who tended to be unsystematic and were minimally influenced by the structuring of the test design suggested by the parallel guide lines of the test design. At the top end of the distribution were persons of the opposite temperament, those who were somewhat stimulus-bound, over-meticulous, too subservient to system, and inclined to be inflexible. Thus, we would have at the extreme low end the disorganized and at the high end the more compulsive individuals. Since consistency and flexibility both had favorable connotations, which we wished to avoid, it was determined to call the scores conformity-variability (C-V) measures, terms with more neutral meanings, and to regard the middle range scores as normal or ordinary. These medium scores indicated reasonable adherence rather than rigid devotion to Pts.

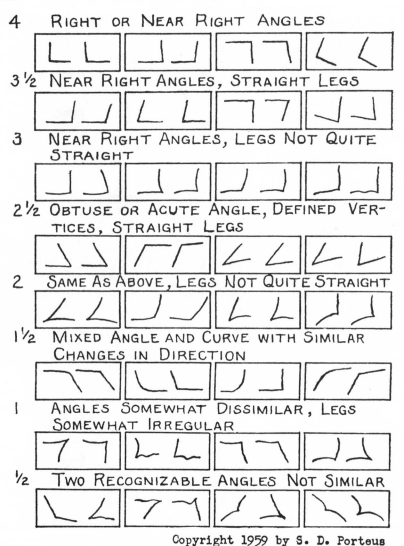

FIG. 5. C-V Scoring Rules and Samples (Similarities)

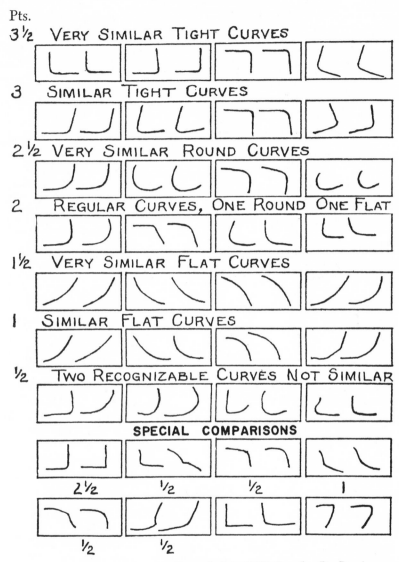

Fig. 6. C-V Scoring Rules and Samples (Similarities)

a pattern of performance, or put otherwise, moderate flexibility. Differentiating personalities along these lines could be of real advantage in clinical assessment.

Though the problem of social value of C-V scores has not been

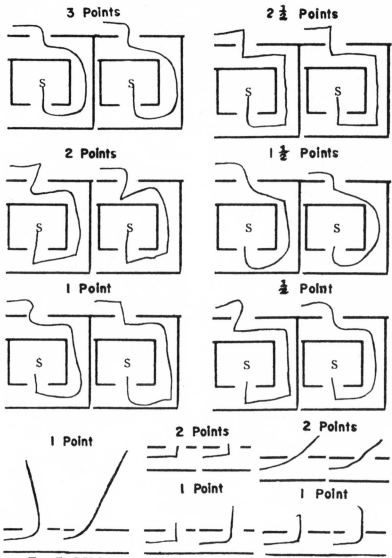

FIG. 7. C-V Scoring Rules and Samples (General Similarities)

resolved by reference to an external criterion, interesting results have been obtained with various groups. With psychotic patients it appeared that routine chlorpromazine medication tended to fixate or re-enforce the repetitive tendency. After a two-month interval between testings, an experimental group did not show the expected fading phenomenon but exhibited a small gain in C-V scores, indicating greater conformity. On the other hand, the mean of the control group revealed a loss of 3.75 points of score. The sum of the differences was 5.08 points (p < .001), using McNemarr's method of evaluating net changes.

On the basis of the idea that the pioneer or the explorer in new territory does not reach his objective without many false starts and misdirections, it is well worthwhile for him to leave behind him some kind of blazed trail, with indications as to which courses lead to blind endings. Future travellers may be saved a great deal of lost effort thereby. In our excursions into the somewhat novel field of the use of part of the XI year Maze as a projective index, we followed the usual course of making comparisons of the scores of various groups, divided by ethnic ancestry, social maladjustment, and sex, only to find that the study of the various means did not advance our knowledge to any very marked degree.

If there is any parallel between subconscious motor expression and other physical and physiological activities over which we do not ordinarily exercise conscious control, it would not be surprising if the comparison of means failed to yield significant differences. Pulse rate, respiration, body temperature are examples of vital activities which are carried on by the automatic nervous system and of which we are only subconsciously aware. The only value, it would seem, in the establishment of norms for these conditions would be to discover the clinical significance of deviations. Once the physician finds that his patient's pulse rate falls consistently between, say, 66 and 78, he looks elsewhere for symptoms of disease. Since subconsciously controlled functions are those that are most immediately essential to survival, there is likely to be a narrow normal range. Thus, the mere fact of being human brings us closer, quantitatively speaking, to our fellow men.

Consequently, if, as we have theorized, the phenomenon of self-consistency in patterns of drawing through a Maze is subconscious as regards ordinary memory and attention, the averages for different groups should differ little; on the other hand, if the activity demands a maximum of conscious attention, then the means of performance could be expected to be wider apart. We have earlier in this volume demonstrated that the average test age in the Maze varies widely as between, for example, Kalahari

Bushmen and Australid aborigines. What is the situation with regard to C-V scores?

Among populations where the use of pencil and paper is common, we find a close grouping of means, regardless of social behavior. For example, for adult criminals in a Hawaiian prison (N 72), the mean C-V score was 15 with 87.5 per cent falling between the limits of 10 and 21 points. Nor did it make much difference if the group were divided into recidivists, serving long sentences, or new arrivals (orientation group) at the prison. Three groups of differing ethnic origins also were found to be closely similar. Part-Hawaiian male high school students (N 53) averaged 14 points, Chinese males 13.7, Japanese males 13.6. Actually, one group of Australids (N 23) in Central Australia scored somewhat lower, with a mean of 12.2 points, probably due to unfamiliarity with the use of paper and pencil. The more acculturated Arunta group averaged 15.7 C-V points. In all groups, distribution percentages falling between 10 and 21 were very similar: 87 for the Australids, 87 for the part-Hawaiians, 82 for the Japanese males, and 79 for the Chinese. Thus, geographical position, education, and social conformity made little difference, with common humanity over-riding all other considerations, and the data tending rather strongly to confirm our belief that the activity in question is subconsciously operated.

Further evidence of the levelling influence of subconscious trends was provided by two groups of girls and boys committed to a correctional facility, most of whom were part-Hawaiians. Males (N 27) averaged 13.6 points, females (N 24) 14 points. A somewhat lesser concentration between 10 and 21 points is indicated by percentages of 74 and 71 respectively, falling between those limits.

It would seem obvious that the main concern of clinical psychologists is not with run-of-the-mill cases but with the deviants, just as in the case of intelligence ratings. If an individual's test quotient falls between 85 and 115, that fact has little educational, social, or psychological significance. If above or below those limits, the chances that he is exceptional are much greater. But again the warning against accepting a single I.Q., or one devised from an inadequately validated battery, should be repeated.

Because of Foulds' observation with regard to obsessional cases, we are inclined to view the percentages falling distinctly above the "normal" limits as marking down the deviant or exceptional.

As will be seen from the data of Table 6, the largest percentages of high C-V scores were for females, a close male group (7%) being the adult criminals. This may have been due to the inclusion of recidivists, who are likely to be somewhat compulsive in behavior. Yet even so, their percentage of scores above 21 was only half that of nondelinquent females.

Table 6

Conformity-Variability Scores

Group	N	Mean	S.D.	Per cent —10	Per cent 10-21	Per cent +21
Adult Criminals Males	72	15	3.85	5.5	87.5	7.0
Part-Hawaiian Males	53	14	3.26	7.5	87.0	5.5
Japanese Males	50	13.6	4.23	12.0	82.0	6.0
Chinese Males	34	13.7	4.25	17.6	79.4	3.0
Yuendumu Males	23	12.2	3.14	13.0	87.0	0
Hermannsburg Males	23	15.7	3.5	4.3	87.0	8.7
Koolau Males (delinquents)	27	12.7	4.84	18.5	74.0	7.5
Waimano Males	20	13.8	4.90	15.0	80.0	5.0
Part-Hawaiian Females	54	16.2	5.15	7.4	76.0	16.7
Japanese Females	49	16.6	4.68	4.0	82.0	14.3
Chinese Females	42	15.4	4.99	11.7	74.0	14.3
Kawailoa Females (delinquents)	24	14.88	4.86	17.0	71.0	12.0
Waimano Females	21	15.95	5.66	7.7	76.3	19.0

Without further information derived from external criteria, we cannot attach social values to this tendency. It does appear, however, that neatness, orderliness, and conformity to the structuring of the test seem more characteristic of females than males. For the present, the extreme C-V scores should be recorded even though they cannot as yet be interpreted in terms of value judgments.

The next steps in research should lie in the direction of examining developmental trends in C-V scores by age, intelligence, education, racial origin, etc. If, as we suppose, these scores do indicate trends such as fixity of patterns, we certainly would like to know whether degrees of self-consistency, devotion to self-standards of behavior, and conservatism are more characteristic of the old than the young, and whether, for example, there are unsettled or unstable periods in men and women when fixity of ideas becomes less or greater. But, as earlier indicated, I believe that much more will be learned from deviant individuals than from run-of-the-mill cases.

Another relationship could be quite easily examined. This is the possible relation of conscious to subconscious memory. We certainly would like to know whether the subconscious contribution to conscious rote memory is important. But there is little need to suggest problems to psychologists, who are far better at propounding questions than answering them. The clinical psychologist, more than his experimental or developmental colleagues, must devote himself to the understanding of the unaverage or exceptional.

That there are no longer opportunities to judge whether psychosurgery would bring about changes in habitual ways of response as indicated in C-V scores must remain a matter for not unmixed regret. However, there can be other means of validation. It would be most interesting, for example, to persuade women to classify themselves in housekeeping ability and to have friends or relatives rate them also for comparison with C-V scores. Business men, also, might entertain questionnaires dealing with their methodical habits. The exploration of other types of compulsiveness, such as alcoholics, or other individuals classified by a dichotomy of political attitudes, liberalism versus conservatism, etc., might also shed light on the subject of rigidity in thought patterns. Whether from the standpoint of confirming or rejecting theories of the usefulness or otherwise of the C-V approach, the fact that it represents a new dimension in projective measures will, I trust, prove a challenge to psychologists. For those wishing to do experimental work in this field, information as to scoring methods has been set forth by the present writer (1960).

SUMMARY

The question of the significance of Conformity-Variability represents what is unfortunately "a loose end." The Rorschach Test is by its nature somewhat restricted as an adequate index of personality. It has to do only with visual perception and interpretation, which is only one outlook on life. It is dependent upon verbal reports by the subject and leaves out any appraisal of his "doing" capacity.

The manner of discovery of the fact that motor-expressive perseveration can be demonstrated by details of Maze Test execution is described, and the reasons for regarding it as a projective phenomenon discussed. The method of scoring is set forth.

The subconscious element in performance is compared by analogy with subconsciously controlled or mediated activities in physical and physiological functions. The fact that means and distribution of scores tend to be restricted as between ethnic, educational, and behavioral groups is interpreted as evidence for the subconscious nature of the newly demonstrated human trend, which is an expression of our common humanity.

The importance of the deviant individual to clinical psychology is touched upon, and the difficulties in the way of a conventional correlation approach are acknowledged. Suggestions for further work and the possibility of setting up relevant behavioral rating scales as external criteria are mentioned.

CHAPTER TWELVE

Porteus Maze Test: Application and Scoring

The Maze Test has currently three forms, known as the Original series or Vineland Revision (Porteus, 1919a, 1933b, 1950, 1959c), the Extension (Porteus, 1955b), and the Supplement (Porteus, 1959a). It should be clearly understood that these are not alternative but supplementary series. The last two forms have been so devised and standardized as to give equivalent scores if applied in the order given above. The object in providing the three forms was to eliminate (or control) practice effects in such situations where the experimenter desired to repeat the tests. One example is research into the effects of drugs, whether stimulant, depressive or tranquilizing. Other kinds of therapy might call for reexamination to measure cumulative effects. Had there been practice-controlled forms available while psychosurgery was in fashion, the error of regarding postoperational effects as transient would have been avoided.

The only series which is standardized from three years upwards is the Original. Because older subjects are much more often involved in therapeutic treatment and research, the Extension and the Supplement series begin with the VII Year design. Since the individuals to whom it is usually applied are older adolescents or adults, and have already worked through the Original series, they are familiar with the appearance of the test designs and know what is required of them. Therefore, leading up to the more difficult test items through experience with the simpler tasks set for young children is no longer necessary.

Summarized in the barest outline, the chronology of Maze Test publications is as follows:

The earliest test series, 1915.

A partially revised form with variations of scoring, The Vineland Revision, 1919.

A small book entitled *Guide to the Porteus Maze Test,* containing also Adult designs I and II, 1924.

A second book entitled *The Maze Test and Mental Differences,* 1933.

A monograph under the title of *Qualitative Performance in the Maze Test,* 1942.

A third book, *The Porteus Maze Test and Intelligence,* reproducing the tests with modification of instructions to allow of qualitative scoring, 1950 (reprinted in 1956).

A monograph, *The Maze Test: Recent Advances,* giving the standardization of the Extension Series, 1955.

A fourth book, *The Maze Test and Clinical Psychology,* containing the Original and Extension series, as scored for test age and qualitatively, with new and formerly current tables of test quotients, 1959.

The Porteus Maze, Supplement Series, 1959, standardized against the Extension Series.

The present volume contains the three current series, Original, Extension and Supplement, setting forth variations in scoring and administration, with particular reference to application to primitive subjects in 1963. For the first time the three forms of the test are now printed together, and include the newest, most concise instructions for their application, the qualitative scoring and the tables of test quotients in current use.

That such a variety of references and cross references has been presented will not be surprising when it is remembered that the Porteus Maze Test has now been in use for fifty years and that during that time there have been some important modifications, not sufficient in extent, however, to change radically the appearance and character of the tests. In other words, the instrument, somewhat crude or tentative in 1914, has experienced further development and evolution by 1965. Changes that have taken place have come about through diversity in its environment of use or application in different fields, such as are described in this book. Without these developments and varied applications in some of psychology's most uncertain areas of functioning, the Porteus Maze Test would not have achieved any maturity or longevity. It is the importance of the problems rather than the qualities of the measure that have ensured its survival and may favor its continuance. Where complete illumination is not possible, mankind uses what light there is.

But without uniformity of form and method, only confusion can result. *It should be emphasized that the method and rules set forth herein are an essential part of the tests themselves.* In other words, the rules make the game. Any methodological change, i.e., giving only one trial at each age level instead of the number prescribed, or adopting a different form of instructions given to the subject, could change the results in such a way that it would no longer be the Porteus Maze Test that is being applied. Strict adherence to the rules is therefore most decidedly recommended, with only such minor departures from method as are approved in the test.

General Rules

Using the Original Series, children under six years of age begin the testing with the design for Year III. With older cases, unless mental deficiency is suspected, the testing begins at Year V. For timid or withdrawn subjects, with primitive individuals or special cases where the language used in instructions is a barrier to understanding the V and VI Year tests can be used for practice. Not until the latter maze design is performed correctly without help should the testing and the scoring of trials go on to the design for Year VII.

In the Extension and Supplement series there are no test designs below VII, and since the individual has already done the Original series, no practice or demonstration is allowed.

With a primitive adult or adolescent, or a frightened child of any ethnic group, it is permissible to have other persons familiar to him in the room, but only while demonstration and practice are in progress. When the Year VII test has been reached, arrangements should be made for observers to withdraw. Only in very rare instances should a parent or friend be allowed to remain and in that case he should sit in such a position as to be unable to see the subject's performance. Verbal comment should be strictly forbidden. Any help, verbal or otherwise, simply makes the subject more dependent.

Every effort should be made to establish a good relationship between the examiner and subject before the testing begins. When a strange adult, a teacher, or a person of a culture alien to the subject applies the tests, special efforts should be taken to establish this *rapport.*

The instructions for application and performance must be strictly adhered to. There are several errors commonly committed by examiners who are beginners in the use of the Maze. The first is leniency in applying the rule that no blind alley may be entered. Crossing by the width of an imaginary penciled line blocking off the entrance constitutes an unsuccessful trial. It is quite common for a subject to make a slight deviation or turn opposite an opening as if intending to enter the blind alley, but if he corrects it in time, only the qualitative error of "changed direction" (CD) is recorded, and the test continues. If, however, the imaginary line is crossed, the test design is immediately removed and an unsuccessful trial is recorded.[1]

Another mistake in application is for the examiner to neglect to invert and repeat a test design if, after the subject has failed in the allotted number of trials in the test for the previous year, he succeeds in passing the next higher test. The rule is that this success —in case it was accidental—is not accepted. The test is reversed and the worse performance of the two presentations, ordinary or inverted, is recorded for scoring purposes. If, for example, a child fails Year X but passes the XI Year test in one trial, the XI Year must be inverted. If he required two trials, a half year is deducted from his score. Failure is recorded if there are two unsuccessful trials below XII, or four in tests above that level.

A third examining mistake is to point out the opening at the end of the VIII Year or a higher test. Frequently the individual will ask, "Where do I get out"? Except in the case of the V, VI and VII Year designs, the subject should be quietly told that he must find his own way out.[2]

Tracing the course with the pencil or finger in the air over the maze is strictly forbidden, as this amounts to a trial or an overt prehearsal. If the subject persists, he should be told to keep his hand by his side until he is ready to begin drawing through the maze.

Detailed Instructions

The examiner, preferably sitting opposite the subject, holds the top of the test design with the tips of his fingers so that it cannot

[1] The inexperienced examiner will sometimes excuse his leniency by saying that the subject allowed his pencil to slip. He has, however, no right to make any assumption of accidental error. Special cases, such as individuals with tremors or partial paralysis, may be accorded lenient treatment in regard to the above rule, but in their case only approximate test ages are expected or attainable.

[2] For very primitive subjects the VIII Year exit may be pointed out.

be shifted in position. The surface of the table should be smooth and a moderately soft lead pencil of medium sharpness should be provided.[3]

YEAR III. The examiner says:

"I want to see whether you can draw all around between these lines without crossing or touching them with the pencil. You draw just like this."

The examiner demonstrates a slow and careful drawing performance between the guide lines, beginning at the arrow and proceeding just around the first angle. He then places a new blank design on the table and hands the pencil to the child. Every encouragement should be given, and in some cases where necessary the examiner should put his hand on the child's so as to guide it around the first angle in the design. Three trials are allowed and the subject is allotted 3 year credit if on any trial not more than three lines are crossed.

YEAR IV. The examiner says:

"Do this the same way. Begin here (indicating starting arrow) and draw right around without crossing any of the printed lines."

Three trials are allowed, and after the second trial, the examiner may point out places where the lines were touched or crossed. Four year credit is allotted if on any trial there were not more than three line crossings.

YEAR V. The examiner says:

"This is what is called a maze and you must draw with your pencil like this." (Examiner takes the pencil and draws about 1.5 inches of the course from the starting arrow near the rat to around the first turn:) "These lines are all supposed to be walls and this rat went in here (indicating arrow) to try and get some cheese." (Point to cheese at the end of the maze.) "Now I want you to draw a line showing me where the rat went to find the cheese. But you must be very careful not to cross any lines or to go into any place that is blocked at the other end. If you go into any blocked place, you cannot turn around and come out. You must start all over again with a new maze.

"One more thing you must remember—you can stop anywhere and look as long as you like, but try not to lift your pencil off the paper until you have drawn right to the end of the maze."

---

[3] A somewhat blunt pencil should be supplied by the examiner. If the point is too sharp, it may dig into the paper or it may make it easier for the subject to avoid touching the lines, an item that is scored qualitatively.

Two trials are allowed.

YEAR VI. The examiner says:

"This is another maze. Begin here and show me where the rat went to get the cheese. But do not cross any lines or go into any blocked places."

Two trials are allowed.

Note: The V Year and the VI Year tests are used for demonstration and forepractice in the testing of older illiterates or primitive subjects. For these individuals the reader is recommended to follow in general the procedures outlined in Dr. Gregor's field notes in Chapter 9. However, allowing observers in the testing area is not recommended except for the practice or demonstration designs. If subjects can be gathered together where the examiner can demonstrate to the group the V and VI Year designs on a blackboard, that is an excellent way to smooth out misunderstandings and obtain *rapport*. In many examining situations this is impossible, but in either group or individual demonstrations, Gregor's introduction or some similar explanation is suitable, using pidgin English or dumb show. Miming can also be used with the deaf or in cases with extreme language difficulties.

YEAR VII. In the Original series for more sophisticated older children not under any suspicion of mental defect, this design is the starting point of the Maze Test application. It also marks the beginning of the Extension and Supplement forms, in which tests for years lower than VII are not provided.

For older individuals the "rat and cheese" introduction is no longer needed by way of explanation of the test. For cases who have already worked through the simpler mazes, there is, of course, no need to repeat the instructions. Otherwise, the VII Year test is introduced in the following terms.

The examiner says:

"I want you to suppose that this is a maze in the form of a street map. All the lines are stone walls. You can imagine, if you like, that you are walking or driving a car in here (examiner points to starting point marked S) and you have to find your way out here (examiner points to exit arrow). But you must be very careful not to bump into any of the walls nor go into any blocked street, because if you do so you cannot turn around or back out. So if you go into a blind street, you must start all over again.

"This is not a speed test. You can stop anywhere as long as you like while you decide which way to go, but try not to lift the pencil off the paper until you are right outside the maze, and don't bump into any walls. Start as soon as you are ready."

Two trials are allowed.

YEARS VIII, IX, X. The examiner says:

"Begin here and find your way out." (Examiner points to the starting arrow, *but not to the exit.*)

Two trials are allowed in each test design.

YEAR XI. The examiner says:

"Begin here in the center and find your way out."

Two trials are allowed.

YEARS XII, XIV, AND ADULT I. The examiner repeats the instruction: "Begin here in the center and find your way out."

Four trials are allowed in the XII, XIV, and Adult tests.

Note: As the tests get more difficult, it will sometimes happen, particularly in the Adult test, that the subject will pause and say, "There's no way out." If at the same time he lifts his pencil, this is scored as an unsuccessful trial, even though he may be on the right course, and the test blank is removed. If he does not lift his pencil after making this remark, the examiner should wait a couple of seconds and then remove the design, substituting a new blank and proceeding with the testing until the allotted number of trials for that Year have been given.

SCORING PROCEDURES

Continue testing until all the designs of a series have been successfully worked through within the allowable number of trials. At any point where a subject draws through an imaginary line across the entrance to a blind street or alley, the design is removed and an "unsuccessful trial," *not a failure*, is recorded. Failure is recorded only if this takes place after the number of trials allowed in the rules has occurred—two in each test design up to and including Year XI, four in the XII, XIV, and Adult. Testing and scoring normally cease after three failures anywhere in the series have been recorded, or two successive failures in Year XI or above.

Occasionally, especially with delinquents, when a complete qualitative record is desired, the rule of discontinuing the testing after three tests have been failed may be relaxed. For example, a subject who failed at IX, XI, and XIV Year levels may be given a chance to do the Adult test. This extra performance is discarded in the test age scoring but can be used in the qualitative score. Delinquents are thus given the chance to augment their chance to accumulate the penalties accruing by reason of Q-score errors.

Crossing or touching lines in the process of drawing is a qualitative, not a test age error, unless a blind alley is entered. Cutting across from one alley to the next to avoid drawing around to reach an opening is scored as a test age error and is at once recorded as an unsuccessful trial.

The general scoring rule is to take as the ceiling of the test the level of the highest test passed in the allowed number of trials, then deduct a half year for every unsuccessful trial. Since four trials are allowed in the XII, XIV, and Adult I test, a subject can lose or gain, according to the number of trials required on each, as much as two years in test age score on each of these higher tests. Below Year XII, since there are only two trials allowed in each test, each failure (i.e., two unsuccessful trials) incurs a loss of one year.

There are no separate designs for thirteen and fifteen years, but two-year credit can be earned if Years XII and XIV are passed on the first trial. If the subject has passed Year XII, but no higher test, his ceiling score from which deductions are made is 13 years. If he passes Year XIV, but fails the Adult, his ceiling is 15 years.

In the case of an inverted test (after failure in the test immediately preceding), the worse record of the two applications is used for scoring.

Among erroneous procedures occasionally followed by inexperienced examiners is that of allowing a subject more than the allotted trials. It is forbidden on the grounds that the extra practice may affect subsequent performance.

Scoring Example 1

Year	Trials	Deductions	Year	Trials	Deductions
VII	1		XI	1	
VIII	2	½ year	XII	2	½ year
IX	1		XIV	4	1½ years
X	2	½ year	Adult	2	½ year

Ceiling score = 17 years less 3½ years (7 unsuccessful trials); Test Age = 13½.

Scoring Example 2

Year		Trials	Deductions	Year		Trials	Deductions
VII		1		XI	Inverted	2	½ year
VIII		2	½ year	XII		Failed	2 years
IX		1		XIV		1	
X		Failed	1 year	XIV	Inverted	4	1½ years
XI		1		Adult		3	1 year

Ceiling score = 17 years less 6½ years (13 unsuccessful trials); Test Age = 10½. When a test is inverted, the worse performance is scored.

Scoring Example 3

Year		Trials	Deductions	Year	Trials	Deductions
VII		1		XI	Failed	
VIII		Failel	1 year	XII	Failed	
IX		2	½ year	XIV	3	No credit
IX	Inverted	1		Adult	3	No credit
X		1				

Highest test passed = 10 years less 1½ years; Test Age = 8½ years.
Test continued for qualitative scoring purpose, but no credit given for Adult and Year XIV successes, because of two successive failures in Years XI and XII.

Scoring Example 4

Year		Trials	Deductions	Year		Trials	Deductions
VII		1		XI		1	
VIII		1		XII		Failed	2 years
IX		Failed	1 year	XIV		2	
X		2	½ year	XIV	Inverted	2	½ year
X	Inverted	1		Adult		Failed	No credit

Ceiling score = 15 years less 4 years (8 unsuccessful trials); Test Age = 11 years.

Scoring Example 5

Year	Trials	Deductions	Year	Trials	Deductions
VII	1		XI	2	½ year
VIII	2	½year	XII	3	1 year
IX	2	½year	XIV	Failed	No credit
X	1		Adult	Failed	No credit

Ceiling score = 13 years less 2½ years (5 unsuccessful trials); Test Age = 10½ years.
Note: To convert test ages into IQ's, 14 years should be used as the divisor for cases at that age or above.

QUALITATIVE SCORING

The qualitative as distinct from the mental age scoring is concerned with errors in drawing or execution rather than in planning. In other words, it has to do with the subject's ability to follow instructions with regard to crossing lines and lifting the pencil, and also takes into account the general neatness of the performance and whether quantitative errors (blind street entrances) took place near the beginning or end of the test design. Qualitative scoring usually begins with Year VII.

The score is intended to reveal any haphazard, impulsive, or overconfident habits of action, or a tendency to become so absorbed in the task of finding the way out of the maze as to neglect other directions for executive performance. The weighting of errors is based on the comparative performance of delinquents, for whom the qualitative score was arranged.

No criticism of the performance is given by the examiner but every error in execution must be rigorously scored. Leniency may change the picture considerably. The higher the Q-score, the worse the record.

DETAILS OF SCORING

The following errors are marked on the face sheet, weighted as indicated and are then totalled for the qualitative score:

1. Any blind alley entrance (test age error) occurring in the first third (FT) of the design, i.e., at or before the arrow marked on each sample of a qualitatively scored maze. Weighting 2.
2. Any blind alley entrance occurring in the last third (LT) of the design, i.e., at or after the arrow marked on the sample mazes. Weighting 1.
3. Cut corner (CC). The error must occur while actually turning a corner. Weighting 1. (A line crossed near a corner but not related to turning is scored as a crossed line.)
4. Wherever the pencil mark *touches* a printed line in a maze, other than in turning a corner, it is scored as a crossed line (CL). Touching a line when going through an opening is similarly scored. Weighting 2.
5. Lifting the pencil (LP) except at the exit is a qualitative error.

The warning against lifting the pencil is given in the initial instructions for Test V (usually children 12 years of age or under) and in the instructions for Test VII with older cases. The warning should be repeated again after five lift pencils in a single test, or after a total of ten liftings in any combination of tests. This is the only allowable interruption on the part of the examiner while testing is in progress. The reason is to prevent the too early accumulation of error points up to the prescribed limits. Weighting 3.

6. "Wavy lines" (WL) are recorded against the subject if his general performance is as irregular in appearance or worse than the performance given as a scoring sample of the test in question. Weighting 2.
7. "Changed direction" (CD), formerly wrong direction (WD), is the notation made when it is evident that the subject started to go into a blocked path but avoided the error *before* crossing an imaginary line across a blind alley opening. Weighting 1.
8. Any qualitative error occurring in Tests VI and VII obtains an added penalty of one point for each such error. A place in the face sheet provides space for recording. Weighting 1.

The Q-score is the sum of the weighted scores in the above list, but there are two important restrictions. *The maximum weighted error score* recorded against any individual in any *single* type of error is 48. This means that only 24 crossed lines or 16 lift pencils are counted. It was found that in some cases, particularly delinquents, so many errors occurred that the score lost meaning for comparative purposes. There are no real distinctions between an individual scoring 100 and one scoring 150. For that reason the maximum recorded Q-score is 100.

Obviously, the subject should not be aware that his performance is being scored. However, the number of lift pencils in any single design should be counted and the notation LP followed by the number should be marked on each test design where they occurred. In some cases the individual lifts his pencil but puts it down again at the same place so that the full number of LPs might not be apparent by later inspection. The "lift pencils" can be summated at the end of the testing.

CHANGES IN FORMER PROCEDURES

In test age scoring, the rule regarding successive failures in two year tests now applies above Year IX instead of Year VIII. This gives some individuals a better chance to adjust to the Maze situation.

The table for reckoning test quotients in the Maze allows cases to obtain a maximum TQ of 135 at each age level. In my opinion, TQ's below 30 and above 135 are of little comparative significance. The practice of including months of chronological age in divisors to obtain ratios between mental ages and chronological ages also seems unnecessary, as it confers an air of exactitude that is not justifiable. In the tables of TQ's appearing in the present volume, chronological ages are given in half years up to and including ten years, in 12-month intervals thereafter.

MAZE TEST EXTENSION

The Maze Test Extension series consists of eight test designs published in 1955 so as to give scores equivalent to those of the Original or standard series. This extension was devised in order to control practice effects whenever it is necessary to repeat the Maze after an initial application. As an example of this use, we may instance studies of patients before and after some special therapeutic measures, such as psychosurgery or administration of tranquilizing drugs, where a practice-free form of the Maze is required.

EXTENSION SUPPLEMENT

A second practice-free series called the Extension Supplement has also now been standardized and published. Testing with the Extension and Supplement series begins at Year VII, and the instructions for application, scoring, and TQ reckoning are those set forth in the present volume.

Appendixes

Note: The scoring samples are intended to provide wavy lines (WL) illustrations with which the subject's performances may be compared. Wherever the latter are equal to or worse than the sample, then a wavy line is scored against him.

The first arrow indicates where, if a blind alley is entered at or before the position of the arrow, a "first third" (FT) should be scored; if he enters a blind alley at or after the second arrow, a "last third" (LT) should be scored against him.

Since it is so rarely necessary for subjects to be allotted Q-scores in the Supplement, no samples are given.

The tests are shown in the position in which they are presented to the subject, except when a test is inverted. See scoring Examples 2, 3, and 4.

The Maze Series reproduced in these Appendixes are covered by copyright of books of various dates—*The Maze Test and Mental Differences*, 1933, revised in 1950 (*The Maze Test and Intelligence*), and in 1959 (*The Maze Test and Clinical Psychology*); The Extension Series by *The Maze Test: Recent Advances* in 1955; the Supplement Series by *The Porteus Mazes: The Supplement Series* in 1959.

The samples redrawn herein are intended as aids to qualitative scoring only. They may differ in size and by the addition of arrows marking "First Third" and "Last Third" errors, etc. from the standard forms distributed by The Psychological Corporation, 304 East 45th Street, New York, N.Y., from which they may be ordered. These last named are correct in form and position.

257

PORTEUS MAZE TESTS — VINELAND REVISION

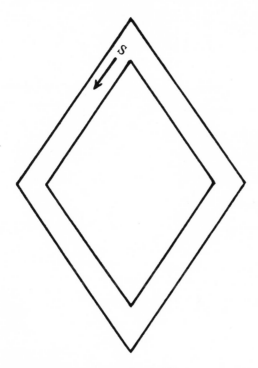

PORTEUS TESTS — VINELAND REVISION   YEAR III

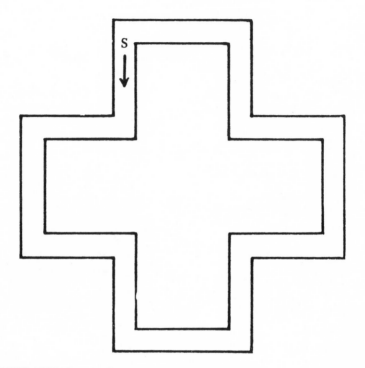

PORTEUS TESTS — VINELAND REVISION   YEAR IV

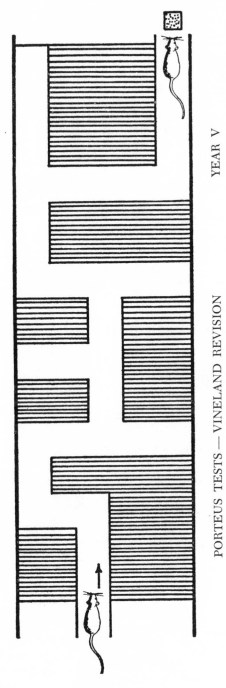

PORTEUS TESTS — VINELAND REVISION   YEAR V

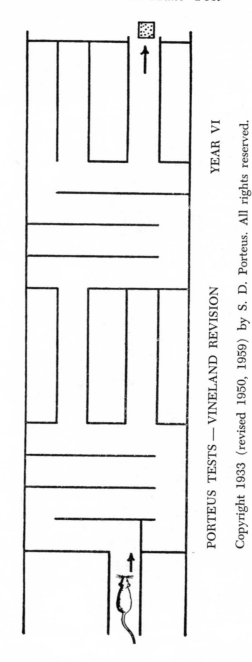

PORTEUS TESTS — VINELAND REVISION   YEAR VI

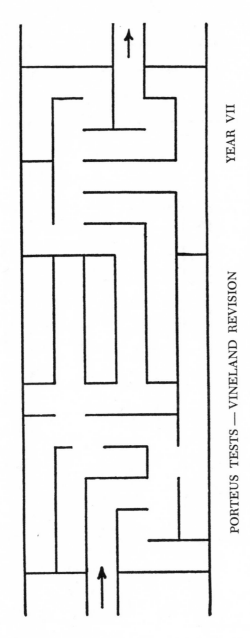

PORTEUS TESTS — VINELAND REVISION   YEAR VII

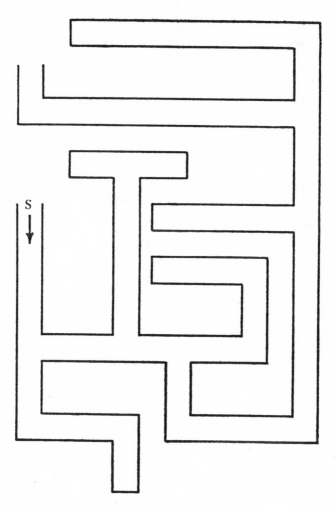

PORTEUS TESTS — VINELAND REVISION   YEAR VIII

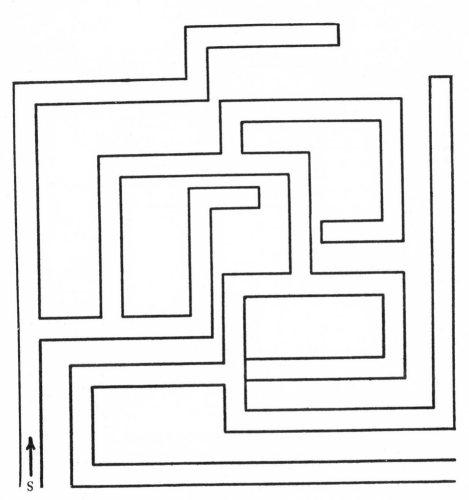

S

PORTEUS TESTS — VINELAND REVISION   YEAR IX

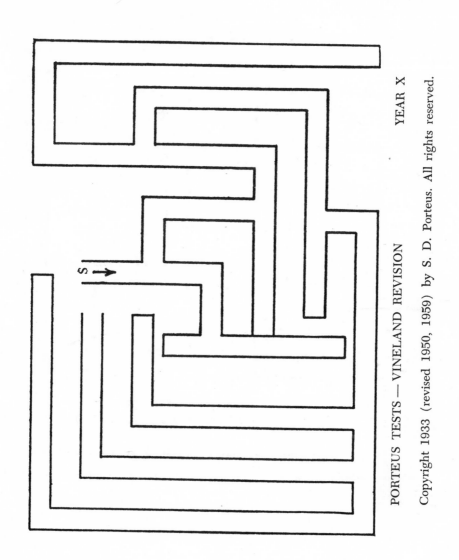

PORTEUS TESTS — VINELAND REVISION   YEAR X

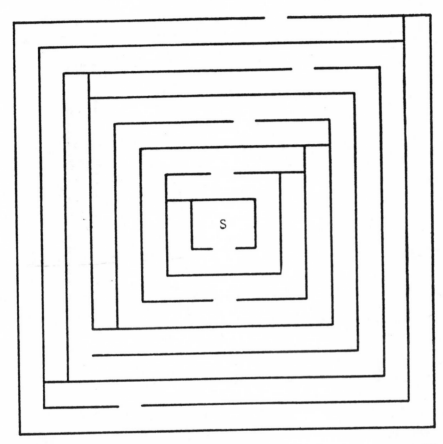

PORTEUS TESTS — VINELAND REVISION   YEAR XI

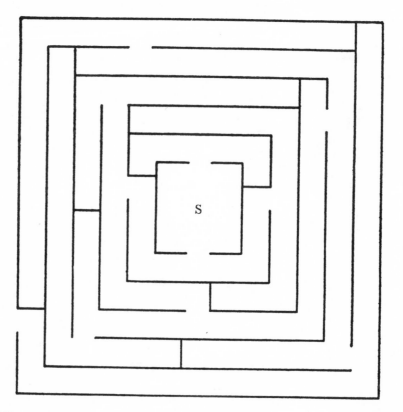

PORTEUS TESTS — VINELAND REVISION   YEAR XII

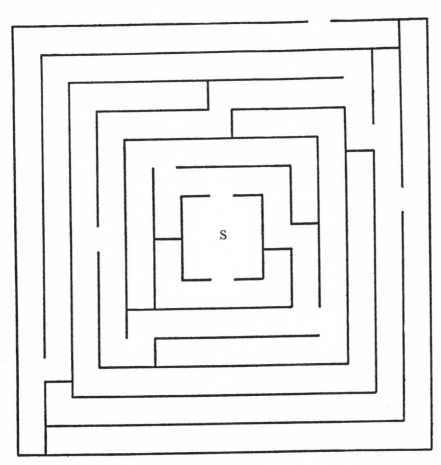

PORTEUS TESTS — VINELAND REVISION   YEAR XIV

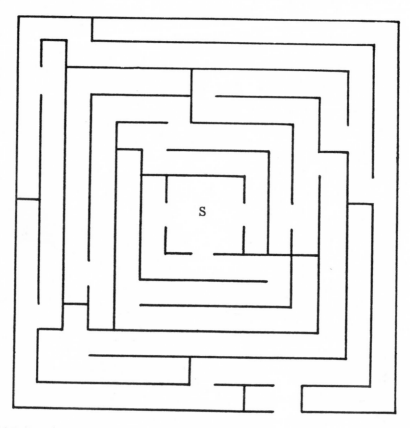

PORTEUS TESTS — VINELAND REVISION   ADULT I

PORTEUS MAZE TESTS — VINELAND REVISION
QUALITATIVE SCORING SAMPLES

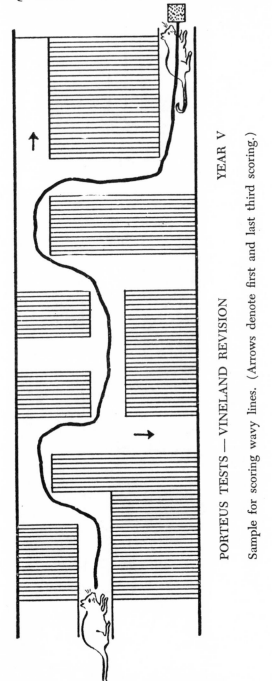

PORTEUS TESTS — VINELAND REVISION   YEAR V

Sample for scoring wavy lines. (Arrows denote first and last third scoring.)

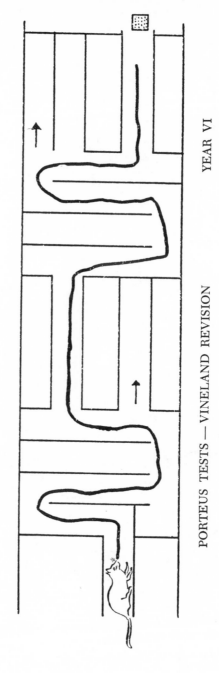

PORTEUS TESTS — VINELAND REVISION   YEAR VI

Sample for scoring wavy lines. (Arrows denote first and last third scoring.)

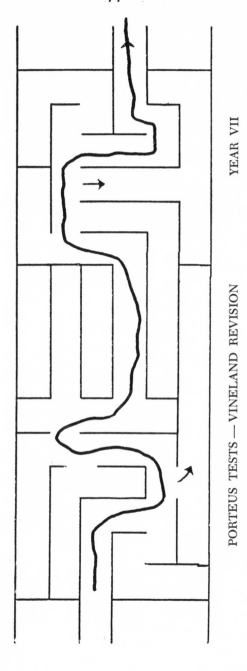

PORTEUS TESTS — VINELAND REVISION   YEAR VII

Sample for scoring wavy lines. (Arrows denote first and last third scoring.)

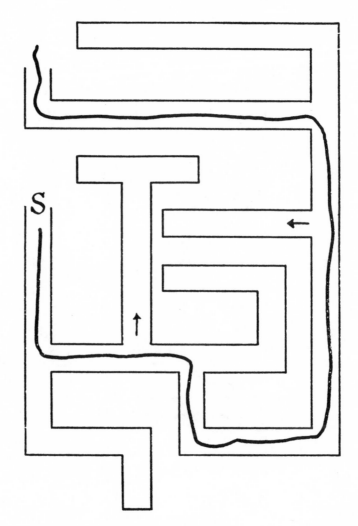

PORTEUS TESTS — VINELAND REVISION   **YEAR VIII**

Sample for scoring wavy lines. (Arrows denote first and last third scoring.)

PORTEUS TESTS — VINELAND REVISION   YEAR IX

Sample for scoring wavy lines. (Arrows denote first and last third scoring.)

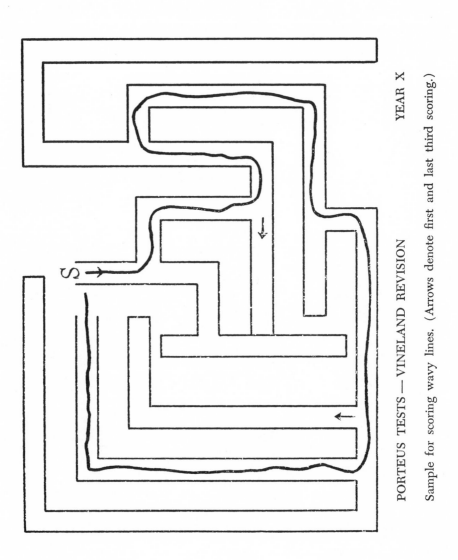

PORTEUS TESTS — VINELAND REVISION   YEAR X

Sample for scoring wavy lines. (Arrows denote first and last third scoring.)

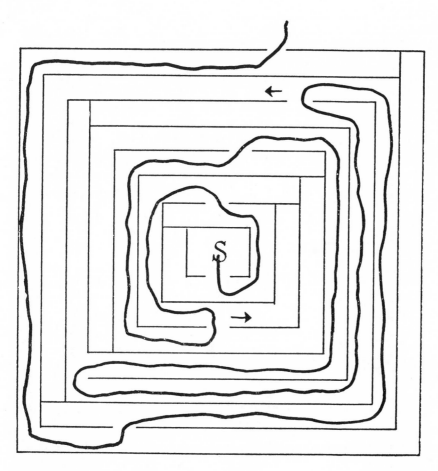

PORTEUS TESTS — VINELAND REVISION   YEAR XI

Sample for scoring wavy lines. (Arrows denote first and last third scoring.)

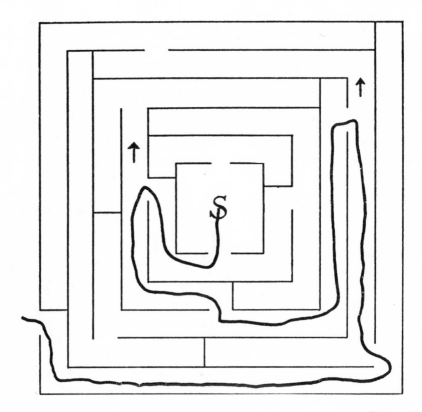

PORTEUS TESTS — VINELAND REVISION   YEAR XII

Sample for scoring wavy lines. (Arrows denote first and last third scoring.)

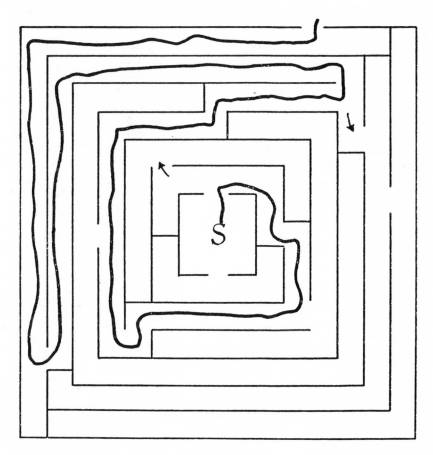

PORTEUS TESTS — VINELAND REVISION　　　　　　　**YEAR XIV**

Sample for scoring wavy lines. (Arrows denote first and last third scoring.)

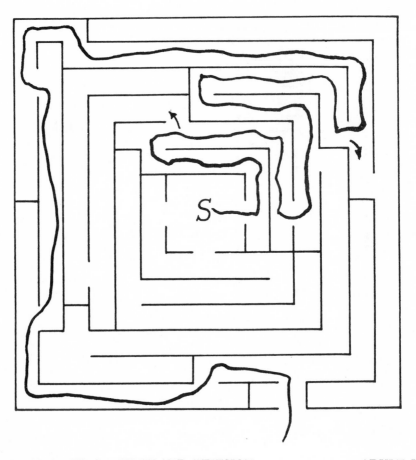

PORTEUS TESTS — VINELAND REVISION   ADULT I

Sample for scoring wavy lines. (Arrows denote first and last third scoring.)

PORTEUS MAZE TESTS — EXTENSION SERIES

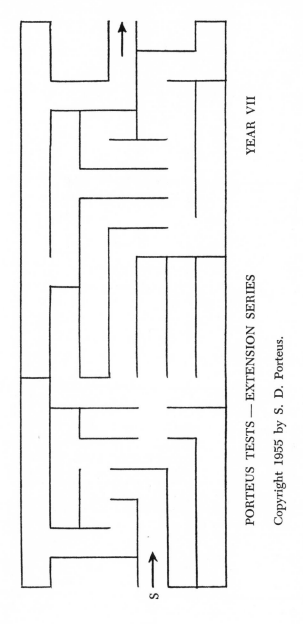

YEAR VII

PORTEUS TESTS — EXTENSION SERIES

Copyright 1955 by S. D. Porteus.

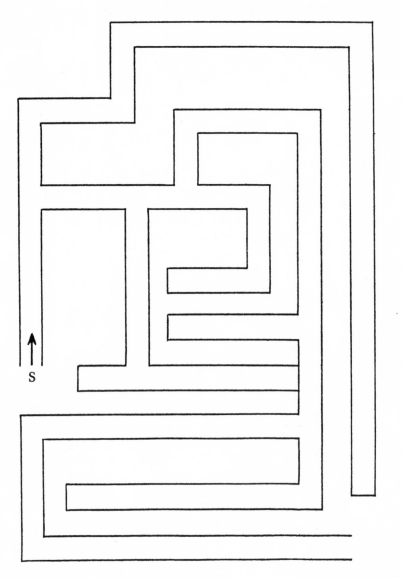

PORTEUS TESTS — EXTENSION SERIES   YEAR VIII

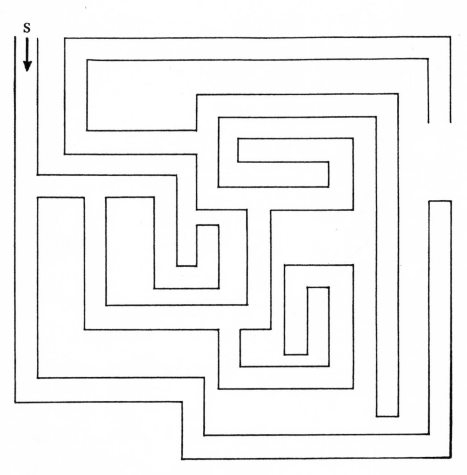

S

PORTEUS TESTS — EXTENSION SERIES   YEAR IX

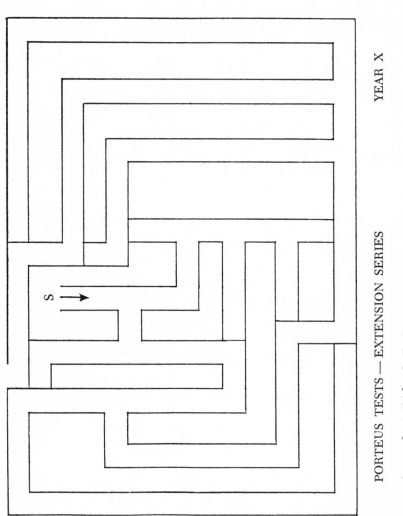

YEAR X

PORTEUS TESTS — EXTENSION SERIES

Copyright 1955 by S. D. Porteus.

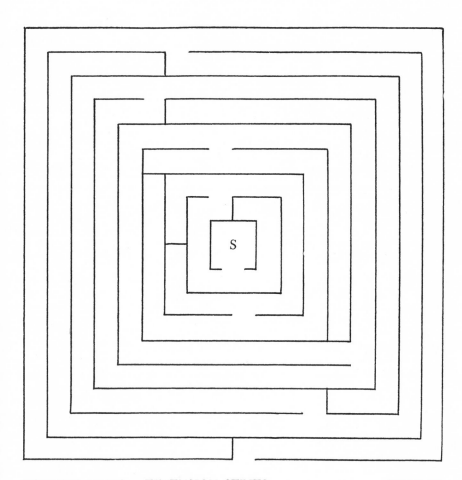

PORTEUS TESTS — EXTENSION SERIES   YEAR XI

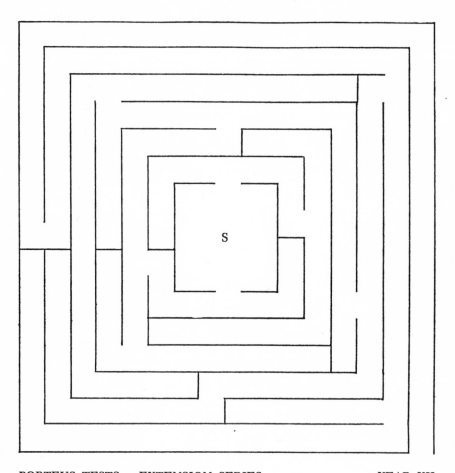

PORTEUS TESTS — EXTENSION SERIES   YEAR XII

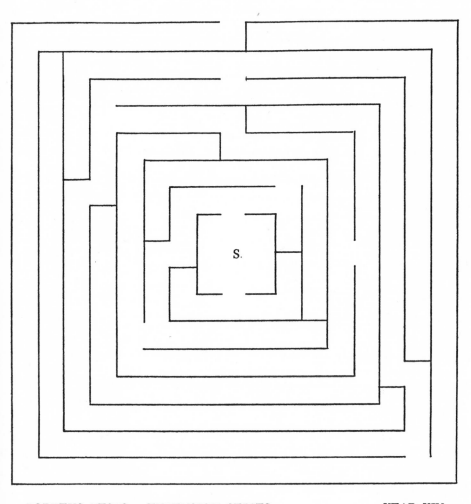

PORTEUS TESTS — EXTENSION SERIES   YEAR XIV

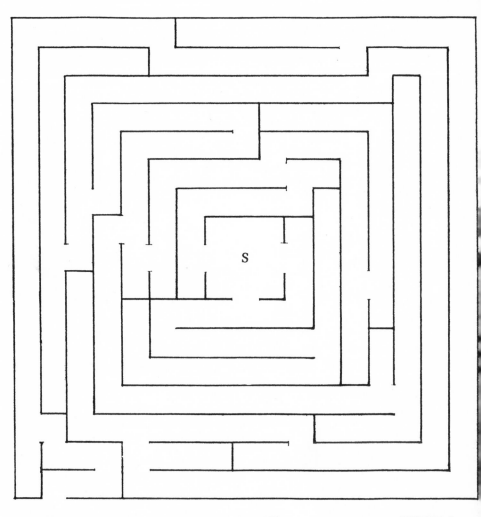

PORTEUS TESTS — EXTENSION SERIES   ADULT I

PORTEUS MAZE TESTS — EXTENSION SERIES
QUALITATIVE SCORING SAMPLES

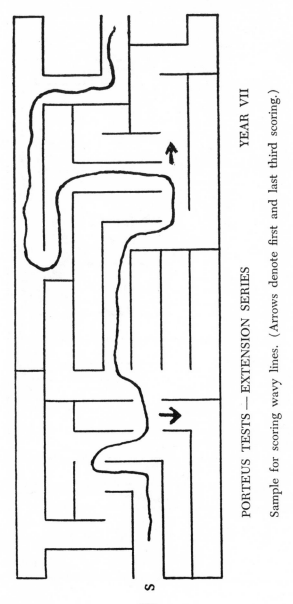

YEAR VII

PORTEUS TESTS — EXTENSION SERIES

Sample for scoring wavy lines. (Arrows denote first and last third scoring.)

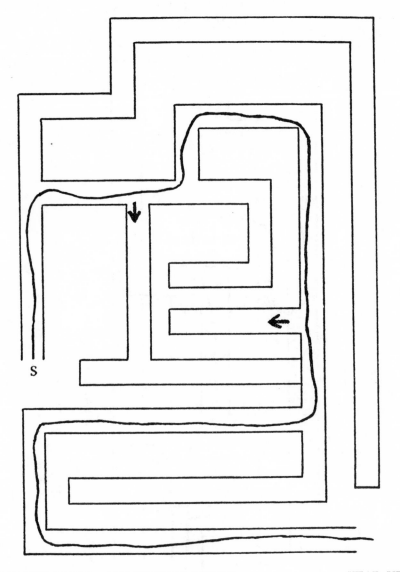

PORTEUS TESTS — EXTENSION SERIES   YEAR VIII

Sample for scoring wavy lines. (Arrows denote first and last third scoring.)

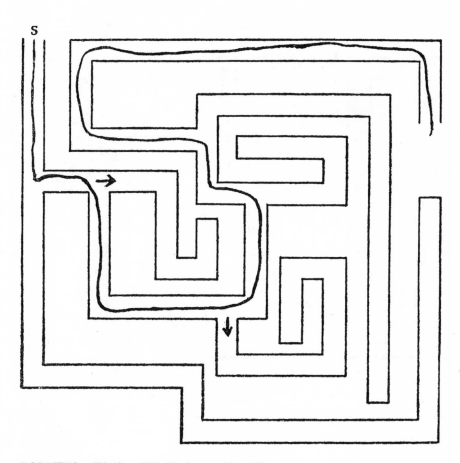

PORTEUS TESTS — EXTENSION SERIES   YEAR IX

Sample for scoring wavy lines. (Arrows denote first and last third scoring.)

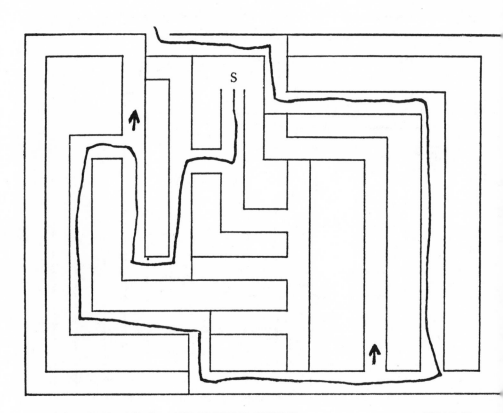

PORTEUS TESTS — EXTENSION SERIES   YEAR X

Sample for scoring wavy lines. (Arrows denote first and last third scoring.)

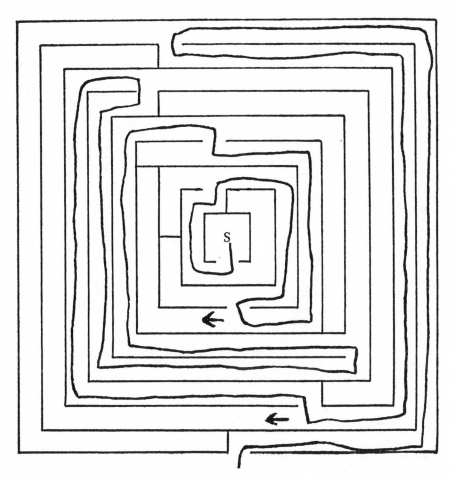

PORTEUS TESTS — EXTENSION SERIES   YEAR XI

Sample for scoring wavy lines. (Arrows denote first and last third scoring.)

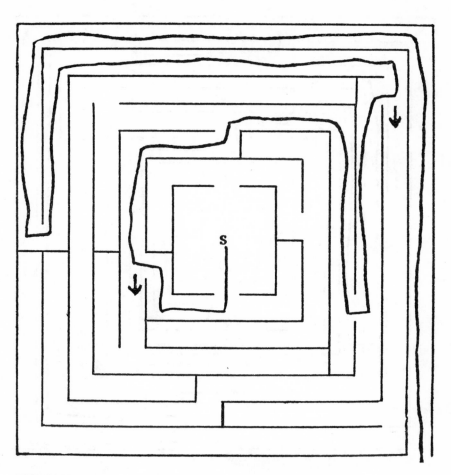

PORTEUS TESTS — EXTENSION SERIES   YEAR XII

Sample for scoring wavy lines. (Arrows denote first and last third scoring.)

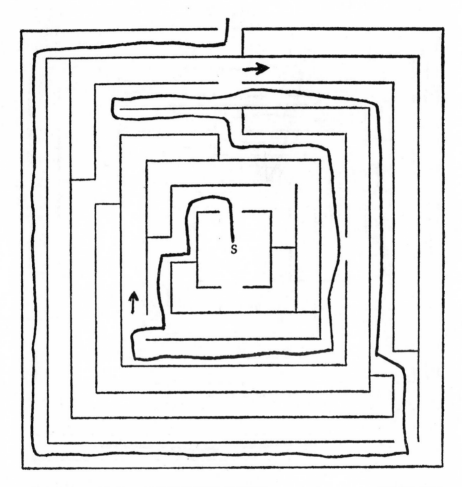

PORTEUS TESTS — EXTENSION SERIES   YEAR XIV

Sample for scoring wavy lines. (Arrows denote first and last third scoring.)

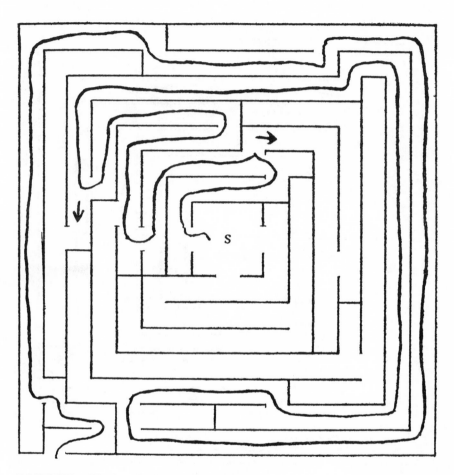

PORTEUS TESTS — EXTENSION SERIES   ADULT I

Sample for scoring wavy lines. (Arrows denote first and last third scoring.)

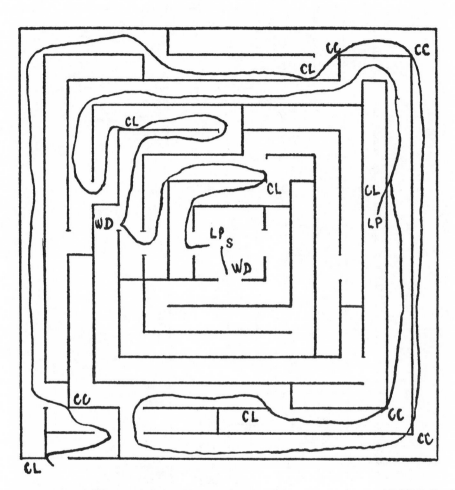

PORTEUS TESTS — EXTENSION SERIES   ADULT I

Qualitative scoring sample.
WD = Wrong Direction   WL = Wavy Line   LP = Lift Pencil
          CL = Crossed Line   CC = Cut Corner

PORTEUS MAZE SUPPLEMENT

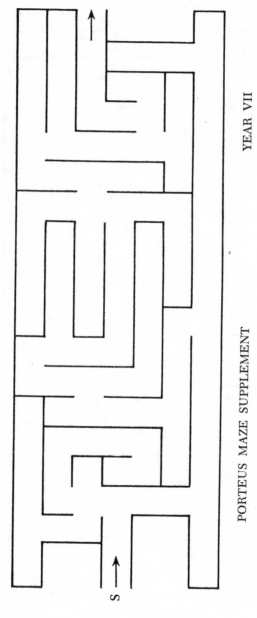

YEAR VII

PORTEUS MAZE SUPPLEMENT

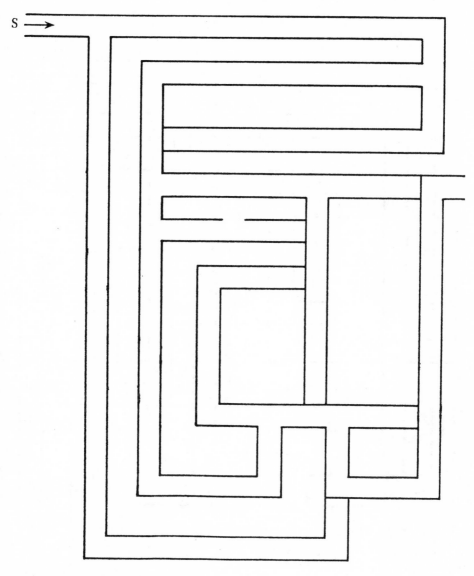

PORTEUS MAZE SUPPLEMENT   YEAR VIII

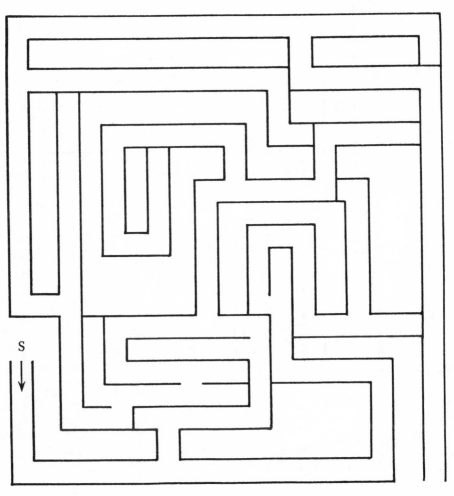

PORTEUS MAZE SUPPLEMENT   YEAR IX

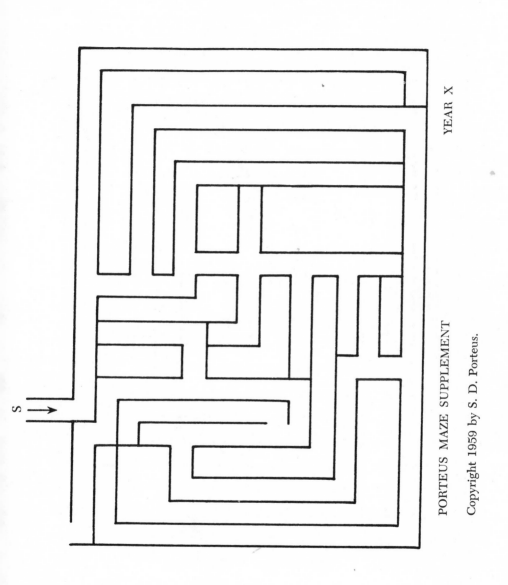

S

PORTEUS MAZE SUPPLEMENT

YEAR X

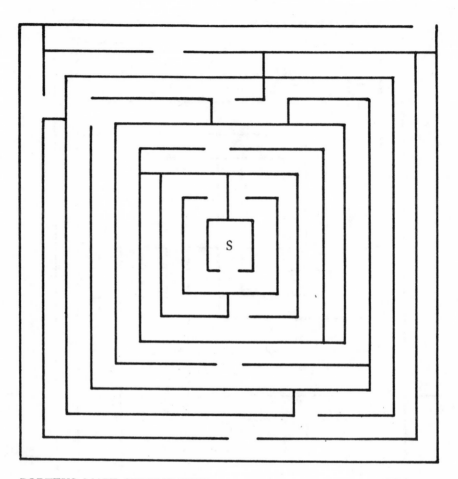

PORTEUS MAZE SUPPLEMENT   YEAR XI

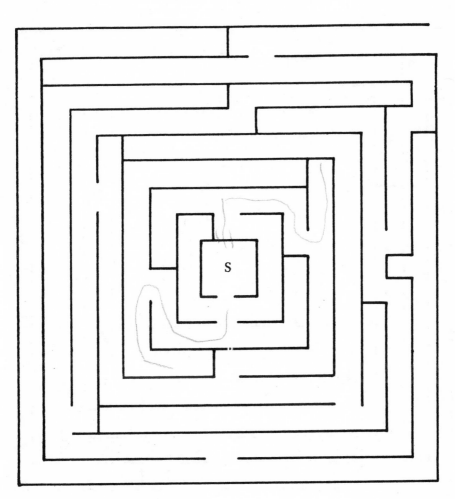

PORTEUS MAZE SUPPLEMENT   YEAR XII

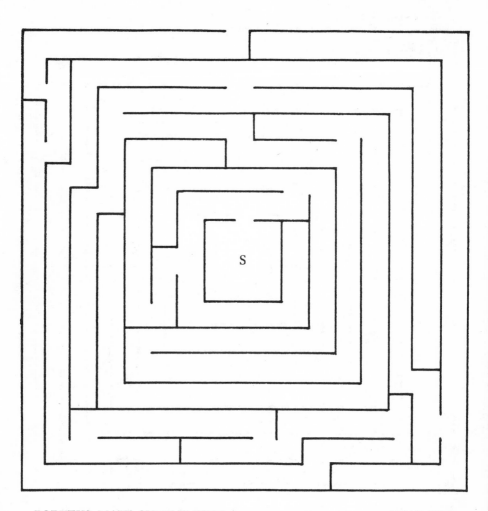

PORTEUS MAZE SUPPLEMENT   YEAR XIV

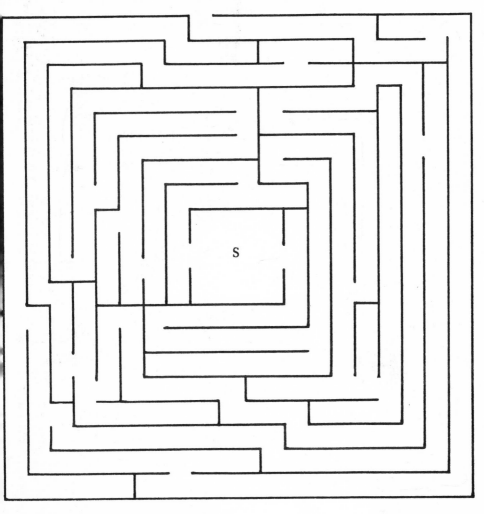

PORTEUS MAZE SUPPLEMENT   ADULT I

Appendix D

TABLE OF MAZE TEST QUOTIENTS

TEST AGES

Chron. Age	4	4½	5	5½	6	6½	7	7½	8
4	80	86	92	98	104	110	115	120	125
4½	78	84	90	96	102	108	113	118	123
5	76	82	88	94	100	106	111	116	120
5½	74	80	86	92	98	104	109	113	117
6	72	78	84	90	96	101	106	110	114
6½	69	75	81	87	93	98	103	107	111
7	66	72	78	84	90	95	100	104	108
7½	63	69	75	81	87	92	97	101	105
8	60	66	72	78	84	89	94	98	102
8½	57	63	69	75	81	86	91	95	99
9	54	60	66	72	78	83	88	92	96
9½	51	57	63	69	75	80	85	89	93
10	48	54	60	66	72	77	82	86	90
11	42	48	54	60	66	71	76	80	84
12	36	42	48	54	60	65	70	74	78
13	30	36	42	48	54	59	64	68	72
14	24	30	36	42	48	53	58	62	66

TABLE OF MAZE TEST QUOTIENTS

TEST AGES

Chron. Age	8½	9	9½	10	10½	11	11½	12	12½
4	130	135							
4½	127	131	135						
5	124	128	132	135					
5½	121	125	129	133	135				
6	118	122	126	130	133	135			
6½	115	119	123	127	131	133	135		
7	112	116	120	124	128	131	133	135	
7½	109	113	117	121	125	129	131	133	135
8	106	110	114	118	122	126	129	131	133
8½	103	107	111	115	119	123	127	129	131
9	100	104	108	112	116	120	124	127	129
9½	97	101	105	109	113	117	121	125	127
10	94	98	102	106	110	114	118	122	125
11	88	92	96	100	104	108	112	116	120
12	82	86	90	94	98	102	106	110	114
13	76	80	84	86	92	96	100	104	108
14	70	74	78	82	86	90	94	98	102

TEST AGES

Chron. Age	13	13½	14	14½	15	15½	16	16½	17
8	135								
8½	133	135							
9	131	133	135						
9½	129	131	133	135					
10	127	129	131	133	135				
11	123	125	127	131	133	135			
12	118	121	123	127	130	133	135		
13	112	116	119	123	126	130	132	135	
14	106	110	114	118	122	126	129	132	135

Bibliography

AARONSON, BERNARD S. 1963. The comparative sensitivity of the qualitative and quantitative Porteus Maze scores to drug effects. *J. Clin. Psychol., 19,* 184–185.

ARONSON, H., & KLEE, G. D. 1960. Effect of lysergic acid diethylamide (LSD-25) on impulse control. *J. nerv. and ment. dis., 131,* 536–539.

ASHLEY-MONTAGU, M. F. 1961. In comments invited by the editor included in an article published in *Current Anthropology. See* Comas.

BABCOCK, H. 1948. Psychologists should study psychology. *J. Psychol., 26,* 83–92.

BALLER, W. R. 1936. Study of the present social status of a group of adults who, when they were in elementary school, were classified as mentally deficient. *Genet. Psychol. Monog., 18,* 165–244.

BATTERBEE, R. 1951. *Modern Australian aboriginal art.* Sydney: Angus & Robertson.

BERRY, R. J. A., & PORTEUS, S. D. 1920. *Intelligence and social valuation.* Res. Publ. 20, Training School, Vineland, N. J.

BLACKWOOD, B. 1927. Study of mental testing in relation to anthropology. *Ment. measurement monogs., 4,* Dec.

BROWN, I. A. FRENCH, L. A. OGLE, W. S., & JAHNSON, S. 1956. Temporal lobe epilepsy; its clinical manifestations and surgical treatment. *Medicine, 35,* 425–459.

BRUNDAGE, E. G. 1943. Private communication.

BUROS, O. K. (Ed.). 1953. *Mental measurements yearbook,* review of the

Maze; quoted from *Brit. J. Delinquency, 4,* 144.

BURT, CYRIL. 1921. *Mental and scholastic tests.* London County Council Publications. London.

BURT, CYRIL. 1923. *Handbook of tests for use in schools.* King and Son, London.

CAMERON, N. 1947. *The psychology of the behavior disorders.* New York: Houghton Mifflin Co.

CAMPBELL, T. D. 1938. Expedition to Cockatoo Creek (unpublished paper).

CLEMENT, F. 1957. In a private communication dated March 3, 1957.

Columbia-Greystone Associates. 1949. *Selective partial ablation of the frontal cortex.* (F. A. Mettler, Ed.) New York: Hoeber.

Columbia-Greystone Associates. 1952. *Psychosurgical problems.* (F. A. Mettler, Ed.), Philadelphia: Blakiston.

COMAS, J. 1961. "Scientific" racism again? *Current Anthrop., 2,* 303–340.

CONNERS, C. K., & EISENBERG, L. 1963a. The effects of methylphenidate on symptomatology and learning in disturbed children. *Amer. J. Psychiat., 120,* 458–464.

CONNERS, C. K., EISENBERG, L., & SHARPE, L. 1963b. The effects of methylphenidate (Ritalin) on paired-associate learning and Porteus Maze performance in emotionally disturbed children. *J. consult. Psychol., 28,* 14–22.

DEWEY, J. 1902. Interpretation of savage mind. *The Psychol. Rev., 9,* 217–230.

DOCTER, R. F., & WINDER, C. L. 1954. Delinquent *vs.* nondelinquent performance on the Porteus Qualitative Maze Test. *J. consult. Psychol.*, **18**, 71–73.

DOLL, E. A. 1917. *Clinical studies in feeble-mindedness.* Boston: Badger.

DU BOIS, C. 1944. *The people of Alor.* Minneapolis: Univ. Minnesota Press.

EARLE, F. M., & MILNER, M. 1929. *The use of performance tests of intelligence in vocational guidance.* London: H. M. Stationary Office.

ELKIN, A. P. 1961. Comments invited by the editor on an article published in *Current Anthropology.* See Comas.

FOOKS, G., & THOMAS, R. R. 1957. Differential qualitative performance of delinquents on the Porteus Maze. *J. consult. Psychol.*, **21**, 351–353.

FOULDS, G. A. 1951. Temperamental differences in Maze performance. *Brit. J. Psychol.*, **42**, 43, 209–217, 33–41.

FREEMAN, W., & WATTS, J. W. 1942. *Psychosurgery* (1st Ed.). Springfield, Ill.: C. Thomas.

FREEMAN, W., & WATTS, J. W. 1950. *Psychosurgery.* (2nd Ed.). Springfield, Ill.: C. Thomas.

FRY, H. K., & PULLEINE, R. H. 1931. The mentality of the Australian aborigine. *Australian J. exper. Biol. and ment. Sci.*, **8**, 3.

FULTON, JOHN F., & JACOBSEN, C. F. 1935. The functions of the frontal lobes, a comparative study in monkeys, chimpanzees and man. Abstr. 2nd Int. Congr., London.

GODDARD, H. H. 1912. *The Kallikak family.* New York: Macmillan.

GODDARD, H. H. 1916. *Feeblemindedness: its causes and consequences.* New York: Macmillan.

GRAJALES, M. L. 1948. Porteus Qualitative Maze Test as a measure of delinquency. M.A. Thesis (unpublished), Fordham University.

GRUETZOW, H., & BROZEK, J. 1946. Intellectual function and reduced intakes of B-complex vitamins. *Amer. J. Psychol.*, **59**, 358–381.

GUILFORD, J. P. 1958. The structure of intellect. *Psychol. Bul.*, **55**, 267–293.

HAVIGHURST, R. J., & HILKEVITCH, R. R. 1944. The intelligence of Indian children as measured by a performance scale. *J. abnorm. soc. Psychol.*, **19**, 419–433.

HEBB, D. C. 1954. *Proceedings of the Third Research Conference on Psychosurgery.* Public Health Service Publ. 21. Washington: U. S. Govt. Printing Office. (*Vide* p. 113.)

HELPER, M. M., WILCOTT, R. C., & GARFIELD, S. L. 1963. Effects of chlorpromazine on learning and related processes in emotionally disturbed children. *J. consult. Psychol.*, **27**, 1–9.

HERD, H. 1923. The Porteus Maze Mental Test. *The Medical Officer*, **30**, 267–268.

HERD, H. 1930. *The diagnosis of mental deficiency.* London: Hodder & Stoughton.

HUNT, W. 1962. In a private communication dated January 23, 1962.

JENSEN, M. B. 1952. Our undeveloped mental resources. Paper presented at the Annual Meeting of the AAAS, St. Louis, Mo., December 29. (Mimeographed.)

JENSEN, M. B. 1961a. The "low-level" airman in retesting and basic training: A sociopsychological study. *J. soc. Psychol.*, **55**, 177–190.

JENSEN, M. B. 1961b. Old age and intelligence (a study of domiciled veterans). *Mimeo. Res. Rep.*, Dec.

JOSEPH, A., & MURRAY, V. F. 1951. *Chamorros and Carolinians of Saipan.* Cambridge, Mass.: Harvard Univ. Press.

JUDSON, A. J., & MacCASLAND, B. W. 1960. The effects of chlorpromazine on psychological test scores. *J. consult. Psychol.*, **24**, 192.

KAINER, ROCHELLE. 1965. The Porteus Maze Test and the delay of gratification. Unpublished thesis, Teachers' College, Columbia University.

KARPELES, L. M. 1932. A further investigation of the Porteus Maze as a discriminative measure in delinquency. *J. appl. Psychol.*, 16, 426–437.

LANDIS, C. 1949, Experimental methods in psychopathology. *Mental Hygiene*, 33, 96–107.

LANDIS, C. 1951. Psychological observations on psychosurgical cases. *Psychiat. Quart.*, 1–9, July.

LANDIS, C., ZUBIN, J., & METTLER, F. A. 1950. The functions of the human frontal lobe. *J. Psychol.*, 30, 123–138.

LEWIS, N. D. S., LANDIS, C., & KING, H. E. (Eds.) 1956. *Studies in topectomy.* New York: Grune & Stratton.

LORANGER, A. W., & MISIAK, H. 1960. The performance of aged females on five non-language tests of intellectual functions. *J. clin. Psychol.*, 16, 189–191.

MARGOLIS, R., ENGLEHARDT, D. M., FREEDMAN, N., HANKOFF, L. D., & MANN. D. 1960. Changes in Porteus Maze performance as a function of drug treatment and level of cognitive development. Paper presented at Eastern Psychological Assoc., April, 1960.

MACLEAN, P. D. 1949. Psychosomatic disease and the "visceral brain." *Psychosom. Med.*, 11, 338–353.

MATHEW, J. 1899. *Eaglehawk and crow: A study of the Australian aborigines.* London: David Nutt.

MCCARTHY, F. D. 1938. *Australian aboriginal decorative art.* Sydney: Australian Museum.

MIRSKY, F., & ROSVOLD, H. E. 1960. The use of psychoactive drugs as a neuropsychological tool in studies of attention in man. In L. Uhr and J. G. Miller (Eds.) *Drugs and Behavior.* New York: Wiley and Sons, pp. 375–392.

MONTESSORI, MARIA. 1912. *The Montessori method.* New York: Stokes.

MORGENTHAU, D. R. 1922. Some well-known mental tests, evaluated and compared. *Columbia Univ. Archives Psychol.*, No. 52.

O'SHEA, H. E., ELSOM, K. O'SHEA, & HIGBE, R. V. 1942. Studies of the B vitamins in the human subject. IV; Mental changes in experimental deficiency. *Amer. J. med. Sci.*, 203, 388–397.

PARTRIDGE, M. 1950. *Prefrontal leucotomy.* Springfield: Thomas.

PENFIELD, WILDER. 1950. The cerebral cortex and the mind of man. Chap. VII, in *The physical basis of mind.* (Ed. Laslett) Oxford: Blackwell.

PETERSON, J., & TELFORD, J. 1930. Results of group and individual tests applied to practically pure-blood Negro children at St. Helena Island. *J. comp. Psychol.*, Dec. 1930.

PETRIE, A. 1952. *Personality and the frontal lobes.* Philadelphia: Blakiston.

PIDDINGTON, M., & PIDDINGTON, R. 1932. Report of field work in northwestern Australia. *Oceania*, 2, 342–358.

PORTEUS, S. D. 1915a. Motor-intellectual tests for mental defectives. *J. exper. Pedag.*, 3, 127–135.

PORTEUS, S. D. 1915b. Mental tests for feeble-minded: A new series. *J. Psycho-Asthenics*, 19, 200–213.

PORTEUS, S. D. 1917. Mental tests with delinquents and Australian aboriginal children. *Psychol. Rev.*, 24, 32–42.

PORTEUS, S. D. 1918. The measurement of intelligence: Six hundred and fifty-three children examined by the Binet and Porteus Tests. *J. educ. Psychol.*, Jan., 13–31.

PORTEUS, S. D. 1919a. *Porteus Tests— The Vineland Revision.* Res. Publ. 16, Training School, Vineland, N. J.

PORTEUS, S. D. 1919b. *A standardized information record.* Res. Publ. 17, Training School, Vineland, N. J.

PORTEUS, S. D. 1920. *A study of personality of defectives with a social ratings scale.* Res. Publ. 23, Training School, Vineland, N. J.

PORTEUS, S. D. 1922. *Studies in mental*

deviations. Res. Publ. 24, Training School, Vineland, N. J.

PORTEUS, S. D. 1931. *Psychology of a primitive people.* London: Arnold.

PORTEUS, S. D. 1933a. Mentality of Australian aborigines. *Oceania,* 4, 30–36.

PORTEUS, S. D. 1933b. *The Maze Test and mental differences.* Vineland, N. J.: Smith Printing House.

PORTEUS, S. D. 1937. *Primitive intelligence and environment.* New York: Macmillan.

PORTEUS, S. D. 1941. *The practice of clinical psychology.* New York: American Book Co.

PORTEUS, S. D. 1942. *Qualitative performance in the Maze Test.* Vineland, N. J.: Smith Printing House.

PORTEUS, S. D. 1945. Q-scores, temperament and delinquency. *J. soc. Psychol.,* 21, 81–103.

PORTEUS, S. D. 1950. *The Porteus Maze Test and intelligence.* Palo Alto, Calif.; Pacific Books.

PORTEUS, S. D. 1955a. Some commonsense implications of psychosurgery. *Brit. J. med. Psychol.,* 28, 167–176.

PORTEUS, S. D. 1955b. *The Maze Test: Recent advances.* Palo Alto, Calif.; Pacific Books.

PORTEUS, S. D. 1957a. Maze Test reactions after chlorpromazine. *J. consult. Psychol.,* 21, 15–21.

PORTEUS, S. D. 1957b. Specific behavior changes following chlorpromazine. *J. consult. Psychol.,* 21, 257–263.

PORTEUS, S. D. 1959a. *The Porteus Mazes. The Supplement Series of Mazes.* New York: Psychological Corp.

PORTEUS, S. D. 1959b. Recent Maze Test studies. *Brit. J. med. Psychol.,* 32, 38–43.

PORTEUS, S. D. 1959c. *The Maze Test and clinical psychology.* Palo Alto, Calif.; Pacific Books.

PORTEUS, S. D. 1961. Ethnic group differences. *Mankind Quarterly,* 1, 187–200.

PORTEUS, S. D. 1963. Namatjira; famous Australian artist. *Percept, and motor skills.* 17, 13–14.

PORTEUS, S. D. 1962. The will to live. *Mankind Quarterly,* 3, 1.

PORTEUS, S. D., & BABCOCK, M. E. 1926.

Temperament and race. Boston: Gorham Press.

PORTEUS, S. D., & BARCLAY, J. E. 1957. A further note on chlorpromazine: Maze reactions. *J. consult. Psychol.,* 21, 297–299.

PORTEUS, S. D., BARCLAY, J. E., CULVER, H. S., & KLEMAN, J. P. 1960. Measurement of subconscious memory. *Percept. and motor skills,* 10, 215–229. Monog. Supp. 2-V10.

PORTEUS, S. D., & BASSETT, D. M. 1920. *Sex differences in Porteus Maze Test performance.* Res. Publ. 22, Training School, Vineland, N. J.

PORTEUS, S. D., & CHING, E. T. 1959. Research with feebleminded. *Hawaii Med. Jour.,* 18, 491–493.

PORTEUS, S. D., & CORBETT, G. R. 1953. Statutory definitions of feebleminded in U.S.A. *J. Psychol.,* 35, 81–105.

PORTEUS, S. D., DEWEY, D., & BERNREUTER, R. G. 1930. Race and social differences in performance tests. *Genet. Psychol. Monog.,* 8, 93–208.

PORTEUS, S. D., & DIAMOND, A. L. 1961. Measurement of psychomotor perseverative tendencies. *Nature,* 189, 691–692.

PORTEUS, S. D., & DIAMOND, A. L. 1962. Porteus Maze changes after psychosurgery. *J. ment. Sci.,* 108, 53–58.

PORTEUS, S. D., & GREGOR, A. J. 1963. Studies in intercultural testing. *Perceptual and motor skills,* 16, 705–724. Monog. Suppl. 7–V16.

PORTEUS, S. D., & KEPNER, R. DeM. 1944. Mental changes after bilateral prefrontal lobotomy. *Genet. Psychol. Monog.,* 29, 3–115.

PORTEUS, S. D., & PETERS, H. N. 1947a. Psychosurgery and test validity. *J. Abnor and Soc. Psychol.,* 42, 4.

PORTEUS, S. D., & PETERS, H. N. 1947b. Maze Test validation and psychosurgery. *Gent. Psychol. Monog.* 36, 3–86.

POULL, L. E., & MONTGOMERY, R. P. 1929. The Porteus Maze tests as a discriminative measure in delinquency. *J. appl. Psychol.,* 13, 145–151.

Proceedings of the Third Research Conference on Psychosurgery. 1954. Publ. 221. Washington: U. S. Dept. Health, Education and Welfare.

RAY, P. C. 1953. Maze Test performance of the Bhil of Central India. *Bul. Dept. Anthrop.*, **2**, 83–90.

Ross, E. L. S. 1921. Vocational tests for defectives. *Studies in Mental Deficiency*, Jan. 1921.

RUSSELL, W. R. 1948. Function of frontal lobes. *Lancet*, **254**

SCHERER, P. A. 1963. *Venture of faith.* Board of the Finke River Mission, Tanunda, S. Australia.

SHAPIRO, M. B., KESSELL, R., & MAXWELL, A. E. 1960. Speed and quality of psychomotor performance in psychiatric patients. *J. clin. Psychol.*, **16**, 266–271.

SHAW, E. R., 1917. Suggestions for child study. *The Kindergarten and First Grade*, **2**, Nos. 3, 4, Dec. 1917.

SHERRINGTON, C. S. *The brain and its mechanism.* London. The Rede Lecture, Dec. 5, 1933.

SMITH, A. 1960. Changes in Porteus Maze scores of brain-operated schizophrenics after an eight-year interval. *J. ment. Sci.*, **106**, 967–978.

SPARLING, M. E. 1941. Intelligence of Indian children—the relationship between Binet and Porteus scores. *Amer. J. Ment. Def.*, **46**, 60–62.

STEWART, K. See Porteus *Primitive intelligence and environment.*

STOKES, J. L. 1846. *Discoveries in Australia.* London: T. & W. Boone.

STREHLOW, T. G. H. 1961. *Nomads in No-Man's-Land.* The Aborigines Movement League Inc. of S. Australia, Adelaide.

TERMAN L. M. 1916. *The measurement of intelligence.* Boston: Houghton Mifflin Co.

TOBIAS, J., & GORELICK, J. 1962. The Porteus Maze Test and the appraisal of retarded adults. *Amer. J. ment. defic.*, **66**, 600–606.

TOW, P. MACDONALD. 1955. *Personality changes following frontal leucotomy.* Oxford Med. Publ. London: Oxford Univ. Press. Pp. 171–181.

VAN DER POST, L. 1958. *The lost world of the Kalahari.* London: Hogarth Press.

VICARY, T. C. 1938. An investigation into the use of non-verbal tests of intelligence in India. Master's thesis (unpublished), Univ. of London.

WAITE, J. H., & NEILSON, I. L. 1919. A study of effects of hookworm infection upon mental development of North Queensland school children. *Med. J. Australia*, **1**, 1–8.

WEBSTER, M. S. 1949. A comparison of the qualitative performance of manic and depressive patients on the Porteus Maze Test. Master's thesis (unpublished), Univ. of Maine.

WECHSLER, D. 1944. *The measurement of adult intelligence.* Baltimore: Williams & Wilkins Co. (3rd edition).

WEISENBERG, T., ROE, A., & McBRIDE, K. F. 1936. *Adult intelligence: A psychological study of test performance.* New York: Commonwealth Fund.

WRIGHT, C. 1944. The qualitative performance of delinquent boys on the Porteus Maze Test. *J. consult. Psychol.*, **8**, 24–26.

ZUBIN, J. 1949. Rorschach test. Chap. 21, Columbia-Greystone Associates *Selective partial ablation of the frontal cortex.* New York: Hoeber.

Index